Praise for
Bringing Your Soul to Light

"Nourishes your heart with inspiring true stories that will echo in your soul long after you put the book down."—Michael J. Tamura, award-winning author of *You Are The Answer*

"In this highly recommended read, Dr. Backman [explores] the process of reincarnation and what is experienced between lifetimes by sharing case material from numerous regression sessions."—Walter Semkiw, MD, author of *Return of the Revolutionaries*

"The case studies in this book are convincing and absolutely fascinating. They demonstrate how past-life and between-lives regression can help people understand themselves and make daily life more productive and happy."—Wayne Peterson, author of *Extraordinary Times, Extraordinary Beings*

Bringing Your

Soul

to Light

About the Author

Dr. Linda Backman, licensed psychologist, has been in private practice since 1978. She also has graduate education and training in the fields of speech pathology, audiology, and special education. After experiencing the premature birth and death of her second child, Dr. Backman discovered the great need for more psychotherapists who are trained and devoted to working with those in grief. She co-founded an ongoing agency in Charlotte, North Carolina, dedicated to serving individuals and families who have experienced the death of children. In line with this work, she was asked to provide the commentary for the book *I Never Held You* by Ellen M. DuBois (DLSIJ Press, 2006).

Since 1993, Dr. Backman has guided individuals in regression hypnotherapy to access their past and between lives. In this way, she helps people to more fully recognize who they are as a soul throughout their many lifetimes and during the time they are not incarnate. Regression hypnotherapy allows clients to understand their soul mission, soul progress, soul relationships, and much more. Dr. Backman's work today includes guiding regressions as well as speaking, writing, and training others in the benefits of soul regression hypnotherapy, both in the United States and abroad.

Dr. Backman studied and taught with Dr. Michael Newton, author of the seminal books *Journey of Souls* and *Destiny of Souls*, and co-created and served on the founding board of the Society for Spiritual Regression (now the Newton Institute) as membership chair and president. In 1997, Dr. Backman and her husband, Dr. Earl Backman, established the Ravenheart Center, a Mystery School in Boulder, Colorado, dedicated to guiding individuals in discovering their path as a soul. In addition, Dr. Backman co-founded the International Between Lives Regression Network in 2005, a network for regression therapists and for the promotion of awareness among the general public, in the United States and abroad, of the benefits and purpose of regression hypnotherapy.

The Backmans have been married for over forty-one years and have two married children and three grandchildren. For further information, please visit www.bringingyoursoultolight.com or contact Dr. Backman at Linda@ravenheartcenter.com.

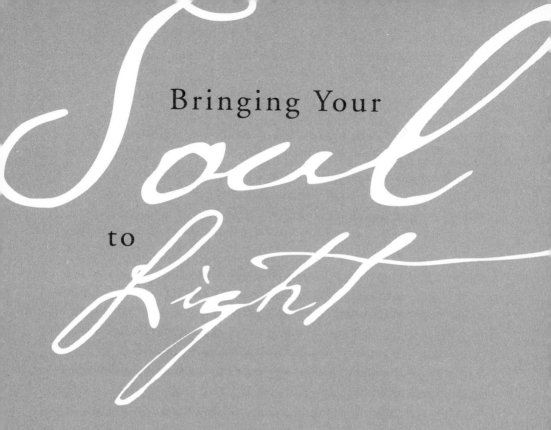

Bringing Your

Soul

to *Light*

Healing Through Past Lives and the Time Between

DR. LINDA BACKMAN

FOREWORD BY C. NORMAN SHEALY, MD, PHD

Llewellyn Publications
WOODBURY, MINNESOTA

FIRST EDITION
First Printing, 2009

Book design and editing by Rebecca Zins
Cover design by Kevin R. Brown
Cover photo from EyeWire

Llewellyn is a registered trademark of Llewellyn Worldwide, Ltd.

Library of Congress Cataloging-in-Publication Data
Backman, Linda, 1946–
  Bringing your soul to light : healing through past lives and the time
between / Linda Backman; foreword by C. Norman Shealy.—1st ed.
     p. cm.
  Includes bibliographical references and index.
  ISBN 978-0-7387-1321-2
  1. Reincarnation therapy. 2. Regression (Psychology) 3. Hypnotism—
Therapeutic use. I. Title.
  RC489.R43B33 2009
  616.89′14—dc22

                              2008043788

Llewellyn Worldwide does not participate in, endorse, or have any authority or
responsibility concerning private business transactions between our authors and
the public.

All mail addressed to the author is forwarded but the publisher cannot, unless specifically instructed by the author, give out an address or phone number.

Any Internet references contained in this work are current at publication
time, but the publisher cannot guarantee that a specific location will continue
to be maintained. Please refer to the publisher's website for links to authors'
websites and other sources.

Llewellyn Publications
A Division of Llewellyn Worldwide, Ltd.
2143 Wooddale Drive, Dept. 978-0-7387-1321-2
Woodbury, MN 55125-2989
www.llewellyn.com

Printed in the United States of America

I dedicate this book to all those who understand
that each and every soul contributes to the
beauty and the becoming of the universe.

contents

foreword

by C. Norman Shealy, MD, PhD

One of the great gifts I received in this life came with the parents I chose. They did not encase me in rigid beliefs that strangle the ability to seek and understand the multidimensional reality of life. As a child, I was often mystified by the hypocrisy of many individuals who professed to be religious leaders. At age sixteen, I was off to Duke University, where my search for knowledge included exposure to Dr. McClellan, the dean of the chapel and a wonderfully broad thinker. Even though I was raised a rather liberal Methodist, I still had all the basic Christian beliefs.

My first major philosophical awakening came in 1967 when I read Craveri's *The Life of Jesus*, a book where the authenticity of the Bible was questioned. Craveri was, of course, excommunicated for stating that several hundred passages had been changed through the years to achieve specific political aims. This is not to deny the existence of Jeshua of Nazareth; certainly he lived, and I later discovered through regression that I was there at the scene of his death. But Craveri's book initiated my exploration of the many varieties of opinions about the foundations of Christianity and the question of life after physical death.

The question of reincarnation was raised in some other books I read, but I remained neutral until 1973 when, sitting in a scientific meeting, I had a spontaneous knowing that I had been John Elliotson, a British physician who introduced Mesmerism into England. Six months earlier, I had written an anonymous novel on the hypocrisy of medicine in accepting new ideas. As I explored Dr. Elliotson's work, I came upon his Harverian lecture given 130 years earlier on exactly the same topic and using many of the same examples I had used in 1972! And a month before I had this discovery, I had begun work on psychic diagnosis, another major contribution of his. Thus began my second major philosophical awakening. We not only reincarnate, but we often carry with us many traits, beliefs, and values. My story of Elliotson's life and my relation to it can be read in Dr. Walter Semkiw's *Return of the Revolutionaries* (Hampton Roads Publishing Company, 2003).

By the time the *Revolutionaries* book came out, I had experienced many spontaneous recalls and at least twenty guided past-life therapy sessions, where more insights came. Many of my spontaneous and revealed lives have been confirmed by one or more talented intuitives. I had also conducted many hundreds of past-life therapy sessions with patients, friends, family members, and students. I consider it to be the most powerful psychotherapeutic tool available to us.

I no longer "believe" in reincarnation: I know this is the reality in which we live. I am writing this brief personal experience of the subject of *Bringing Your Soul to Light* to emphasize my rapport with this critical scientific foundation. I have explored progression into the future with some success and with a few remarkable examples of precognition. Although I have not yet explored time between lives, this additional aspect of our continuity obviously has to be an essential part of the whole.

Bringing Your Soul to Light is a wonderful introduction to fill that gap in our understanding of the complex interrelations we share with each other. I think you will want to take advantage of Dr. Backman's message that an exploration of life between lives will enable you to experience:

- release from the fear of death and any presupposition that there is nothing afterwards;
- understanding of the soul's overall purpose and of the purpose of the incarnation under review;
- awareness of members of one's primary soul family or current cohort;

- meeting one's spirit guides;

- receiving a nonjudgmental evaluation of current soul progress;

- receiving information on choices made for the current life, such as body, parents, spouse, life circumstances, etc.;

- receiving energetic healing on a physical and/or soul level; and

- simply and poignantly re-experiencing the reality of residing in the spiritual realm.

What glorious potential. I encourage you to read and then to experience. Your life will be forever changed—for the better!

C. Norman Shealy, MD, PhD
President, Holos University Graduate Seminary
President, International Society for the Study of
Subtle Energy and Energy Medicine
Founding President, American
Holistic Medical Association

Dr. Shealy is a neurosurgeon who developed a number of innovative approaches to pain management, including Transcutaneous Electrical Nerve Stimulation (TENS). He is the author of over 300 papers and twenty-five books, including *Life Beyond 100*.

acknowledgments

*W*ith a body of accounts that is beginning to grow exponentially in the field of soul-regression therapy, ever more light is shining on the great mystery of birth, death, and rebirth. I believe this is neither an accident nor a surprise, and that humanity is coming into a new and more subtle consciousness of itself and of all the kingdoms, seen and unseen, that surround it. It is a privilege and a blessing to be able to offer this book as a window onto the soul and a bridge into the spiritual realm of all that is and ever will be.

It is truly impossible to offer thanks to every incarnate and discarnate soul whose involvement has served as the seed, the soil, the air, and the water to allow these pages to come into reality. However, I would like to begin by honoring the number eight. Eight indicates regeneration and progression and is an apt description of the current times we are experiencing. Eight special people, special souls, in my present incarnation provide incredible warmth and joy in my life.

To Joel, my son; Teresa, my daughter-in-law; Braydon, "Curly," my grandson; Toni, my daughter; Randy, my son-in-law; Daniel, "Mr. D," my grandson; and Gabrielle, "Precious Face," my granddaughter: you are beyond important to me. The love of my life (and of other lives as well) is Earl, my husband of more than forty-one years. Earl and I have walked many roads

side by side and are partners beyond this earth. I give thanks to the divine;
Baruch Hashem.

Many others deserve recognition and thanks, but it's likely this book
would not have seen the light of day without the special contribution of two
precious beings who have graced my journey in this life and gone before into
the next. I thank our second son, Adam, who came into our lives for just
an hour or two at birth. With the wisdom that has now been granted me, I
believe his death was a soul agreement lovingly and in greatest compassion
preincarnationally conceived between Adam and Earl and me, his parents.
It opened the floodgates to my understanding of grief as one of the greatest
teachers of all.

And I also thank my dear friend, colleague, and business partner in psychology, Dr. Lynn F. Greenlee, Jr., who will always be Bud to me. Soon after
his passing in 1993, I began having the spiritual experiences that were my
first "window on the soul" and that led me to pursue my research and training in soul-regression therapy. I will be forever grateful to the spiritual realm
for having known and lost from earthly life these two special ones.

Allow me now to simply acknowledge by name, and in no particular
order, those people who have contributed the "bricks" to build this book:
Chris, my first between-lives soul regression client; Dr. Mark "Mordechai"
Cohen, who believed in me and the work of soul regression; Mary, my wise
advisor and sounding board; Dr. Michael Newton, who brought this work
to the planet; and all the students and clients of the Ravenheart Center who
have studied and trained to anchor this new approach in the world. The
names of so many of you float into my mind, and my heart is filled with the
love of your souls.

Many client examples and case studies are included this book. All client
names have been changed to protect their confidentiality. I take this opportunity to express my deepest gratitude and warmly thank them for sharing
their insights and stories to provide you with this window onto the soul.

Lastly, I send heartfelt thanks to Carrie Obry, acquisitions editor at
Llewellyn Worldwide, who found me; to Diana Holland, my private editor,
who is truly a "godsent"; and to all of the others who have traveled the path
with me, offering enlightenment at every turn.

author's note

$\mathcal{T}$he more people I meet, both in my personal life and in my practice as a therapist, trainer, and speaker, the more people I find who believe in reincarnation. Over and again, I get questions like:

- What is the purpose of my current life?
- What happens when I die?
- Does experiencing *déjà vu* indicate that I have lived before?
- Do I have past lives that are affecting my present life?

As you have opened this book, I assume you are at least curious about reincarnation, and that you may even know for sure you have lived before. Some people come into the world with that certainty. The journey from "maybe" to "acceptance" took me a number of years. The same may be true for you, or you may discredit reincarnation altogether, or even be sublimely indifferent about it one way or another.

It doesn't matter. The intent of this book is not to prove or disprove the truth of reincarnation. Based on thousands of first-hand accounts, this book simply explains what happens when we gain access to past lives and to the between-life continuum though the process known as regression hypnotherapy.

Welcome to *Bringing Your Soul to Light*, an exploration of the soul's journey. Undergoing a soul regression allows you to access and experience aspects of your past lives and also the period when you exist as pure soul energy between lives. Here you can discover the true nature of your soul and get details about your soul's journey. You will receive information about what lies on the other side, and guidance is often given on the plan for your current life, its purposes and progress. Whether you choose to experience a soul regression session now or ever, it is my hope that reading this book will assist you in advancing your soul understanding and progress.

Details of a soul regression, including the length of a session, information on locating a trained regression hypnotherapist, and what to expect can be found in the Resources section of this book.

For practitioners, the between-lives soul regression induction process is highly specific, with particular hypnotic commands, sequencing, and instruction. Please be sure to receive appropriate training and practice in the methodology before attempting to guide a client to access the soul state. For details on both past-life soul regression and between-lives soul regression training, see the Resources section at the back of the book.

I believe that the soul is pure energy, an essence of light and color that emanates from the divine and innervates matter. To use an analogy, it is the gasoline that activates our car body as we breathe moment by moment. When we die, our soul is released from the confines of being human. It reunites for a time with our higher self, the eternal and essential part of our being that is its holographic counterpart in spirit, before resuming its physical journey and life lessons by incarnating again.

To begin this work, I would like to share with you how I discovered that soul energy does indeed carry over from life to life, a phenomenon known as continuity of consciousness.

I was being trained in the work of soul regression at the time, and I remember that day with great clarity. I had just left the hotel room of my student partner, where I had experienced a practice session serving as the client. My mind was sifting through the various details I had received. Suddenly, as I was walking along the hotel hallway toward my room, I latched on to an amazing correlation between the past life I'd just examined and my present life.

During the past life, I was a teenage female who had been taken to a concentration camp during the Holocaust. Many images of the past-life events continue to be crystal clear in my mind. My beautiful home had been stormed by soldiers and ransacked. Elegant crystal objects fell to the floor in pieces like broken hearts. Our nightmare journey to the camp was in a tight, dark space, where I clung to my beloved uncle as if he were my lifeblood.

Because I was young and capable, I was assigned to work in the makeshift camp hospital. The beds appeared to be rectangles of heavy fabric stretched between four pegs in the ground. My daily task was to walk from bed to bed tending to the seriously ill and dying. All I could do was to wipe their faces beaded with sweat, attempt to remove what I could of the putrid-smelling vomit, urine, and excrement, and soothe these dear souls in whatever manner possible.

I came to a bed where an emaciated man lay close to death. This skeleton clothed in skin was my dear uncle with whom I'd come to the camp. My heart knew what was needed. Cautiously, I slipped into the bed to lay parallel to my uncle, facing his back. With my arms wrapped like a blanket around his body, I held him tightly until he exhaled his final breath. I had no fear of sharing this priceless moment with him. My student partner asked if I recognized my uncle as anyone I knew in my current life. Within an instant, I spoke the name of a cousin who is very dear to me today.

After reliving my time in the camp and completing the soul regression, I stepped into the hotel hallway and turned right to walk the short distance to my room. Suddenly, I realized an uncanny parallel between that life in the late 1930s or early 1940s and my life today. (In my present life, I was born in 1946.)

In 1960, when I was fourteen years old (approximately the same age I had been when my uncle died in the camp), the phone rang around dinner time in my home. It was my aunt, instructing my mother, father, and me to come quickly to their home a few blocks away. My favorite uncle in this life had suffered his second heart attack.

That night, for the first time in my current life, I experienced observing the end of a life as my uncle took his final breath. The details are inextricably written in my core. The cousin that I named in my practice session as the uncle in my Holocaust life is the son of my uncle who died in 1960.

I relate this story to you because it was at that exact moment in the hotel hallway, as I completed compiling these analogies between my past and current life elements, that I became a true believer in the continuity of soul consciousness. I knew for myself that soul energy does indeed carry over from life to life.

Whether you choose to experience regression hypnotherapy for yourself or are simply curious, may this book be for you a window on the soul.

chapter 1

I did not begin when I was born, nor when I was
conceived. I have been growing, developing, through
incalculable myriads of millenniums. All my previous
selves have their voices, echoes, promptings in
me. Oh, incalculable times again shall I be born.

—*Jack London*

What Is Soul Regression Hypnotherapy?

Regression hypnotherapy is a mechanism, or tool, that allows an individual to access the memory of past lives and of the period when we are pure soul between lives. It is an experience of stepping back and forth, rather like a seesaw, from a place in current time where there is a past and a future into a timeless space where we are, and always will be, pure soul energy.

During soul regression hypnotherapy, we function simultaneously in body and in the spiritual realm, experiencing our higher self, that holographic counterpart of our deepest essence that resides permanently in spirit. During this encounter, we are gifted with the ageless and eternal knowledge of who we truly are: pure soul.

Regression hypnotherapy is thus a powerful tool. In simple terms, it refers to the use by a trained practitioner of specific breathing techniques, guided imagery, and other noninvasive means to guide the client into a natural state of relaxation, or trance hypnosis, that is conducive to accessing information beyond that of current life data.

All of our past lives, and therefore information about them, are believed to be held within the Akashic Records. *Akasha* is a Sanskrit word meaning sky, space, or aether; the concept of Akashic Records was developed in the nineteenth century. It is believed that these records are real but energetic, existing in a nonphysical plane. While in trance, the client is able to utilize intuition to become aware of past-life events and details.

The regression covers two distinct areas: a past-life soul regression is a regression into a past life. A between-lives soul regression includes a past-life regression to the death scene and beyond, where time and space are one, and the client steps into "now" time. Thus, past-life and between-lives regressions can be and often are conducted separately, but the between-lives soul regression includes both.

The vast majority of regression hypnotherapists use the standard methods of trance induction listed above to guide the client into an altered, meditative state, just as they would do in any other general hypnotherapeutic session, be it for insomnia, pain control, anxiety, or related psychobiological needs. In addition to a standard trance induction, past-life and between-lives regression include a specialized induction for the purposes of soul-regression hypnotherapy.

General hypnotherapy can be utilized for many purposes, including weight loss, smoking cessation, improving self-esteem, easing childbirth, and the aforementioned examples. Basically, general hypnotherapy is tied to utilizing our embodied self via an altered state of consciousness to focus on and alleviate or improve a current physical or emotional issue.

Regression hypnotherapy is often labeled transpersonal hypnotherapy because there is a metaphysical or spiritual component, where clients experience themselves from the soul level, where the core of our being resides. In regression hypnotherapy, any desired present-life alteration stems from a conscious and unconscious process led by the client's higher self and their team of spiritual guides and teachers.

The end result of all regression hypnotherapy is therapeutic, serving to aid clients in understanding themselves on a soul level, thus benefiting their current lives through releasing energetic and conscious remnants of past-life trauma. And so the dual components of this work, past-life soul regression and between-lives soul regression, may also be referred to simply as soul therapy.

Having practiced general psychotherapy for approximately half of my thirty-year career as a licensed psychologist, I find the work of regression hypnotherapy to be fascinating and powerful. Though I by no means suggest minimizing the value of general psychotherapy, I have discovered that the holistic spiritual perspective innate to regression hypnotherapy offers boundless depth and dimension as a healing instrument. I invite you to spend a few minutes reading Appendix A: Practitioner Notes for some important general considerations.

Now let me take you through a between-lives soul regression to give you a sense of what takes place during it. A session generally lasts about three to four hours, and in the first step, the client is guided by a trained regression hypnotherapist to first move through a past life, gaining whatever details of that incarnation come into awareness. Ultimately, the client is guided to move to the final moments of that life and describe what happens.

With the therapist's subsequent instruction to progress beyond physical dying into the spiritual realm, a spirit guide will appear in about 80 percent of cases to aid in healing the client. Our team of spirit guides and wise elders will be discussed later at length, but I mention their appearance here because the between-lives portion of the soul regression technically begins at this juncture. At the end of the session, the client is gently guided back to the present life and present moment to finish up with a debriefing.

Neither the client nor the therapist has complete control over the session. It is the client's team of guides and teachers in the unseen world who determine the content of the regression. However, clients may bring to the session a short list of questions. More often than not, the therapist is able to assist them in making a request to obtain the desired answers. Frequently, all queries will be answered, while on other occasions, only certain questions receive a response. What is most necessary for clients to be made aware of is benevolently determined by the higher wisdom of their spirit team.

The most common question that prospective or new clients ask is, "How often do you find someone who cannot go into trance?" Most clients' greatest concern is that they will not be able to relax sufficiently to access the memory of past lives or the period of time they are pure soul between lives.

Light trance, or the slowing of mental activity to a light alpha brain wave state, which is discussed elsewhere in greater detail, is all that is needed for past-life soul regression. It is extremely rare when I have a client who cannot achieve the necessary trance state. In fact, no more than 1–2 percent of my clients have any difficulty moving into a light trance. Technically, the client must be in a somewhat deeper trance, either deep alpha or upper theta brain wave state, to gain memory of the period between lives. Only a slightly higher percentage of my clients, approximately 3–5 percent, are unable to move into this depth of altered state of consciousness.

In other words, the vast majority of people have little or no difficulty allowing themselves to be guided to the levels of trance state required for past-life soul regression and for between-lives soul regression—and rightly so. Shifting our brain waves into reduced arousal mode is a completely normal occurrence that happens every night as we move toward relaxation and into the sleep state.

Returning to our description, the regression therapist begins the session with a complex, lengthy induction to guide the client into trance. The first stage includes guiding the client back in time in their present life, moving all the way to the time of being in their mother's womb, and ultimately to the accessing of soul memory.

Next, the regression therapist uses past-life induction to assist the client in discovering an important past-life scene. There are many different means to accessing a past life. Most often, I use the image of a hallway that is called the Hall of Wisdom or the Hall of Records. There are many doors on both sides of the hall. Each life story is behind a particular door. The client moves through the past life they have accessed, retrieving knowledge concerning important people and significant events, including where, how, and with whom their dying happened.

So what do clients say actually happens at the point of death?

People undergoing soul regression describe their physical departure in myriad ways. By some accounts, the leave-taking occurs in a single, simple breath. For others, it is a complicated, intense disturbance. For many, there is a sense of expansion and even exhilaration as the soul escapes the confines of the flesh.

Whatever the nature of the relived death, once the soul has expanded outside of the body, the experience and related shock of dying seem to melt away. We simply leave our physical container behind, increasing our energetic vibration as we release the past-life body and step into the spiritual realm.

So at the outset, let me calm any concern about moving through the dying experience on the last day of a past life while a soul regression session is in process. Regardless of the cause of physical death—whether by illness, a plane crash, stabbing, or any other sudden or painful means—the client will not experience the level of pain that we imagine would be associated with the death trauma.

The manner in which clients move through reliving the past death also varies greatly. Some choose to simply watch the dying scene without being entrenched moment by moment. Other clients will sense, to some slight degree, the physical trauma. For example, if a client dies from a respiratory illness, there may be minor coughing or pressure felt in the chest. Finally, some clients process the experience more abstractly and will simply tell the therapist something like, "I have died, and my soul is leaving the body in the past life."

While past-life soul regression may include some slight vestige of traumatic events, between-lives soul regression is never focused on trauma. On the material level, the soul is simply pure energy, consisting of waves of light and color. When we die, our soul is released from the confines of being human. This soul energy must increase in vibration in order to exit the body and reunite with its holographic counterpart in spirit.

Through thousands of soul regression sessions, individuals have encountered—and described in vivid detail—what a profound experience it is to experience their essential being as a soul unencumbered by the trappings of the flesh. They use words like *misty, peaceful, quiet, a kaleidoscope of color, free,* and *expansive* to describe the sensory experience of crossing into the spiritual realm as the soul exits the body and begins its voyage home.

The following is a direct transcription of a client session beginning on the last day of the past life.

*S*arah: THE FINAL DAY

I'm out milking the goats. And I know this is the day I am leaving. John, my husband, is around. It feels like we are going to go together. I don't know how you do that. I let the goats go free after I milk them. I go inside and cook breakfast. I do the daily chores. I am old—in my nineties. There is something wrong with my legs. I can't figure out what it is about the legs. John is in bed. He did not eat much breakfast. He is sick. He has lost a leg. He lost it in his work. I tend to him and make him comfortable. He is dying.

I am going to go with him, to die with him. My life is done. I did good work. I am old and creaky. It is okay… okay to go. I make a sweet tea. It has bitter herbs. I make it sweet. The tea will stop the heart.

John has now died. I am in bed with John when I drink the tea. I took care of everything. Everything is clean. The animals are taken care of. I am now gone.

Dr. Backman: "Your soul knows exactly what happens at the point of physical dying. Where are you now as a soul in relation to your body?"

It feels peaceful. I am hovering over my body. John has left already. He will be up there. I feel much emotion now. (Tears come.) The peace is wonderful. To be with somebody I love and who loves me. I did good work in that life. I am going to have peace in my current life like I have had with John.

The soul is holographic, or divisible. When we incarnate, a portion of our soul energy steps into the body, while a mirror-image complement remains in spirit.

Here is another client's account of the soul leaving the body and finding her way home at the end of a past life.

Jonathan: I KNOW WHERE I AM SUPPOSED TO GO

I have pneumonia. My young apprentice is mixing herbs and plasters. I do not want to die in the work room and contaminate the herbs. There are blankets all around me to keep me warm. I am having trouble breathing. I can't get enough air. My apprentice is with me. I die. It is just like a sigh. My apprentice is watching. She seems sad. She knows I am not completely gone. I will help her sometimes. I will jog her memory.

Now I feel very floaty. I feel a nice pulsing. It is misty and foggy and mostly white. I do not feel alone, but there is no one specific with me. I am moving now. I know where I am supposed to go. There are more colors in the fog. Someone is here now. I feel at home. I feel a welcoming. I hear the words, "Glad you are back."

Numerous clients ask whether their passage into spirit upon death will be assisted by a loved one who has died many years ago and may even have reincarnated. The answer is yes, because a quantity of our soul remains always in the spiritual realm. This is our higher self.

I suspect that many of you reading this book would say you have sensed on this side of the veil the presence of a loved one who has left the earth. Do any of the following client statements sound familiar? If so, you know what I am describing.

"My phone rang three times in a row, and no one was there. It was the day of my father's birthday."

"Every time I decided to hike on that trail, at the very same location a butterfly would appear."

"The lamp that always worked beautifully in the past starting turning off on its own."

"I simply felt her presence in the room."

"I smelled her perfume while I was completely alone."

"To my surprise and amazement, the clock in the hall had stopped at the exact time of my father-in-law's death."

When you recognize the soul consciousness or feel the embrace of a special person who has left the earth, the strength and beauty of that presence is palpable. It is as if we can taste, touch, and even smell it. The soul is the mediating, or bridging, principle of consciousness. Believing that our loved ones who have died maintain soul consciousness affords us a link, a means of continuing to know that their energy remains.

Regression can provide an amazing opportunity to commune with a loved one in spirit. Deborah's story is a good example.

Deborah: AFTER-DEATH SOUL COMMUNICATION

Deborah came for a session hoping to discover why her beloved husband, Sam, had left the earth and herself behind. As Deborah described their

*former soul bond in the current life, it was graphically clear how this couple
fit together like hand in glove.*

*Deborah initially scheduled a past-life soul regression, in which she dis-
covered a previous life where Sam was a comfortably melded life partner
who offered her strength and protection. Under hypnosis near the start of
her session, Deborah "crossed through the gateway" into the soul regression, with words like* bright, warm, tingly, *and* twinkling lights. *Deborah then
stated:*

There is someone here. He feels like "home." He is always there with
me. He has to learn something, and so do I. He did make the clock fall off
the table in our present house after he died. All souls can't move objects,
but Sam can.

He takes me to a table with something rolled up on it. These are the
"blueprints" of my current life. I will have to learn how to deal with grief. I
did not do that well before. I must learn to not be so dependent, to care for
myself. We never say goodbye. Life always continues. He's there to help
me until my life is over. Sam was done. There will be no more incarnations
for Sam. I wasn't ready to be done. I must stay to help our son deal with his
grief, and other people too.

Sam will assist from the other side. He is the soul I am closest to. We
teach each other. We travel together, guide each other, and sacrifice for
each other if needed. I will be happy again.

Following the regression, having been able to feel his presence again, Deborah knows at a core level that Sam's soul energy remains near to her in the
spiritual realm. While the physical loss of a loved one can be unspeakably
painful, the concrete knowing that their soul energy is eternal offers indescribable comfort. I have spent many years working with bereaved clients
where the loss of a loved one has been profoundly devastating, and I know
this to be true.

Let us now continue our description of the soul regression session by moving through the between-lives portion.

Whatever the precise circumstances, at the completion of the past life, the
client recognizes that the soul leaves the body, the physical container where

it has been housed during that particular embodiment, or lifetime. The client's soul may choose to take a brief time for energetic closure in the past life. Then, with a sense of autopilot, the client's soul travels onward into the spiritual realm. Many relate that the experience of soul expansion is nearly indescribable.

In fact, the client will virtually never be able to verbalize the level of detail and the sensory experience that unfolds. Not only is there a rapid and rich tapestry occurring, but at the same time, the human language is incapable of capturing the full taste, touch, and smell of the soul-level experience.

Past-life soul regression may or may not include a review of traumatic instances that occurred during that life. Between-lives soul regression, as an extension and further evolution stemming from a past-life soul regression, brings in the death scene and steps us into the period of time when we are discarnate, or without a body. In simple language, during the between-lives segment, clients experience who they are at their core soul level rather than who they are in various lifetimes.

Between lives in the spiritual realm, the client is first met and greeted, usually by their spirit guide or by closely associated souls. To reiterate, it is technically at this point that the actual between-lives portion of the session begins. Occasionally, when a client is unable to move into the time between lives, it is not due to lack of trance depth, but rather that their guide has chosen to block them from experiencing the interlife period.

In such cases, the guide will generally state what work the client must accomplish in life before being allowed to access the soul state. When clients are informed by the guide why they cannot travel into the between-lives state, they are hardly ever surprised. Many have already been aware of the personal introspection or other change that would benefit their life. The experience is one of loving support; there is never any blame or recrimination from our team of spirit guides and wise elders.

Numerous possibilities open up for the individual once greeted: there may be time spent evaluating the past life; deep and powerful healing may be provided to support the client both in the present incarnation and following the past-life experience; the soul family may present themselves; very often the wise elders will appear to guide, support, and offer current advice to the client; and the client may learn the purpose or reason behind their preincarnational choice of body, personality, and relationships for today's life. Some clients have reached a juncture in their current incarnation where a visit to the spiritual realm is like a meal to someone who is nearly starving. They get to deeply remember that they are truly a soul.

We are always loved and accepted in the spiritual realm. Upon arrival, having concluded another lifetime, we often come immediately into our soul family, the group of souls with whom we've been the most familiar from the very start of our soul journey. Clients seem to know this has been their base of operations starting from day one as a spark of divine energy.

Further information on the soul family can be found in chapter 5. For now, here is a taste of one client's soul family reunion.

Gary: PASSING OVER

I am in bed. My hair is white. My great-niece, great-nephew, and children are there. My sister and mother have died. I am not ready to forgive. A thickness holds my soul in my body. I need to go up and through. The people in the room hold me. They are frightened. They do not believe I will go to a better place. I embrace them. They let my soul leave. I ask for spirit to come. There is a lot of light. There are hands on my arms gently pulling me. I sense heart-like crystals in my body break loose.

I am becoming more diffuse. I'm drifting, and it is getting brighter. There is lots of light. Everything feels familiar. I feel a welcoming. A blue light envelops me. Now there is a greeter with me. This is the one who oversees the guides. I am welcomed back. I am told that I did okay.

First, I am encouraged to rest. After a time, there is a cluster of lights. I feel joy and excitement. There are fifteen lights. This is my group. They are in front of me. We square dance, moving in and out. We reintegrate by weaving together and rubbing our edges. This is gentle and playful. Now I feel more settled, less strange. I am enclosed by the group and held. I feel floaty, peaceful, full of sweet love and nourishment.

Every between-lives soul regression is different and characteristic of the client's present needs. The possibilities related to what is received are endless, as Nan's experience shows.

Nan: A REPRESENTATIVE CASE

In regression, Nan is experiencing the last day of her past life:

I am in a room with friends. I am grateful for no pain and for peaceful quiet. Nobody is upset with my going. I am ready to go and feel blessed by the support of these dear people. I feel the energy of grace in the room. This has been an important life. I feel emotional pain, but I accept this pain and the help from others. All is okay.

Now I feel pulsations and twinkling. The light becomes strong and steady. There is one bright blue light in the center. I hear, "I am." This is my guide. I feel his warmth and his welcome. He walks with me with his arm around me. We're going somewhere. He exudes joy, and we're celebrating.

Now I am with my council of wise elders. They say, "You are ready for the Ascension. Peace on earth is the potential. You are ready to create it. The earth is ready, and you are ready. Carry the light. This is your life purpose. You can be peaceful in chaos."

They continue by saying that I am giving away too much of my power. They tell me to nurture myself first. They say, "You have the answers. Be brave." There is a huge potential for the earth when I carry the light. Carrying the light is not easy. "You must balance your need to fix along with being a healer," they add. "There is no true healing with fixing." I will be guided to where I am needed to hold the light. Now I hear beautiful, vibrating tonal music. I am to know that music can be healing.

Nan's case highlights key soul elements that are useful for all of us. Often at the end of life, there is a palpable sense of spiritual grace in the room. As dying occurs, the presence of loved ones already gone ahead provides a clearly marked pathway for the soul to exit. The experience of ending a life can, and often does, feel perfectly okay.

As with Nan, a smooth crossing occurs for most clients, whereby the soul exits the nonfunctioning body and travels into increasing light. With ease the guide arrives, and the client welcomes a conscious renewal of the bond with their "spirit buddy."

Nan learns from her wise elders that her purpose in life is not something pragmatic like "be a better computer programmer or attorney." It resonates deeply when she is told that her role is to carry the highest energy, described as "light," to assist in expanding peace on our planet.

Nan will be shown when and where she is to offer her work. It is not her job to "fix" or "cure" anyone; her role is to hold love and the highest energy of spirit at her core. In a loving but firm manner, she is reminded to take care of herself first. The underlying message is that it is not self-centered to remember to meet our own needs.

Before starting the regression portion of a client session, I explain clearly that the spiritual realm is in charge of the content that will be received. At times, our personal team of guides and teachers will speak in just the manner Nan's did and provide some esoteric detail, but like Nan, most clients have no difficulty comprehending and registering what was directed specifically to them. (Chapter 4 offers fuller details concerning one's spirit team.)

The power and impact of past-life soul regression and between-lives soul regression to illumine one's soul journey is very profound. The vantage point I hope you have glimpsed is that a soul regression can provide myriad details and information.

Following are one client's comments after experiencing several sessions:

Clara: THE FREEDOM THAT COMES FROM FORGIVENESS

For most of my life, I've experienced a feeling of not belonging. When the feeling struck, I felt as if I was in a world in which I just didn't belong. There was even a day when I was in my late teens when my mother said to me, "You are not like the others (meaning her other children); you think differently from everyone else."

At the time, I was perplexed by her words because even though I felt different, I didn't think it showed to anyone else. Her words stayed with me throughout my adult life. It was not until I read *Journey of Souls* and

Destiny of Souls by Michael Newton and eventually met Dr. Backman that I would find the answers.

My experiences with past-life soul regression and between-lives soul regression have been so profound, and they have brought me a sense of peace about myself. Finding the connections to people that I know in this lifetime, to other cultures and, more importantly, to other worlds, has allowed me to embrace that feeling of not belonging.

There is always one universal thought that is revealed in each session. It is that love is more important than anything else we experience.

One particular session stressed this very strongly. As often happens following a session, it took a few hours to process what I had learned. After this particular session, I went home and sat in front of my computer and allowed the message to come through as I typed.

I was told to remember that the pain experienced here is temporary and that beyond the pain is forgiveness, and that beyond forgiveness is pure, honest love. That is the process...that is the lesson.

When we give love freely, we allow ourselves to be vulnerable as humans. That vulnerability will lead to pain; at some time, in some way, there will be loss. Through the pain we grow, as long as we forgive and remember with love as we move forward. Our backward glances should always be through the eyes of love.

We humans place much too much significance on our actual life, when the life is what is so temporary. The beauty of forgiveness, the freedom that comes from forgiveness, and the love that follows—that is what is eternal.

For some clients, a soul regression session is a once-in-a-lifetime event. For others, a return visit occurs more than once. As a soul regression is intended by the client's spirit guides and wise elders to serve the client's current life needs, each session is timely and distinct. General benefits are discussed in the next chapter.

We've covered many ideas about soul regression in this introductory chapter. Many of them may seem strange and possibly overwhelming. Appendix B: Basic Tenets of Soul-Regression Hypnotherapy gives a very clear summary of the belief structure that supports past-life and between-lives soul regression. Consult it now and again in the course of reading this book—say, just before you begin a new chapter—and you may begin to deepen your understanding of this profound subject.

chapter 2

Good for the body is the work of the body,
good for the soul the work of the soul, and
good for either the work of the other.

—*Henry David Thoreau*

The Benefits of Soul Regression

*P*ast lives can affect our current life in every imaginable manner—from the physical to the emotional to the behavioral. Regression into past-life memory "opens the curtain" on specific important scenes and events that we have lived in different times and places, providing an opportunity to unlock our emotions, thoughts, awareness, and energetic blocks stemming from them.

Simply stated, regression hypnotherapy is a precise and powerful tool you can use to access and deepen your understanding of your core self. It can open a unique window on any number of issues and life circumstances, including:

- fear of death;
- health challenges;
- emotions;
- phobias;
- career choices;
- geographic location of residence;
- relationships;
- grieving; and
- karmic situations.

Another benefit of the experience is that during the regression, clients are operating from both an intellectual and an intuitive level, and so they verbalize information stemming from their own intuitive altered state of consciousness. Thus, the outcome and usefulness of the session stem from both thoughts and emotions. At the same time, a powerful and inexplicable process is also generally at work whereby healing is occurring on an energetic level, whether clients are aware of this facet or not.

The karmic benefits of regression hypnotherapy can also be very profound. Uncovering the details of a past life affords us the possibility of cleansing, or releasing, old energy in order to advance. When such energy is cleared, we no longer carry it in our spiritual DNA. Thus, our body, mind, and spirit can function from a lighter, more elevated perspective.

Clearing past patterns can repair and restore our physical well-being, emotional health, relationship challenges, and spiritual understanding. This clearing is what occurred for Dorothy, an herbalist and intuitive healer in her fifties, who stated two main reasons for doing her soul regression: to understand her primary purpose in this life and to get to the source of her feelings of fear, panic, and sadness about teaching herbalism.

Dorothy: LESSONS LEARNED

I am an adult man wearing a belted robe to my knees. I am youngish. My hair is chestnut brown and curly, and I have a beard. I'm wearing a helmet with feathers on top. It feels like I am in the Middle East, in a place with narrow streets where the buildings are narrow, close together, and have arched tops. I feel strong but anxious. This is not my home. I know that something will happen today.

It is later. I am inside a building and underground. I feel alone even though I know there are people around. I do not know the other people well. Everything keeps becoming nebulous. I feel unsure of myself. There is something I do not want to see. There is something taking place that I need to be sure happens. I'm conflicted about the task and the responsibility. I do not agree with the task. I became a soldier because everyone was becoming a soldier. There is an open area with a mob. (Dorothy suddenly feels a lot of grief and sadness.)

This is the crucifixion of Jesus. I feel overwhelmed by the emotion of the crowd. The crowd is upset. There is a quality of illusion going on. They are getting caught up in the mob thing. People are taking the emotion as a guideline for how to act. Each person would be different by themselves. They are in an open area of the street. I am looking down from a hill. I feel strong emotions of grief and sadness. (The client tries to not presuppose the outcome.)

Now I am moving into the mob. I have a soldier's job, which is partly to let the mob take over and partly to control them. They make way for me because I am big. I feel like I am going to burst. I can feel the crowd's energy, and I feel my duty. But what is taking place feels all wrong. This behavior does not jibe with my heart. Some guy is getting railroaded.

The guy feels important to me. We have met before. What happens to him feels unfair. I push the crowd back. I am moving from my heart and caught up in my own emotion. I am trying to stop the whole thing. This makes the crowd angrier. Other soldiers are not happy. They knock me down. They are stomping on me. I cannot get up. They are not letting me up. A spear ends my life.

My death is inconsequential to the whole thing. There are so many forces at work in the whole scene. The events are bigger than me. But my life is not inconsequential. In the end, I went with my heart. This was a good thing. But it was too little too late. Still, this was an important shift for me. I continue to watch the scene about how energy or forces came together to produce that event—what one person can and cannot do. What I did changed things for me, but not for the event. I am sad for Jesus.

During our routine processing time at the end of the session, Dorothy explained how reliving elements from the past life during her regression allowed her to recognize that something there mirrored her sense of ambiguity and confusion today about following one's emotions and being assertive.

As the soldier, she had acted on her sense of duty and her need to fit in. She had involved herself in the use of physical and political power to "railroad" an important figure. At the same time, the behavior of the people in the crowd grew out of emotions that Dorothy felt did not serve a fair outcome. The crowd followed one another's feelings, which seemed disastrous. The Roman soldier followed his heart, thus honoring his truth even though he died in the end.

Dorothy has struggled for most of her current lifetime with viewing assertive behavior as inappropriate. In examining the soldier's dilemma over whether to do his duty and use his strength to perpetrate something wrong (thereby fitting in) or listen to his internal feelings and attempt to quell the mob, she was able to realize that in this lifetime, she can be strong and follow her deeply held emotions at the same time.

By now, you may be wondering, "Why would I want to experience a soul regression? What would it do for me?" If you asked ten clients following their regression, you would likely get ten different answers. The following responses cover a representative range of benefits.

1. Grief Reduction

For some clients, a lessening of grief over the physical loss of a loved one can be the primary gift. Amid the emotional upheaval that ensues, many people have a powerful desire to know where the loved one is following that person's death and to communicate with him or her. Serving as an initial greeter and potentially a conductor into the between-lives portion of the session, a beloved father or significant other who has been sorely missed in everyday life can arrive as the regressed client is crossing into the spiritual realm.

Virtually every time a client has asked the loved one in spirit how he or she is doing, the response has been a resounding "I am completely fine." Even though the client may have previously presumed the loved one was doing very well in the spiritual plane, substantiating this belief is a significant comfort to many. The effect can be almost medicinal.

When the soul of a loved one appears early on, or once the client completes the past life and steps into the time between lives, it is fair to assume that the soul of the loved one and the client's soul are familiar with one another. They have likely incarnated together more than once before and may easily belong to the same soul cluster, or soul family. Chapter 5 discusses the notion of soul family in detail.

2. Experiencing the Spirit Realm

At the end of their soul regression, other clients will describe their time swimming though the spiritual realm to be a profoundly enriching and confirming journey. As incarnate souls, regardless of our spiritual awareness or acumen, moment by moment we operate by melding our human brain and our soul nature.

We may "know" with our brain that our loved ones continue in the unseen, divine realm, which our spiritual understanding trusts is real. Nevertheless, while we are in moderate to deep trance during the soul regression, our perception is in the intuitive mode, meaning that we primarily feel or sense rather than think.

If you have ever had what could be described as a "spiritual experience"— where neither your body, nor time, nor anything else human mattered—perhaps you recognize what I am attempting to describe.

Palpably returning to the spiritual realm while we are still living our current life serves as an indescribable buoy for many clients. Others may be still struggling to unlearn a previous rationalistic, scientific, or religious perspective whereby this life, this body, are all we have and ever will have.

For those who have only recently begun to understand and accept the reality of soul consciousness, walking through the graphic, sensory experience of being a soul leaving the body at the completion of a lifetime and encountering elements in the spiritual realm can be of immense value.

At the opposite end of the spectrum, clients who have long since accepted soul continuity may find life on earth to be frequently unbearable in its apparent senselessness and cruelty. A visit to bask in their "true home" can allow such clients to carry on with everyday life. Of course, there are numerous clients in between, who leave their soul regression sensing they have tasted, touched, heard, and even smelled the reality of their soul. It never hurts to spend some time in the Promised Land, even when we are already believers.

3. Receiving Healing

Many would agree that we store the memory of past lives in our spiritual DNA, or spiritual cellular memory. Thus, we hold remnants of past-life experience and trauma that affects our current life in simple yet profound ways. One soul regression client described a burning in his throat from which he had suffered for many years and that no medical personnel had been able to diagnose or cure.

As the details of a past life began to coalesce, it became obvious that this client had died in the Holocaust by breathing the noxious fumes of the gas chamber. Following the regression, the client's symptoms were considerably lessened, if not fully alleviated. Soul regression often serves in healing imbedded trauma from past-life ordeals.

4. Reviewing Significant Lives

Each soul regression client receives their own "tailor-made" session detail, which is designed and coordinated by the person's guides and teachers, the team of discarnate souls who assist us in daily life, both within and outside our awareness.

A particular past life may have been significantly complex and left behind emotional, physical, behavioral, and/or spiritual remnants. One soul-regression client describes a past-life experience as follows:

Denise: A HEALING SPIRIT GUIDE

Client: "I am an American Indian female looking out over the cliffs. I feel sad. I've seen the death of animals and people. I talk to Spirit, saying, 'O Great Spirit, why?' There is too much sadness."

The client's spirit guide appears and says, "You have done well. You have carried the sadness of your people." The guide holds his arm over the head of the native woman as she kneels, and he seems to assist in healing her.

Client: "My people died of sickness, of health issues. They starved in the cold Wyoming snow. I wear something on my chest. It collects pain for all time."

The guide takes off the breastplate. The plate turns silver and rises into the sky as a bright star.

Client: "My guide is healing me. I have scars. He's touching my chest. He erases each of the names on my chest."

In this example, the client accesses the story of a past life and also receives healing from a spirit guide.

5. Encounter with the Spirit Guide

Chapter 4 provides details concerning the purpose and value of a spirit guide. At this point, a simple explanation is that we each have such a guide to direct and support us. Our spirit guide is most often more advanced than we are but never uses that advantage to judge, blame, or punish.

Many clients who come for a soul regression want specifically to meet their spirit guide and confirm that they indeed have a "spirit buddy" in the unseen spiritual realm. An encounter of this nature does occur about 80 percent of the time, since a key general function of the spirit guide is to help the newly deceased soul to travel within the divine realm and negotiate the transition. When a spirit guide does not appear, it is generally an indication that the client's soul is relatively advanced.

6. Encounter with the Soul Family

During their pre-session interview, many clients express a desire to meet members of their soul family during their soul regression. In simple terms, our acquaintance with these comrades begins in our spiritual "homeroom," and we incarnate frequently with these souls. Many clients wish to validate an acute sense of familiarity they have in their current life as well as possible past-life connections with particular people/souls. Such details about former relationships can be enormously useful in explaining the quality of present-life interactions (more on this topic in chapter 5).

The following is one client's journey of dying, leaving the earth, and encountering his spirit guide and soul family during soul regression to learn his true character as a soul.

Bob: MY SISTER'S KEEPER

I am going to a white temple with columns. There is a waterfall there, and it is cool. My entire group is there. My spirit guide manages a group of precocious children. The temple gives us an enclosed space in which to communicate. If we don't have an enclosed space, we just dart around. We need a container.

There are twelve in my group. We are a group, a team. We like each other. We're very energetic, changing, and silly. We're hard to manage and adventurous in a mental way. We're not easily corralled. (Seven souls are identified by current life name and their soul color identified. This topic is discussed in chapter 9.) When I meet any of the others in my current life, I will know them. Some are not incarnate. Karen from my soul family is my sister in this life, and she is giving me quite a ride this time.

My spirit guide says: "You needed to be challenged in this life to accept Karen not being so good. Karen sees this as an adventure. She is trying on a non-pristine life."

We are all a team. We help each other. We are all so serious on earth. We need more time to relax, which we do now. I am now being taken to a classroom, where I will sit at a desk and learn how to not be so serious and to be more like my true soul nature.

7. Encounter with the Wise Elders

A primary focus of the soul regression can be an encounter with one's council of wise elders. For the majority of clients, the bulk of the guidance and advice received during the soul regression session stems from the spirit guide, the wise elders, or both. Each of us, as a soul, has our very own conglomerate of these high-level teachers who provide guidance, support, and all-loving acceptance (chapter 4 provides further information).

Here is an example of time spent by a client meeting with his council. The elders generally appear in front of the client, seated at a table of some formal nature, often on a raised dais. It is relatively unusual for the council to be seated on the floor, as in this case. In this particular example, it is an indication that the client is a highly developed soul.

Maya: A LIFE REVIEW

We are in a Greek-seeming temple with a rounded dome and open sides. There are four or five of them, all in robes and sitting on the floor. They tell me I've been in lives before where it was easy to be myself. This time, I have chosen a life where it is more difficult to be truly who I am. I am quite an accomplished soul. This time, I will have to work to find a way to honor the truth of my soul's advancement. I have chosen a difficult family to be born into.

My task is to find my own light and let it shine and not be bogged down or align with the style of my childhood family. Many of my soul family are in my present life. We have or will find each other. Then I can truly be myself. We can come together and create very bright light. This is an exciting life with much adventure. I haven't truly let my light shine yet. I've taken the difficulty of this life much too seriously.

I need to work with energy. As a soul, we get too caught up with the story of each life, but it is just a story. I must remember who I truly am. This will change who I am in my work. I must just be myself. I spend too much time covering up who I am. I am doing pretty well but need to simply shine more.

Wise elders are never punitive or judgmental. Having a meeting or an audience with souls of great wisdom generally provides input as to how you are doing in your current life, along with support and guidance in your daily process of moving forward moment by moment. Chapter 8, Life Direction, presents details from soul regression sessions concerning the question, "Are we ever off-track in our current life?"

8. Life Purpose and Plan

The most common question clients would like answered during their soul regression is, "What is my present life purpose? In other words, for what key reason did I step into this life?"

This topic is discussed at greater length in chapter 6, but for now, let us cover a few main points. Each life does have an overall intention. Some lives are designed for an explicit reason, while others have a more generic intent.

The overarching purpose of our soul, and therefore of our lives, is to progress as an individual soul and, in gaining individual wisdom, to enhance universal consciousness. Each of our lives serves as a crucial element in the ocean of the universe. Here are some glimpses of soul purpose during the current life as described by different clients:

- This life is about not being concerned about money. I need to be focused on a good, clean, and kind universe, where life is functioning well and healthily. I need to be focused on universal values.

- You are to move into creative healing. Be less narrow in what is important in your life. Relinquish your current status quo regarding (corporate) work and income. Part of your remaining with the status quo is the drama there. Let go of the need for the drama, and you will be released from the energy outlay of the drama. Do not scatter your energy: be more focused.

- Your life purpose is not about changing the world. You are to affect people in your space, in your immediate life. You are to be a good person. You are to be understanding and loving. You are to be a good mom. You are to be happy.

In some lives, we "take a rest," which is often well-deserved. When you notice that somebody else seems to be leading a life more carefree than yours, please do not judge. You cannot know the complexity or difficulty of other lives that person has led. As souls, we are all advancing at the perfect speed for our journey at any point in time.

Other clients discover their life purpose to be highly painful and complex. Perhaps it involves dealing with loss of loved ones, loss of physical health, and other similarly challenging life circumstances that befall us. Soul regression sessions can, and often do, provide soul-level explanations for such seemingly cruel or heinous current-life events.

Life purpose—whether seemingly simple, quiet, complex, or in the limelight—is always designed to create and enhance the tapestry of each life. Free will exists, both during the phase of developing life details prior to birth and as we progress moment by moment through embodiment (chapter 7 offers further discussion on free will).

THE BENEFITS OF SOUL REGRESSION

Regression into past-life memory allows us to access key scenes and events from past lives and generally offers one or several means to resolve mental, emotional, and energetic blocks stemming from them. Your present can influence your past.

By the same token, past lives can affect our current life in myriad ways—from the physical to the emotional to the behavioral. During presentations, I share the following list to help people discover hunches, if not powerful clues, to circumstances that have centrally affected their past lives. Consider how attracted you may be to the various indicators below or whether you feel any powerful aversion to any particular:

- geographic locations in the world;
- historic periods or events;
- ethnic foods;
- historic figures;
- people in your life; or
- styles of clothing.

Any such "charge" may be significant. For further clues to your past lives or activities, examine your phobias, fears, desires, and health concerns today, as well as your current type of work and your relationship issues. You may be quite surprised—or possibly not at all!—when correlations surface during the course of a soul regression. For many clients, certain things about their life suddenly seem to "fit" and make sense. The insights can prove significant in any number of ways.

For example, the sense of release and relief that can stem from the uncovering of past-life details—be it intellectual, emotional, spiritual, and/or energetic—is often more powerful than I have words to express. The following account, Bill's story, is a good example. Uncovering your own significant past lives would be the best way to experience it for yourself.

Bill: A SOLDIER'S LOT

During Bill's initial interview, he explained that a military background is not part of his current life and stated clearly his feelings that war is not the way to peace. In the opening scene of his past life, he is wearing a dark blue uniform as a young man in his late twenties. An officer in the Union Army during the Civil War, he is involved in a meeting with his superiors at the end of a difficult battle.

Hundreds of Confederate soldiers were slaughtered. Some Union soldiers were also killed. Bill, as the young officer, is rebuffed by the general and colonels after he states the war needs to be over, that there is too much "useless killing." A lieutenant, he goes back to his responsibility to lead the troops under his command. His wish is to defect, but duty prevails.

Another battle is being strategized where a Confederate camp will be boxed in by Union soldiers and taken by surprise. This next battle is, again, a massacre. During the fighting, Bill encounters a Confederate lieutenant like himself. The two look into each other's eyes, and Bill sends the unspoken message, "We've got to stop this war." He is shot by the opposing lieutenant in the leg and stomach and is severely wounded.

While in the hospital, Bill is visited by a senior officer who praises him as a "hero" and bestows on him a medal. Bill does not want the medal and considers handing it back. He believes that stopping the useless killing is impossible. Discharged at his own request, Bill returns home feeling despair and depression. He finds it impossible to release his overpowering memories of the horrific war. One day while working on the farm, he simply sits down at the base of a tree and wills himself to die of a broken heart.

In examining the past life, Bill points out that it felt wasted. He did not understand the politics of war, which was said to be about glory and ego, but in effect turned out to be sad and senseless. As a young person in his present lifetime, Bill was determined to have a military career but soon chose not to pursue this vocation. He found the notion of war excessively uncomfortable, and he knew he could not fight in a battle. When friends in his youth invited him to see war movies, Bill would repeatedly decline without being able to explain why.

Finally, during the regression, the pieces fell into place in his mind and heart, and he understood his reasons for avoiding the military life and war. "War is useless and never leads to peace," he explained. Furthermore, he was able to identify the soul in his present life who was the Confederate lieutenant. This recognition provided an additional release for Bill.

Clients and other people considering having a soul regression often ask, "How will I know if the details of the past that I uncover are accurate?" Here are some indications of validity for the client to consider:

- Does the client resonate deeply with the components that show up in the past-life experience?

- How vivid and uncanny is the recall of past-life details? For example, does the client provide specific details like the color of clothing worn, facial expressions, knots in the wood of a table, etc.?

- Does a powerful emotion suddenly occur for the client during the session?

- Do the components of the past life shed light on details of the client's present life that were unexplained before? An example would be the fear of swimming in someone who previously drowned.

- Can the client remember the graphic details of the past life for days, weeks, and months following the session?

Such indicators generally serve as benchmarks that the recall of past-life details is accurate. On the other hand, whether or not the regression assists the client in moving forward in their current life is the key. Some clients prefer to view the past-life content as metaphor and tend not to be too concerned about complete accuracy of details. To them, if the elements of the metaphor help them to grow, then there is value to the experience.

Spontaneous Regression

Past-life memories can be spontaneously triggered in both children and adults. Contributing causes include exposure to once-familiar sights or smells, the return of significant dates, particular locations, movies, events, people, and the like.

When past-life memories intrude on one's thoughts and feelings, it can be a complicated and difficult experience. They can even provoke significant anxiety. I vividly recall one night in Mexico when I was staying with my husband in a hotel on the water and awoke in extreme fear. After some time struggling with my emotions, I calmed down somewhat and began "seeing" images in my mind. They were of a past life near water where trauma with a man (my husband in current life) was ongoing.

When a spontaneous regression occurs, it is critical to trust that any strong feelings associated with it are occurring for a reason and not to dismiss, deny, or run away from them. Instead, focus on becoming quiet and centered so that you can discern what your inner self is attempting to learn, unblock, or release through this experience. In my case, identifying elements from the past life I was able to access while visiting Mexico unlocked an extremely important door for my husband and me. As a result, our personal and work lives have progressed more smoothly since.

Reasons for Regression

The impetus for my clients to come for a regression is varied. For many, a life trauma or loss is the driving force that compels them to seek out the story of their soul. In 1993, a new client, Carla, arrived in my office for an initial interview. She began by describing how she had pulled over on the highway one day to check on her back tire. As she walked around to the rear of her car, she was struck by an 18-wheel tractor-trailer truck. Flown by helicopter to a nearby hospital, she was twice pronounced clinically dead.

Carla then recounted having what is called a near-death experience (NDE). During one of the episodes when her heart stopped, she could describe in detail the picture below as she observed from a vantage point above her body lying in the hospital bed. The scene my client described was the moment her husband walked into the room with both of her young children. In fact, she was able to delineate what was said and describe the clothing her family members were wearing at the time.

Many people who have sustained a near-death experience and made the choice to return to their body do so with their view of life forever altered. Most of them adopt a more spiritual view of existence and believe wholeheartedly that we are souls having a human existence one life to the next.

Children and Past-Life Memory Recall

Concerning the influence of past lives on the present, it is especially fascinating when children spontaneously provide details of their past lives. A friend shared with me a time when her four-year-old son placed his hands on her cheeks, stared into her eyes, and said, "You have been my mommy before, but you looked different." An example of spontaneous recall is that children riding in a car have been known to point out where they lived in a previous life. Some vividly recall people or events. One of my clients knew from childhood that he saw a dirigible crash into the ground during World War II.

I find it unfortunate that parents and caregivers will often dismiss past-life statements made by children. Researchers have listened to hundreds if not thousands of detailed accounts from children of where they lived or what occurred, and these stories have been verified.

I strongly recommend that as a parent, you neither ignore nor coax your child to talk about past-life memories. If he or she spontaneously shares information, simply listen. However, should you feel the child needs help to cope with or release the effect of a memory, please seek assistance from a qualified regression hypnotherapist.

The Last Word

Another point I wish to make here is that people nearing their final curtain call often say very profound things. How well I remember walking into my elderly grandfather's room just a few days before he died, only to find him struggling to pull on his trousers. When I asked what he was doing, he emphatically explained, "I have my train tickets, and I must go meet Freda." Freda was my grandmother who had died thirteen years earlier.

Often the dying will literally see or sense the presence nearby of loved ones no longer alive. Others report hearing angelic music or an ethereal chant like something from a fairy land not far off. As the veil thins, we sometimes get a glimpse of the pure, radiant realm that awaits. Many NDE accounts speak of a tunnel of light.

Soul Wisdom

Some soul regressions carry inexplicable wisdom for the person concerned. I can attest to this firsthand. When I was a young, married woman of twenty-five, our second child was born fourteen weeks early. He lived an hour or two and died. For many years, I have been fully convinced that the timing was perfect for my life to shift in the direction of knowing grief. More and more, with acute hindsight into the life's work that now engages me, I can almost see the Akashic curriculum guide in front of me containing the preincarnational agreement I had made to go kicking and screaming into understanding death, particularly the death of a child.

Spiritual Practice

How to best benefit from a soul regression session is a question I am often asked. For many clients, engaging in some form of regular spiritual practice will often boost their ability to move into a trance state. Spiritual practice can take many forms, and there is not an exact formula. In fact, there are myriad means we can use on our own to gain ease and a smooth means of moving into altered states of consciousness.

My definition of "spiritual practice" thus includes any activity that assists us to relax and gain either a conscious or unconscious connection with our spirituality. Aside from formal meditative practice, this would include listening to music, hiking, walking, gardening, sitting quietly, watching a burning candle, or doing drumming or any other traditional shamanic journey practice using percussive sound. Ten people will likely have ten distinct styles of spiritual practice. It really doesn't matter what practice is used.

Higher Wisdom

Before we bring this chapter to a close, let us examine another soul regression. The scene opens for a female client in her fifties.

Dana: ANCESTRAL LEARNING

The buffalo have been slaughtered. The young ones talk of war. We are part of s Sioux tribe holding the ways of the Mother and the Father. There is so much anger. We have been forced from our lands. Our livelihood has been stolen. The children are starving, and the women cry. We have no game. The young men hate the situation.

I am a holy man known as Eagle Thunder. The elders try to maintain leadership, but the War Council begins. The young braves ride off. The land has changed. We are powerless. Our health has been affected. People have died.

We begin the Flute Dance. Many of us have died. We cannot defeat the white ones. We must join them. They now inhabit our land. We must teach them our ways of the White Buffalo Calf Woman. I must learn to love. The lower part of me is sickened. The lower part will dance. The higher part will find oneness. I have to go very high. The Eagle Medicine bears me to the heavens to see the bigger picture.

This is a time we have prepared for. We must hold close our ways. We must leave a piece open for newcomers. If we do not, we will perish. We must have faith. The way ahead will be tough. I have completed my life and my contract. I can feel my ancestors in the Milky Way. They no longer need me here. I have completed my responsibility. They are capable of carrying on. I feel lighter now. I have released a thread of guilt.

The client shared the following comments about her current life: "I have feared becoming a spiritual leader and letting people down. I did what I could for my people as Eagle Thunder. I must honor myself here and now." In doing the session, she came to understand her current life attachment to learning the ways of the Sioux and also her feelings of shame at not living up to her leadership commitments. After the session, she did some research and found that a Sioux medicine man by the same name had existed. While historical corroboration may not constitute absolute proof, it can provide added confirmation for the client.

As the previous story illustrates, the soul has an innate drive to gain higher wisdom through its own evolution but also to contribute to the collective evolution and consciousness. Reincarnation thus serves a fundamental purpose. As we step forward through each life and from one life to the next, we fulfill the soul's intention both to purify our "selves," its vehicle, and to assist in the refinement of other souls with whom we share lives.

Each incarnation is designed in a team approach between the soul and its complement of guides and teachers who serve in an intimate, supportive, ongoing relationship. The specific nature of each embodiment is crafted in minute detail. As discussed in chapter 9, elements that are predetermined for each life include the body, ethnicity, and brain that sheathe the human personality, the emotional and physical health, as well as the mother, father, family members, and friends, and numerous life circumstances and events.

To describe all of the potential experiences a client can gain during a soul regression would require innumerable pages. Please accept that the regression is a tailor-made journey tied to the present-day needs of each client. In simple terms, it affords an individual a certain amount of "human" time in which to experience the spiritual realm and have a tangible experience of who and what we are as pure soul. The topic of who and what we are as pure soul is the subject of the next chapter.

chapter 3

You have a purpose, and your Higher Self
will see to it that you carry out that purpose,
whether it's done in a few hours or a hundred
years, whether you do it kicking and screaming
all the way or having a delightful time.

—*Serge King*

The Higher Self

There is a great dichotomy in life: our soul is timeless, while our human minds have difficulty comprehending the absence of time. Yet, if we can simply accept that our soul comes from and remains in a place where time and space do not exist, then, and perhaps only then, can we hold in our conscious mind and awareness that nothing else matters. The purity of our soul stems from the divine, no matter what human terms we use to label the unknowable, ineffable highest realm and energy of wisdom and love.

We begin this chapter with the regression experience of Nadine, a sixty-year-old real-estate broker. During her preliminary interview, she stated that she wanted to learn two things from her session: how she could reconnect with her past lives and what was the block keeping her from sensing guides and teachers on her own. As her session unfolded, it gave her a glimpse of the radiant nature of her higher self, that ineffable presence that is her core. Our account opens as Nadine dies in the past life and travels onward into the spiritual realm.

Nadine: A GLIMPSE OF THE HIGHER SELF

My soul goes whirling off. It is like a spiral dance as I go up into the light. I am free and expanding. There is a sense of awe as I reach out and connect with God, the energy field of the Source. I feel ecstatic and complete. Now I have to go to be processed. Beings will guide me.

Angelic beings take away the old residue. I have come away from a life which had so much responsibility. Now I am in eternity. I do not need to do anything. I must let go of needing to always do something. It is enough to just be.

I start growing. It is as if I've been resting like a seed in the ground. In this place, I can grow as big as possible. I need to go reconnect with my group soul. All I have to do is put my mind on it.

These beings live in a mountain range. My teacher, Leo, who died in my current life, is there. This is a group of ascended masters that includes Saint-Germain and the White Brotherhood. I am part of this group soul with the mission to bring consciousness and light to open people's awareness.

Why can we not make more of an impact on earth? We forget who we are. There is a downward pull on this level, on earth, where we need love and acceptance. Therefore, we adapt. It is easy to have self-doubt and hard to maintain our soul experience.

This is a mythic realm in the mountain, where there are symbols that are a powerful language to represent consciousness and the alchemy of energy. We can create symbols to help us to remember who we truly are and to resonate with the deepest sense of the universe. I need to go deeper into the knowledge of consciousness that I have. I have pushed away the images of this realm because the stress of the material world is too great. I want to resonate with the human world, so I forget my knowledge of the greater universe.

It is time to get into my own power and to act by putting my knowledge and understanding out to the world. "You must believe that your group exists both in spirit and in body." I am told that when I believe I am part of a group, I will meet others on earth like myself.

Now I am taken to a place where there are desks and ancient books. There is someone there to guide me. These are not really books to be read:

they are realms where we can go. I travel into the book of the nature realm that is about all of the beings associated with flowers and plants.

This is a delicate realm where I can be very tiny, even getting into the space between the atoms. It is hard for me to go here because of the pain I feel about the destruction of flowers and plants. I am told these beings are not so solid. They are not destroyed when their habitat is ruined. It is natural for these forms of beauty to exist and manifest for just a short time.

The questions Nadine brings to her soul regression session indicate that she is spiritually very aware. She realizes that she has constricted herself and forgotten who and what she is as an advanced soul. Her session allows her to renew her grasp of the core of her being. Traveling to share time with her advanced group in the mountains gives her some extra perspective on the advanced knowledge and capability she does command. Among other things, her higher self comprehends the minuscule forms of energy in nature and can also recognize the symbology, or energetics, of consciousness.

The universe, including our planet, is constantly reminding us how crucial it is to heighten our collective vibratory energy, if only to improve broad-based health. By availing ourselves of tools like soul-regression therapy that allow us to experience the spiritual realm while we are still incarnate, we have an opportunity to enhance and transform our emotional, physical, and spiritual health toward greater wisdom.

The earth's base frequency, or "heartbeat" (the Schumann resonance), has been discovered to be rising dramatically. Science does not fully understand why this alteration has occurred. At the same time, however, while the earth's "pulse" is rising, science has also demonstrated that the strength of her magnetic field is decreasing.

What effect will an altered field have on us? Many believe that this shift will make it easier to access higher states of vibratory energy and consciousness. The cells of our body will work to attune to or match these energetic shifts, as occurs with a tuning fork. We are likely to be more aware of emotional vibrations, both our own and those of others. All emotions will be felt with increased intensity.

As emotions become more palpable, we have the opportunity to bring in a new age of increased vibration. Our higher self—whether we refer to it as soul, love, intuition, or God Self, to name a few examples—must serve as our master and not our servant. Grounding soul energy into our seemingly mundane everyday life is critical.

We are in a preparatory time of healing through awareness. Many say these alterations will allow greater access to awareness of the fourth dimension and beyond, energy outside of time and space, also known as the non-local.

For those who are not familiar with the concept, let me introduce a brief explanation of these terms as posited by physicists, mathematicians, metaphysicians, and others who study the quantum dimension.

Third-dimensional reality (3D) is the sum total of what many view as "life." It is the everyday life that exists in the material realm and our linear mind, the world of bills, daily chores, appointments, and so on. All too often, we become identified with our bodies, our minds, and our daily routines and rituals in this dense energy space we call earth.

Higher consciousness, the realm of divinity or spirituality, tugs at our deeper awareness. Sometimes a dream will indicate that a loved one is near who is no longer physically present. The birth of a new being, a new soul, reminds us of the miracle of life. A sunset attracts our eyes to the beauty and the glory of nature.

As the current life or incarnation progresses, many of us come to recognize the impossibility of grappling with the events it presents us from a grounded, earthly, and logical perspective only. Life's traumas, particularly those related to loss, sometimes make no sense at all. Death, divorce, health issues, job, relationship, and other such concerns seem to require a deeper, more spiritually focused explanation.

The fourth-dimension perspective (4D) is that of the astral plane, or the energetic vibration just beyond our physical, incarnate existence. In the astral existence, recently "departed" souls can pause before traveling forward into the spiritual realm to send an energetic communication to loved ones. In this manner, via our inner, or deeper, more intuitive senses, we can send and receive communication outside the human third dimension.

Many begin their spiritual awareness with an initial recognition of the non-local, the world outside of time and space. Premonition, telepathic communication, and after-death communication are common examples of energy transfer outside the third dimension.

When we first encounter these non-grounded, non-literal information pathways, it is not uncommon to experience shock and disbelief. On the other hand, it is precisely such experiences of the non-local that lead many of us onto the seeker's path of higher consciousness and higher wisdom. As a seeker, we progress from third-dimension earthly density to an exploration of the fourth dimension.

But while 4D contains elements of telepathy, out-of-body experiences, magic, mysticism, and enchantment, it is not the ultimate spiritual destination or the endpoint of our soul journey. On the contrary, our spiritual path will serve the highest good and assist in heightening the vibration of our individual souls and that of the planet only if we strive to experience, through our intuitive awareness, the fifth dimension (5D). Ego remains with us in 4D and continues to use the physical, the mental, and the astral bodies as tools to achieve ego purposes. In Buddhist terms, the fourth dimension is the world of "I am" and the fifth dimension that of "all that is and ever will be."

But as the earth continues to shift, allowing us greater access to higher vibrations and higher wisdom, we, as embodied souls, must assist ourselves in opening to greater knowledge and healing as individuals on this planet and within the universe. It is our mission to move forward into higher consciousness while incarnate in the third dimension—using the fourth dimension as a bridge into experiencing and gaining awareness, knowledge, and behavior reflective of the ascended wisdom of the fifth dimension.

The fifth dimension is the realm of pure soul, pure love. When we speak of the divine, we speak of the fifth dimension. It is where our spiritual team of guides and teachers reside, and it is the abode of our higher self, our holographic counterpart in spirit, that eternal and essential part of our being. We leave the fifth dimension to incarnate into a body on earth.

Various means exist for each of us as conscious beings to merge with and hold the highest light and love of the divine, including Kabbalah, shamanism, past-life soul regression, and between-lives soul regression.

In its own unique way, each of these modalities assists individuals to get in touch with their higher self and realize their soul existence. Through these magnificent portals, each of us has the opportunity to broaden our perspective beyond the mundane details of daily living, to recognize the ascendancy of love over fear and to dwell for a time in the eternal, primal light of the fifth dimension as the higher self.

But how does our embodied consciousness, or intellectual process, participate in this merging and assist in the healing, or soul progression, that these tools of perception make available? In all four modalities, an altered state of consciousness (ASC) is the means of communing with the non-local, or spiritual, realms outside of time and space.

Humans need consciousness to contemplate the Tao, the universe, and even themselves. Without consciousness, there is nothing. But consciousness is more than the awareness of our physical surroundings. It is also an awareness of our innermost subjective feelings and thoughts.

There are hundreds of theories put forth to define consciousness, but none has fully managed to explain it. Consciousness is not a physical entity even though it manifests through the brain. Modern science has begun to understand the altered state of consciousness to be at once a structural arrangement of the brain cells and a biochemical process in the brain, and it has been able to demonstrate consciousness as a function of the brain's electrical activity.

There are four levels, or states, of brain-wave activity, and each of them is designated by a Greek letter: beta, alpha, theta, and delta. Electroencephalogram (EEG) equipment measures these brain waves. The beta level is defined as our normal waking consciousness, the one most used in third-dimensional living. About 75 percent of waking consciousness is consumed with monitoring the body's physical functions. The other 25 percent of the beta state deals with the thinking and planning state of the mind. The brain waves range from 14 to 27 cycles per second.

The alpha state is the "resting state" of the brain, a passive state where one is noncritical. Listening to music and relaxing are activities that reflect this state. Mystical states of consciousness happen in the alpha state, generally occurring prior to and just after sleep. The alpha state also occurs voluntarily during light hypnosis, meditation, biofeedback, and daydreaming. The brain-wave activity ranges from 8 to 13 cycles per second.

The theta state is the "reverie state" of consciousness that opens the door to intuition and inspiration. "Here and now" stimuli such as heat and cold are often ignored, and one is unaware of physical surroundings in this state. Theta occurs during light sleep. It is also accessible during biofeedback and meditation. The brain-wave activity ranges from 4 to 8 cycles per second.

The lowest level of brain-wave activity is the delta state, in which the individual is unresponsive to any stimuli. The delta state usually occurs during deep sleep, and the brain-wave activity ranges from 0.5 to 4 cycles per second.

Each and every day, we move from beta through the full range of brain-wave states, arriving at delta as our consciousness is altered to the point where we fall asleep. Hypnotic trance induction generally slows the pattern of activity from beta into alpha and theta. Alpha state generally allows us to access the fourth dimension. Theta takes us into the fifth.

As we reported in chapter 1, the vast majority of individuals are quite capable of attaining this depth of relaxation and accessing an altered state of consciousness during the course of a between-lives soul regression. While remaining within their third-dimension existence, clients move through 4D and into 5D, or the spiritual realm. My term for this experience is *ascension*.

Chanting, dancing, praying, repetitive percussion sound, and hypnosis are examples of the varied means by which Kabbalah, shamanism, past-life soul regression, and between-lives soul regression enable us to access these higher states of 4D and 5D consciousness.

For centuries, through chanting, dancing, and praying, shamans have tapped into the energy of *non*-form in order to assist human life by *in*-forming our bodies, minds, and souls. Using a repetitive percussive beat similar to the rhythm of the human heart that is evoked during regression hypnotherapy, shamans have shifted into an altered state of consciousness to gain awareness and communication with the unseen 5D realm. Through intent to heal, shamans utilize an energetic connection with the force of the universe to benefit their community and its individual members. They are often termed healers.

Medical doctors of today at times serve a similar purpose. Unfortunately, some of them tend to relate in a way that creates a negative, fear-based mindset in patients rather than laying the groundwork for positive healing. This can and often does result in alienating both the MD and the patient from tapping into beneficial universal energy.

Soul-regression therapy utilizes the altered state of consciousness, a change in brain-wave activity, to access both past-life and between-lives detail. The client generally receives specifics of one or more past lives in the upper alpha state. Between-lives soul regression requires an altered state of consciousness at the level of deep alpha and upper theta, which includes clarity of consciousness. In order for the client to reach this deeper level of trance, the hypnotic induction is generally lengthier for between-lives soul regression, and the vast majority of clients respond successfully.

Most between-lives soul regression clients recognize they are benefiting from a higher level of consciousness and guidance, and they receive concrete validation that each incarnation is both finite and purposeful. They get to know and experience, even kinesthetically, that we are each far more than this life, this body, or these current circumstances. This realization can lead to an altered view of life itself by highlighting that our particular life circumstances, as well as each and every day, add to this life's pearls of wisdom.

Lenore: HIGHER-SELF BASICS

Lenore, a client in her sixties, is an advanced soul who has experienced two very large traumas in her current life: the chronic mental illness of her husband and the significant physical disability of her adult son. As we come upon her in this account, she has completed a past life and has arrived at the place where guides and teachers provide a review of the past life.

Lenore asks her spiritual team, "Did I ever deliberately hurt anyone? I felt that I did not do enough," and the answer she receives is, "You did no harm." Having this affirmed seems to alleviate Lenore's inner struggle with not offering enough to others in her present life. She repeats what she hears: "I have not done harm."

"Do no harm" is a key tenet of soul existence while in body, a bottom-line statement from the spiritual realm as to how to live our lives. Following are two more between-lives soul regression experiences highlighting soul purpose while incarnate.

Fowler: HIGHER-SELF CONTRACTS

A male client in his early sixties gains knowledge in a preliminary past-life soul regression of having lived in a concentration camp during the Holocaust. He survives and is freed around the age of fifty-five. He dies a free man, acutely aware of the deep wisdom he developed while living in captivity.

The same client then moves into the between-lives soul regression, the first step of which turns out to be an added past-life experience that culminates in his dying and ascending into the spiritual realm as pure soul. In this "added" lifetime, he appears as a teacher and mentor, and he is wearing Asian-style clothing. He has spent the bulk of his adult life providing a depth of learning to students, often without speaking. Death comes from an arrow as he is involved in a religious war.

As he moves further and further, higher and higher above the earth, he is struck by the "power of the vastness, the power that creates me, a unique kernel of sand." Then he reaches what he calls the "distribution point," the location where souls are seen coming and going, back and forth, either returning from or stepping into incarnation. "There is a force that wills my movement," he adds.

During the past life as an Asian teacher, this soul gained an understanding of spiritual principles and the value of honesty and integrity. Upon meeting with his panel of ascended guides, his soul purpose is described to him as mentoring and serving others. Service to others is to take priority over material possessions. He is satisfied that "that life fulfilled my contract."

Michaela: HIGHER-SELF WISDOM GATHERING

Michaela, a female client in her mid-forties, arrives for a between-lives soul regression explaining that she feels a bit lost in regard to her future. She has left her governmental position and moved across the United States, and she describes experiencing some degree of loss over that as well as the uncertainty concerning her unsettled future.

A past life is discovered where she is discontent with her marriage and leaves the relationship. In her sixties, she finds peace and pleasure: there is a home surrounded by nature and a comfortable love relationship. Upon transcending into spirit, she is met with a hug from her very familiar and positive spirit guide, Fandameer.

Immediately she is taken to her soul group, the cohort of souls with whom she repeatedly incarnates. Her arrival unfolds in a joyful atmosphere and lots of excited sharing. A discussion ensues about how mediocrity triggers boredom and discontent in her. Fandameer reminds her to "lighten up" and leads her to a private den where a door opens onto the moonlight. Subsequently, she is guided to meet with her council, or panel of wise beings.

Initially, she is anxiety-ridden over the interview, which leads to her moving into a lighter trance state. Following hypnotic deepening and her return to the wise elder scene, the council members become very informal, which is rather unusual, and information is provided that suggests this client to be an extremely evolved soul.

She is reminded of the privilege of—and the progress that can be made by—facing and coping with the ups and downs, the highs and lows, the joys and struggles that are possible only through incarnation as a human being.

Both preceding cases illustrate the particular form of "enlightenment" a soul can gain from regression therapy. Each regression session is tailor-made by the spiritual realm to encourage conscious awareness in the living 3D being, along with advancement of the client's soul.

Bonnie: GUIDANCE ON FOLLOWING ONE'S BLISS

"Fear is created through a disconnect from the soul," stated Bonnie during her between-lives regression. She is a fifty-four-year-old client working in the corporate sector. In recent times, Bonnie has discovered a new passion for incorporating stones into lovely jewelry of a high energetic quality. Some would go so far as to call this work "alchemy." One of Bonnie's key questions during her regression was whether she should leave her corporate job and move exclusively into jewelry making.

Bonnie's answer continued. "The physical person needs to be supported in all ways possible for their success to achieve their soul contract. Few are awake, but many are coming awake. The planet earth and its inhabitants are slow to change. Those of you who can assist with change carry a higher density, or vibration. You need to trust what you are drawn to do. Many stay in discomfort out of fear. For those that move out of fear, it is a true revelation. Unpredictability triggers fear. Alchemy is needed on the earth."

Essentially, spirit is supporting Bonnie to follow her heart and her passion. She was deeply encouraged during both between-lives soul regression sessions she did with me to trust her intuition and follow where she feels guided. In this way, she will be allowing her truth and her passion, stemming from divine awareness, to shine forth.

For many, by the end of the bird's eye view that a soul regression provides into the depths of our core soul nature, everyday life is powerfully and significantly altered. Having the courage to heed that higher consciousness and transcending earthly material values both provide unspoken rewards. And while the individual soul is receiving huge benefits from a regression experience, the earth and the universe simultaneously reap a positive, literal, and energetic evolutionary change.

Numerous scientists and authors continue to expound on the relationship between science and spirituality, examining via quantum physics the truth that our energetic selves can exist outside of form. Quite simply, we know that emotion and intention guide our physical bodies, our DNA, and our life experience in total. Many seek to consciously understand and explain the quantum space of uncontaminated divine force where our higher self resides.

One between-lives soul regression client discussed the "neural net," or the nervous system of universal consciousness, during her session:

> The way I would describe the neural net is that it is the structure of consciousness (or the structure that consciousness creates) which physicality connects itself into … the framework, or grid, if you will. It reaches through all creation, enlivens it, brings spirit into matter. I believe that it is by connecting with this basic framework, similar to how the soul "sings" to the body at the time of ensoulment, that creation occurs. In learning to connect with consciousness through the neural net, we begin to be able to "move" matter, manipulate matter, become multidimensional and work with creation, space, and time. It is through this medium as well that we connect with our soul, or higher self, while we are ensouled.

Clients of late have begun describing the energy matrix of the universe. I believe that more such information is coming forward at this time because we need to more deeply understand who and what we are as souls embodied and existing within a massive universe.

Another client explains:

> The strain, or "DNA of the Tao," that a soul possesses is the drop that is his or her individual portion of the immense ocean that is the Tao. (*Tao* refers to the basic, eternal principle of the universe that transcends reality and is the source of being, non-being, and change.) The energy of the Tao is both vibrant and static; it is that which is absorbing, growing, learning, and at the same time, it is that which is unchanging, steady, immutable … the reliable "is." The dichotomy of Tao, DNA, or soul is both positive and negative, moving and still, progression and stasis.
>
> Within the individual spark of the Tao, the power of soul DNA informs every created thing. This simply is because the human partakes of creation. At the energy level of higher self, the connectedness of soul and Tao DNA is apparent to those who have the ability to discern it. The farther a soul moves along the path of progress or advancement, the closer it comes to apprehending the spiritual DNA that informs it. The energy that it rec-

ognizes as Tao energy is perfect love. Tao DNA does not have purpose or intention, it simply is.

Metaphorically, the Tao is the ocean. The drop that is the individual soul resides as pure energy and love within the ocean. There are very minor adjustments being made in the DNA of the human race, preparing it for a longer life less burdened by physical infirmities. These alterations are very small but will, in time, become observable to humans. These changes will exhibit as more people have the probability of living to an exceptional age and that the end years are not marred by physical decline that would make such a long life hell.

Our DNA serves as the container of all that is and ever will be. In other words, knowledge of the past, present, and future are timeless when examined from the wisdom and knowledge of our DNA. Two strands of DNA lie lovingly beside one another, entwined in an exquisite tapestry. These energetic filaments, sparks of the divine, carry our connection with Source, or the Tao, along with our personal connection with self. These strands are divine and individual, linking our unique soul energy to the universal matrix of energy. Our DNA is not stagnant. As we change in vibration, color, melody, and knowingness, our DNA flows and changes with us. Think of this like a computer constantly downloading updates for our programs.

Regression hypnotherapy affords clients an opening into the higher vibration of positive universal energy in order to achieve a mental understanding and a spiritual awareness of their soul—the eternal, affirmative nature of who and what they are. The process allows each client to swim consciously in the ocean of their soul within the greater universe while retaining memory of the experience after the regression is complete. Utilizing trance, the individual taps into personal and global DNA.

What a gift to be able to experience, while in body, the awareness of who and what we are as an individual soul within the realm of the divine! Each of us as a soul is exactly the same and distinctly different simultaneously. We are nothing more, and nothing less, than pure love.

We are each on our own expedition as we traverse from body into spirit form and back again. And with every singular incarnation and interlife, we are learning, growing, developing, progressing, and advancing for the greater good of the Tao. And we are not alone in our quest.

The vast majority of between-lives soul regression accounts—in fact, the totality of cases I have personally gathered with my clients—attest to the fact that we have a full complement of spiritual guides, teachers, and companions. I invite you to meet some of them in the next chapter.

chapter 4

What the inner voice says will not
disappoint the hoping soul.

—*Johann Friedrich von Schiller*

Spirit Guides and Wise Elders

*O*nce physical death has occurred at the culmination of a past life, the soul is released from the container of the body. The client's soul may recognize the need to remain close to the death scene for a brief time at the moment of dying in order to provide energetic comfort to loved ones left behind or closure to the past life.

When completion has taken place, the client's soul travels onward into the spiritual realm, receiving whatever input and support are necessary for crossing the threshold. Data from thousands of past-life and between-lives soul regression sessions confirm the following scenarios.

Clients may be met by a large number of souls, often called a welcoming committee. Frequently, the client determines intuitively that these are "greeters," which are seen as numerous small, bright lights. Some clients are met by higher master souls like Buddha, Jesus, Mary, archangels, and the like. Another common occurrence is for loved ones who have crossed over to meet the client.

While loved ones in the spiritual realm can and do serve as a type of guide, we also have spirit guides who are generally souls we have not known in earthly life. More often than not, the client is met by their spirit guide, whose primary role at this time is to assist the soul to acclimate and adjust to being "home."

Once the client comes upon the spirit guide, I will ask, "What is the name of your guide?" While some clients cannot determine their guide's name, most will be able to give me a name of some sort. At times, the name is relatively ordinary, like Sam or Mary. The guide may be making it easy for the client by using a name that is part of their language.

On the other hand, the spirit guide's name may sound something like "Ah-nah-wah-nee." I will always ask the client to spell a name they perceive as sound. At the same time, it is important to note that the name of the guide is truly energetic. Therefore, the client may be working hard to pronounce phonetic sounds that are unfamiliar.

Finally, the guide may wish to offer a name that speaks as a metaphor to the client. For example, the name may represent softness the client is needing to achieve, or strength if that is what is needed, or a sense of playfulness if that will benefit the client.

Each of us as a soul has what I like to call a team of advanced souls assisting us. It is comprised of one or more spirit guides and a number of wise elders who form our panel, or council of advisors. They coordinate and manage the spiritual realm and our interaction with it, including our return to it at each time of transition. All of them have developed a degree of spiritual acumen and wisdom significant enough to qualify for this role. This chapter contains observations from a representative group of clients concerning encounters with our guides and wise elders in the spiritual realm.

Daniel: LEAVING THE PAST LIFE AND MEETING A SPIRIT GUIDE

I feel pulsations. There is a twinkling light coming toward me. The light becomes more steady as it moves closer. The light is bright blue at the center, and I hear in my mind a voice that says, "I am your spirit guide." I feel his warmth. He welcomes me. He walks with his arm around me. His name is "Sha-bah-lah." Now we're going somewhere. He exudes joy. We're celebrating being together again. He takes me to meet with the souls with whom I am most connected. This is my soul family. He tells me that I know what to do. He tells me to "just be" and enjoy this.

Ian: COMFORT FROM A LOVED ONE AFTER THE PAST LIFE

Dying is very easy. I am entering a hallway. There is someone there. He is simply there to let me know where I am and to refamiliarize me. I am in a hall that is a half circle, with doors to different rooms. I feel comfortable. This is like a comforting white hospital without much detail.

Then I go up two marble steps to a room with a high ceiling and pillars. Now, someone keeps popping up in front of me. He's trying to get my attention. He's dressed in a white Greek toga. It's my granddaddy. He gives me a big hug. I barely have strength to hug back. Earth takes a lot out of you. His presence gives me strength. I feel a sense of relief as the anxiety I felt about decisions I made in my past life fall away. We welcome each other back here quite often. We've been a source of strength for each other.

He wants me to relax in a courtyard with a beautiful garden. There's a fountain with grass, flowers, and foliage. This is a beautiful place to decompress. He stays with me to help me cope with my past life as a woman with little means and great physical demands. Granddaddy acknowledges the difficult decisions that I had to make.

To reiterate a cardinal rule of regression hypnotherapy, the client is never prompted or told by the therapist what must happen or should occur during a soul regression. Following the enactment of the last day or death scene in the past life, the vast majority of clients spontaneously move onward into the spiritual realm and recognize the arrival of their spirit guide.

Once the spirit guide makes an appearance, the client, as a soul moving within the spiritual realm, is directed step by step by the spirit guide, who conducts the entire regression experience. It is the spirit guide who pilots the journey for the client, not the therapist.

All communication in the spiritual realm is telepathic, including what transpires in the course of a between-lives soul regression session. Generally, clients will not specify at this point in the regression whether they are "hearing" or intuiting the messages received. The information is simply a flow of energy that is verbalized by the client. The guide's role is to support, assess, and answer questions the client may wish to ask. Such questions can relate to any topic of interest to the client in their current life. Questions will be answered that the guide deems pertinent for the client at present.

Our spirit guide may present itself as energy or in human form. If the guide presents itself as energy, it will usually be defined with shape and color. Blue is most often the reported color. When the guide's soul color is not blue, it will generally be purple, gold, or sparkling white.

Guides are perceived as male, female or androgynous. Having a specific gender or not relates to the needs of the client. For example, some clients will be more comfortable with the soft and gentle nurturance of female energy. Occasionally, the spirit guide will appear in animal form, similar to the notion of shamanic totems but never in a harmful, demonic, or monstrous form, no matter how brutal or despondent the recent death.

While a guide could be described as a wise elder, generally speaking, spirit guides are somewhat less experienced or less advanced than elders. Your spirit guide is a bit like an older brother or sister who treats you with the utmost kindness. You might also view your spirit guide as you would a teacher in school, as opposed to the wise elder, who would be principal.

On a scale from one to ten, the spirit guide may be eight or nine steps more experienced than the client. On the other hand, the spirit guide may also be only half to one step more advanced if the human soul is quite progressed. Spirit guides can be labeled as either chief guides or apprentice guides, depending on their level of knowledge and experience. Thus, the more experienced client, one who has accumulated significant wisdom, may interact more often with an apprentice guide, while a less experienced soul might need the knowledge and guidance of a chief.

In my practice, it is rather uncommon to have clients who are very new souls, as a person embodied at the junior level would probably not have any interest in regression. I note this because some clients arrive for their session with the assumption they are not very advanced. On the contrary: in order to easily comprehend the detail of past-life soul regression and between-lives soul regression, it is likely the client is somewhat further along in their soul journey. Not surprisingly, many soul regression clients are what might be termed "old souls."

As souls, many of us have more than one spirit guide because we have completed, to one degree or another, some broad developmental stages in our soul journey. We begin with an original spirit guide. This is similar to having a first-grade teacher who assists us in establishing our most basic academic skills and learning how to cooperate with other students.

Once we have reached grade six and developed greater skill and maturity, our teacher does not need to hold our hand as frequently. From grade six forward, we require more complex instruction with perhaps less individual guidance. Additional teachers or spirit guides who have developed special skills in areas directly related to our soul's purpose and goals arrive to assist.

As I mentioned previously, once we have gained a certain level of clarity as a soul—when our human self has become more closely aligned with our soul self—our spirit guide may be only slightly more experienced than we are. At this stage, the guide and the incarnate soul may occasionally reverse roles from life to life.

No matter where we are along the universal path of soul progress, our spirit guide can be thought of as our "spirit buddy," something like a sponsor in Alcoholics Anonymous. Both are like a best friend, mentor, and older sibling all rolled up into one and available anytime a need arises.

Your spirit guide is present even when you think they are not. Many of us who are seeking to acquire a conscious connection and awareness of our spirit guide come to recognize a singular guide's presence. It is not uncommon for clients to come to me because they want to have a sensory experience of their spirit guide, to "meet" the guide and perhaps find out their name. Souls have one original spirit guide; we take on many other guides as we progress. Therefore, there are many times when the client feels a group entity, which is a number of spirit guides. Consequently, we do not necessarily sense a singular soul energy that guides and facilitates our lives day by day.

Arlene: DETAILS OF A PAST LIFE

I have an argument with my husband about our daughter. I go to my room and cry. I am not happy with myself. I want to be more loving and show affection better. I've made a mess of things and feel very alone.

(A few days later) I like to make it look like I enjoy baking in my kitchen. This makes me appear important. People think I am a good person. People think I am happy when I am not. My marriage is not okay. Now I've burned my hand. I do not want to be fake anymore. I want my life to be over and start again. I think about killing myself, but I do not. It is a sin to suicide.

(Some years later) I am in bed, sick and dying. I feel sick at heart. My husband is here. He does care for me. He is sad. He regrets the lack of love in our marriage, as I do. How can two people so alike be so far apart? It is all my fault. Life did not go okay. I made others miserable. I tell him I am sorry, and he understands. I have wasted a life and messed up. I've kept too much inside of me. I did not accomplish much. I had to marry and felt guilty about it. My daughter was deaf. She loved her father more than me.

(The client dies in the past life.) I am going higher. I cannot see my body any longer. It is dark all around. Now I feel like I am being pulled. I relax and let it happen. I am in a clearing. It is getting lighter. This feels very relaxing; I am stretched out. Now I see where I am supposed to be. I am coming into a globe or a dome of sorts with points all around it. This looks like country-side.

There is intelligent energy here. I see familiar people smiling at me. There is a big building with steps going up. I can go in, but I want to just wait and relax on the grass. Now there are a lot of friends coming. Some look human and others do not. I recognize only some of them. Now my husband and daughter are coming toward me. (When we are incarnate, a portion of our soul energy always remains in the spiritual realm, which can be labeled our higher self or our superconsciousness.)

My guide arrives and says, "I am right here, where I always am. I've been here all along. My name is Swallow. (The guide is a dark reddish-blue color.) I am the guide for your soul family."

Swallow tells me I had a bumpy ride in the last life. She feels sympathetic, not angry or disappointed in me. She assures me there are more opportunities ahead. "Do not get bogged down with 'shoulds.' There is more good in the last life than you think. The guilt was so overwhelming for you that you could not recognize the good. You were so focused on what you did not like in that life. You'll feel better soon; it is all okay."

If there is such a thing as a handbook for spirit guides, I assume it contains a mandate printed in bold that emphatically states: "A spirit guide is required to behave for all eternity in a loving and forgiving manner." While this statement may seem tongue-in-cheek, it is not. Through a significant amount of past-life trials and tribulations, these highly experienced souls have achieved a degree of wisdom that allows them to fulfill their roles as guides and teachers. Therefore, loving, forgiving, all-accepting behavior is the norm.

It is our judgmental human mind and our socialized system that label behaviors as suitable or heinous. Our spiritual team ardently desires our spiritual growth, but it supports us regardless of our trespasses. Once any one of us as a soul is nearing or has reached a level of progression akin to that of our team, we also portray in body the qualities of loving purity and closer alignment with the divine.

Annabelle: THE LAST DAY OF A PAST LIFE

I am old now, approximately eighty, and I'm frail. There are good smells as I sit on my porch. My dog sits beside me. This has been a good life. It has gone well. I have a sinking feeling in my bones. I'm alone in my bed now. The window is wide open. My soul simply rises up and out; it is freeing. I look back and see my body below me.

I'm moving away from earth. All is good. I am coming out of a stormy sky and am coming to a bright light. I'm in a room now where the light is changing from white to gold and back again. It is beautiful. This is a place of rest. I sense that I am told the past life was good and complete. It was a bit physically demanding, and I was loving and giving.

Now my guide is here. Her name is "Tish-ma." She has no form exactly, but she seems to be like a grey triangle. She tells me to be quiet now, to not be abrupt. She wants my soul to unfold gracefully in its own time. She calms me. Now she is going to answer questions and share insights.

"Tish-ma" says: "You tend to forget and become drawn to outer worry and fear. Just remember who you truly are. You are a loving and complete spirit. You are afraid to own your voice. You have waited a long time to be outwardly who you truly are. It is time to stop editing yourself. Speak your truth. Be free. The stage is set for you. Do not put a lid on your own boiling pot of beauty. Things that seem frightening are there to show you there is nothing to fear. Your soul family is always there to support you. Feel their energy."

Imagine the most powerful and loving cheerleader, and you have discovered the quality of a spirit guide. Sometimes the guide may find it useful to communicate through chiding, needling, and teasing. Frequently, humor is also a component of the guide's presentation style. As a privileged witness and fellow sojourner during hundreds of past-life and between-lives soul regressions, it is clear to me that many of us are much too serious and heavy with ourselves as we sit in judgment of our behavior in life.

Chapter 14 illuminates more of the messages sent by our team as they tease, cajole, and otherwise insist that we lighten up. They point out that rather than leading life from our heart, we function day by day allowing our mind to rule us. Thus, we are never sure we've done enough, and we continue to berate our self internally, pushing with more zeal rather than listening from the feeling and intuitive core of our soul self.

Brad: ON ENTERING THE SPIRITUAL REALM

I have died. I move through a tunnel and through clouds. Two energies greet me and bathe me with love. They have been with me forever. They are angels of different, beautiful colors, and their names are Ashanti and Bella. Now there is another energy here. This is Miss M. She visits me on earth. She's a purple, iridescent goddess. She takes me to a beautiful, peaceful place where there are gardens and birds. I feel healing now.

Miss M and I are like twins. We teach one another. I am in body when she is not, and vice versa. I incarnate more than she. It is very dense here on earth. She does not like the veil which exists between earth and the spiritual realm. I can come into body more easily than she. Her specialty is different from mine. She goes to places more evolved than earth, where she develops different aspects of her soul. Learning compassion for humans is my specialty. I have served as Miss M's spirit guide.

The method for between-lives soul regression that I practice and teach includes guiding the client beyond the last day and final death scene and into the experience of the client's soul exiting the past-life body and beginning the voyage into pure energetic existence in the spiritual realm.

Commonly, the benefit and beauty of encouraging the client to move into a state of pure divine power is for that person to know that they are first and foremost a soul. Once the client has disengaged from the past-life body, this is technically the point where a between-lives soul regression actually begins.

As mentioned at the beginning of this chapter, the spirit guide oftentimes comes forward following the moment of death in the past life. For many clients, the next timely step is for the spirit guide to facilitate a healing process, using both discussion and the power of divine forces. Descriptions of the location where the healing takes place vary from brilliant prisms of light, to an exquisite bubble containing a purple shower, to vast expanses of meadow with a light breeze and the sound of birds, to ancient chant, and more.

Following the session, clients will sometimes ask, "Did healing serve to lessen the difficulty from the past life, or was it meant to sustain me in my present life?" I usually just answer, "What do you feel is the answer to your question?" In my experience, the answer may be either or both. Such is the beauty of regression hypnotherapy: the spirit guide and spiritual realm provide inexplicable, impeccable understanding and kindness. They funnel into our consciousness the height of seen and unseen generosity for our soul and its upward and onward travels.

Before moving on to discuss the wise elders who offer guidance to each of us, I would like to make one final point concerning spirit guides. It is common for between-lives soul regression clients *not* to experience their spirit guide during a session. Why does this happen? The answer is very simple. Frequently, such clients are experienced souls who, while they certainly have guides in the spiritual realm, do not require the "conducting" which is a guide's primary role to provide as the soul traverses the higher ethereal sphere.

Consider a road trip from Los Angeles to San Diego. If you have lived in L.A. all your life, you have surely driven between the two cities more than once. You do not need a detailed map of the main artery between these two metropolitan areas to get you there. The same holds true for between-lives soul regressions. Even when a spirit guide does not appear, the experience is generally rich in detail and almost always includes a reunion with the client's council of wise elders.

Entering this part of the regression experience is not unlike the honor, pleasure, and excitement you felt as a child knocking on the door of your most respected and loving grandparent, aunty, or other beloved older relative or neighbor. You immediately, palpably recognize the qualities of your wise elders. Some descriptive words are *wise, loving, accepting, non-judgmental, supportive, honoring, unwavering, providing guidance,* and *caring.*

In sessions, I have been privileged to hear a variety of titles attached to a client's esteemed group of elders. These include wise ones, wise beings, senior counselors, and senior advisors. Each of us has a panel, or council, of these highly progressed souls who have attained the level of soul knowledge where they are no longer required to incarnate.

We begin our soul's path of progression with an original group of wise elders numbering approximately four to seven. As a soul, we develop further along our trajectory of learning, and periodically, additional elders (usually with specialized expertise related to that stage or focus of our soul journey) augment our "grandparent panel." Like our guides, they can appear in humanoid or energetic form. When they appear human, the wise elders are most often "viewed" as men wearing robes, but there can also be female members in the group.

In the majority of between-lives soul regression sessions, the guide accompanies the client to meet with the wise elders and usually stands behind and off to the left throughout the encounter. The building where the wise elders are found is generally described as a "temple-like" Greek- or Roman-style building with white pillars.

The wise elders' chambers are often described as circular, ornate, and generally include some form of special table where the elders are seated facing the standing client. The ceiling is open, allowing a flow or ease of connection with spirit, and it is often dome shaped. (Scientifically, we know that a round space contains energy more evenly and easily than a square container.)

The wise elders can be described as our high court, but not with a sense of chastisement or judgment. Their role is to provide guidance, support, love, and specific direction to augment our soul progress. During a between-lives soul regression, these higher souls provide the client with leadership, direction, and an infusion of divine love. The client may wish to ask questions, and these will be answered at the discretion of the wise elders.

Brenda: A MEETING WITH THE WISE ELDERS

I arrive at a rounded sort of building. My spirit guide, Annie, is with me. She is familiar, androgynous, neat, not wimpy, not feminine, and strong. My panel is sitting at a curved table. There are four or five members. There is a woman in the middle who seems to be the chairperson. She is authoritative, kindly, and gives off warmth at the same time.

They all have my interests at heart. There is a man next to the Chair who behaves like a teacher and is a little bit gruff. He has grey hair, a blue robe, and a square face. Another one sits back a bit, and she has a green robe and red hair. She is just listening. The blue robe indicates more seniority in regard to knowledge than the green robe. The last two do not say very much. One is very tall and has a pointy head.

The one with the green robe wears a circular pendant that looks like the sun with rays. The sun indicates wholeness, health, and joy for me. The sun feels so warm and wonderful. The Chair wears a pendant that looks like a gibbous moon, a moon that is past half but not yet full. The moon is part silver.

The Chair's pendant is to indicate to me that something in my life is moving toward fruition. I was born under a gibbous moon. I always feel that I fall short and am never good enough. This moon pendant assures me I will achieve what I desire. The Chair's blue robe suggests that being a teacher is a possibility for me in the future. The green robe presents the option that I could also serve as a healer. I am not sure in which direction I will go. I am told it is my choice and that either is perfectly fine.

The tall one is concerned about my hermit tendency. I am afraid of being in a relationship because I could be hurt. I am told that I can work on that in another lifetime. The Chair says I need to work with my emotions more, even though I am already making progress.

I offer you these client examples to provide an idea of the difficult-to-describe beauty and energetic content of a visit with our elder beings who offer us direction, always with love. Here is another account:

Chuck: ANOTHER EXPERIENCE OF THE COUNCIL OF ELDERS

My guide, Shirlee, takes me to beautiful room, where I stand in front of a marble table. There are six lights, six souls, at the table. This is my panel of elder beings. The leader in the middle appears white with silvery threads and a pulsating blue hue. The others are less blue in color. They are all chattering among themselves when I arrive.

The leader welcomes me. He says, "I know you have read all the spirit books, and we want to give you assurance that you are not making up this experience." They are all of high intelligence. They ask me, "Why, each time you are here, are you surprised? Why do you underestimate your soul potential? Deep within, you have significant ability, and there is much you can offer to others." I do not like to appear that I know so much. He tells me that I have come a long way.

My guide is chatting with the elders. My soul color is violet. Those of us who are experienced souls are powerfully needed on earth. There is an accelerated rate of growth going on on the planet where I now live. We need experienced souls to create balance. We need violet souls to empower others. More violet souls are coming in because people are waking up quicker these days.

My team has had a hard job with me. I am told that I have a filter and will only take in what I choose. I am like a golden oyster waiting to be opened. They tell me I need to withdraw the pearl inside and open up the horizons that lie deep within me. I feel totally supported and need to open more to my life purpose.

Chapter 6 illuminates how our life purpose is determined prior to embodiment and held within each of us as a soul.

Jennifer: A SAMPLE EXPERIENCE OF THE COUNCIL OF ELDERS

My guide, "Ag-mar," travels with me to meet with my panel of wise ones. There are ten members of my panel seated at a large oval table. My guide and I are also seated at one end of the table. At the opposite end is the facilitator of the wise ones, who are all wearing purple robes.

Each robe has a different color around the neck. The facilitator has gold around his neck. The color gold tells me to both lighten up and light up. They tell me that I also need to keep working on being more consciously spiritual. The one with gold is so pleased that I now am aware of "Ag-mar." The woman to his left has blue around her neck. Her name is Eka. The blue tells me that I am gaining in wisdom.

My guide holds up a mirror for me, and I see that I am different shades of lavender. I was not required to incarnate. In my current life, I brought 80 percent of my total soul energy into my body. The remaining 20 percent is in the spiritual realm. This was an experiment to see if I could connect with the spiritual realm with so much of my soul energy contained within my physical self.

I am improving and not getting so bogged down with my mental mind. I could have become more obviously spiritual earlier in this life but was afraid of the opinion of my family and others. Now no one can stop me from being who I truly am. My heart needs to be open so that I will not be so mental. I need to be around more of those people who are consciously tied to spirit. It is good that I have found my own way to meditate.

Council messages can be likened to what Americans call an interstate, the French refer to as an auto-route, and the English label a motorway. When we follow the guidance and advice offered by our wise elders, we learn the most direct means of accomplishing our current life's journey, or "trip," as we seek to progress from one level of wisdom to a higher level. Secondly, these main cross-country thoroughfares have two more lanes, taking each of us in the direction we need to be traveling.

To be more specific, as the elders offer input during a between-lives soul regression session, two general frames of reference are provided. One focus is wisdom that applies to everyone but is by no means insignificant. Here are three examples of such messages from the two above council sessions:

- Often, as an incarnate soul, we underestimate our capability and knowledge.
- Humans need to develop the means of "listening" to input from spirit and trusting what we receive as truth.
- On earth, we can easily become too serious.

The second focus, or the other lane on the highway of council detail, relates to idiosyncratic information concerning the individual client that is presented during a between-lives soul regression. Elders will specifically tailor advice to the recipient, shedding light and providing explanations and recommendations that are unique to that client. The two previous council examples offer the following:

- An explanation as to the client's level of soul development, explaining the need for such capability and wisdom on the planet.
- A description of the client's difficulty in receiving and believing spiritual input.
- A definition of the amount of soul energy brought into body during incarnation, and how a relatively large amount of energy being embodied causes the client to have difficulty being aware of spiritual connections.

The next client finds herself at a white temple and discovers that her panel of wise elders is present in this space. They are described as "sitting in robes on the floor," an uncommon experience as these lofty, experienced souls generally are seated at a powerful and important-seeming table facing the client.

Leena: REALIZATIONS DURING A COUNCIL MEETING

I have been in lives before where it was easy to be myself. This life I have chosen for it to be hard. I will have to work to be true to self. Others will not see that I am different from them. Once I discover who I am and honor that, I will find my own group. Being a lesbian in this life is about finding out who

I truly am. I have to propel myself, on my own, out of the situations I was born into with others who are not like me.

When I find the light in myself, I will know it in others. I was born of good people who are on a different wavelength. I have found my group, but we are not yet a team. When we get together, we will make a beacon. I have chosen in this life to be very mental in order to have to work hard and not to forget about the heart.

There are four or five on my council of elders. We are all in robes, sitting on the floor. This life is exciting and energetic as I find my true self. It will be fun and definitely not boring. We will be assertive and self-directed. We might even learn how to play. I haven't let my light shine yet; I have taken life and its happenings too seriously.

The abuse that I suffered as a child is not my story. We are not to get caught up in the story of each life. We must remember who we truly are as a soul. If I am not fearful, my light is brighter. In past lives, I could retreat and be solitary; in this life, I do not have that option.

There is powerful learning to be gained during a life when we are in alignment with our soul's truth. It is often our most difficult lives, where we are challenged not to become stuck or blinded by the complexity of life circumstances regarding either our own physical maladies or the behavior of others, that provide the most notable progress.

Jacelyn: TRUSTING COUNCIL GUIDANCE

I have died in the past life. I feel reoriented now to being in the spiritual realm. There are four or five ascended masters here now; they hold great wisdom. There is an inner group of wise ones and an outer group of seventy-five who learn from the inner group. The energy of the inner group is purple. The inner group, most of the time, does not leave to return to embodiment. They teach the outer group how to be in the world, helping us to attune to inner guidance while in body. They say that we must "walk our talk."

I am welcomed back by the teachers, who embrace me and are lighthearted. They evaluate the life I've just completed by saying I did practice what I taught and was a little impatient at times. They say the impatience was minor but to simply be aware of the situation. They assist me to expand my energy now that I am back in spirit.

They say I am now ready for the next part of my current life. I have shown that I will not falter. The life I had as an oracle and teacher was to prepare me for my life now.

"You have chosen many different types of lives to blend experiences so that you can see the wisdom in it all. You are to continue some of your regular business work in a modified way. This will take a natural course as you integrate your life teaching to shift people's perspective and consciousness into higher alignment with spirit.

"It is time for you to consistently trust in your attachment with the soul realm. You have sufficiently experienced this in your current life and do not need to worry about returning to lack of trust in spirit. You have total support from the higher planes from which we speak. Do not be afraid. You have come miles. Be sure to have fun at the same time you are teaching."

Frequently, clients are told they must trust what they feel, know, and believe in their innermost core. Any of us can easily become sidetracked by human nature, by our thought processes pulling us into skepticism concerning what we know in our heart of hearts to be true. We can easily get caught up worrying about things like financial stability and what others might think. Our guides and teachers encourage us to remain steadfast and to trust that the guidance we need will be there always.

The client account that includes Miss M pointed to the fact that our guides sometimes incarnate for a special purpose, and that we can even "alternate" with them to some extent. This next account reveals that even wise elders incarnate on rare occasion. When they do so, it is always for a particular reason with a very precise mandate.

Manuela: COUNCIL MEMBERS EMBODIED

There are eight members in my panel of elders. Some are male and some female. The female members feel like a mom with lots of love. I feel a sense of recoil from this reunion with the elders. It is difficult to leave a life in the body and quickly cross into this sanctuary of contentment. This is such a distinct place with a different feel from many of my past lives.

The elders drop their formality. They are like friends of mine. They take off their robes and encourage me to take mine off too. The purpose of my current incarnation is to continue my research. The elders have compassion for the struggle I have endured in this current life. They tell me I have had the privilege of being in the human realm with all its earthly struggles.

I am able to recognize the divine nature of incarnate souls. I feel great love for these souls. I am in body to examine the beauty of the symphony of life, the surprises and disappointments. There are seeds I can plant to assist humans with their pain. My current life will not end for a while. I can serve as an instrument with others. I need much aloneness and separateness. It is hard to get close to people and their human energy. It is difficult to remain so separate. I must acknowledge and honor my own sensitivity to the pain of human life.

The elders are all in everyday street clothes. We all are sitting cross-legged on the floor. I am told that I too am a council member. I needed special permission to incarnate this time, and I may not incarnate again. I came to earth to understand human struggles from a deeper perspective in order to bring this information back to the spiritual realm. It is difficult to be in body and to acknowledge who I truly am, to access my divine nature without feeling that I am a freak. There are others who are council members embodied on earth. We are not superior. It is all about love.

"Symphony" is defined as a harmonious combination of elements; what a fascinating term for the elders to use to describe the variety of elements that coalesce during a human incarnation. The surprises and disappointments in life, the highs and the lows all combine to weave a tapestry of learning on the road called soul progression.

When we can surrender to the flow of life, guiding our soul within its physical boat down the river of possibility, we have the opportunity to lessen, if not abolish, the fear of the unknown. We can surrender to the mystery of what lies ahead instead of building fortresses out of sand to withstand it. If we can hold in our consciousness the belief that "all will be well," if we simply hold our positive intention, then life takes on a beauty, a symphony of harmony.

At birth, each soul arrives with its own signature soul experience, the energetic imprint of all experiences forged in previous lives. Each person you come upon will have a distinct soul color, which ranges from one end of the rainbow spectrum to the other, as the badge of its soul journey from the very beginning to the current end. Each soul maintains its own script, its own deeply focused intention throughout life, a soul plan developed in concert with its spiritual team.

Our soul energy is holographic and can be split into two or more mirror-image portions. Prior to incarnation, we determine an amount, a percentage of our soul material, to carry into the new body container. Once incarnate, we are unable to alter the amount of soul energy we have. Our soul standing and life script contribute to our decision as to how much energy to bring with us. First and foremost, a portion of our soul always remains in the spiritual realm.

When we can stop judging and shaming ourselves and others, then, and only then, are we in spiritual accord with love. As we have seen, highly experienced souls who function in spirit as guides and elders do incarnate at times, carrying a mission of profound import. Other embodied souls are at an earlier step of their learning curve. All is good. All is in perfect order, as it is now and always.

Clients often ask how they can be more aware or how they can recognize the presence of their guide or elders. First, let me suggest that you simply focus your attention on connecting with them. I say this because many people believe it is the guide's job to make their presence known. As I have previously noted, whether your conscious contacts are frequent or far between, your guide is like a "spirit buddy" ever at your side—one who is there for the asking, no matter your degree of soul progression.

In actual fact, the more advanced you are as an embodied soul on the incarnational journey, the more likely you work with a group of guides rather than just one, and the less frequently overt contact and guidance may be required. Consider taking some quiet time to relax and to access your guides as a composite of energy or that "oomph" that provides omnipresent support.

Trusting and listening to your intuition is the key to receiving input from your spirit guides. Some of my clients have been aware of communications from them since they were young children. Others, like me, only began to be aware of our guides during adulthood.

Tools to be able to tune into your guide or guides include, first and foremost, having a spiritual practice. "Spiritual practice" is any regular form of time set aside to step into a deeper awareness. What is your preferred means of quieting and allowing your mental processes not to be dominant? Examples include walking, hiking, singing, listening to music, daydreaming, cooking, and shamanic journeying with percussion, as well as meditation of any sort. Include any activity that assists you in "getting out of your own way" as a demonstration of what I mean.

My final strong suggestion would be to set a specific and regular time for your spiritual practice, in order to assure that you honor your desire to be more in alignment with your soul.

An additional tool to gain awareness of the intended messages that our guides and elders are sending us is to examine uncanny circumstances in our daily life. For example, I have had clients who suddenly found a spiritual book on their shelf, not knowing how it found its way there. Or you might have three different people, in the span of one week, mention a speaker coming to town. Examine any of these seemingly unlikely occurrences as a gentle or not so gentle push from spirit offering you a new perspective.

Experiencing the unconditional love and acceptance that our spirit guides and elder teachers pour into us during a soul regression can be, and often is, life altering. It is all too easy to live incarnate and forget from whence we came and the truth of who we are. During trance regression, however, we have the opportunity to experience ourselves as a soul having a human experience, rather than the other way around. The trials, tribulations, and woes of everyday life often fade into perspective once we know we have a guidance team residing in the spiritual realm who is always there for us—once we realize that we are truly never alone.

chapter 5

The life I touch for good or ill will touch
another life, and that in turn another, until
who knows where the trembling stops or
in what far place my touch will be felt.

—*Frederick Buechner*

Soul Family

*I*n the spiritual realm, we are never alone. Upon conception as a new soul, we join a small group of fellow souls, perhaps six to fifteen in number. These are the spiritual personalities with whom we are most closely affiliated—our soul cluster, or soul family, as it were. When we are between lives in the spiritual realm, both our time in spiritual process and our playtime are spent within the context of this small complement of souls, and we interact primarily within this group.

Soul family members, while possessing unique soul characteristics, are bound to one another by their similar core nature. The much smaller hub of our soul family, which generally consists of two or three souls, is called our core soul unit. These are the souls with whom we are the most profoundly attached and have shared the most lives.

Our most intimate and well-known soul friends—those with whom we are the closest—are those who reside with us in the spiritual realm and are committed to "be there" for us. The souls with whom we have incarnated most frequently are almost always those familiar friends, so we know them well on "this side," too.

When the call comes for us to select a new embodiment and related script, more often than not we pull from this family group like pulling a card from the deck onto the table. The "card" we lay out is there for the taking by our fellow soul family member, who has free will to say yea or nay to our request to be with us in our next incarnation.

As we cast the roles for our upcoming lifetime, we may find, however, that not every key "position" can be filled from within our soul family. We then have the option to cast our net farther afield and invite in a soul from another soul family who is more fitting to play that particular role, such as having a given trait or skill we require in our next mother, for example.

Often, but not always, when an appropriate "cast member" is missing from within our own soul family, we move outward one step to an adjacent soul family, a bit like going to the next-door neighbor's house to borrow a cup of sugar. In most cases, we have at least a passing acquaintance with the people who live next door. In the spiritual realm, our "neighbors" can potentially play a role in our upcoming life script.

Each soul family has its own flavor, style, interests, and such, just as it does here on earth. One soul family may focus on music, while another loves books; one may be more serious than the next, etc.

Imagine a moderately small boarding house, where each soul family member has their own room, and where you eat, discuss, and play together. A spirit guide is assigned to operate as the benevolent parent, or "house mother," to each soul family, providing the guidance, support, and love of a more advanced soul. Each of us receives from our spirit guide the time and support we need for soul development.

In our initial soul family, the members advance at differing rates of progress in gaining knowledge, skills, and wisdom. At a certain point in our soul development, we begin to spend less time with them as a "bunch." We move into working in closer alignment with approximately three to five members of our soul family who have achieved middle- to upper-middle levels of knowledge and are at a relatively equal stage of soul development. This smaller group of progressing souls is called our advanced family cohort. Its specific task is to focus on learning and teaching more advanced energetic lessons.

The advanced specialist group is the third step in advancement (from soul family to advanced family cohort to advanced specialist group). This group generally has two to three members. It may include some souls from our original soul family as well as souls we have never met. An advanced specialist group will have a core purpose that is quite advanced and generally tied to energetic healing.

When a client describes their membership in an advanced specialist group as part of the between-lives soul regression experience, that person will often explain that the other colleagues are not presently in body or that they no longer incarnate.

By reincarnating time and again, we gain greater knowledge and wisdom as souls, and the more we advance, the more we accept responsibility for furthering and sharing this knowledge with others. Our mandate is to provide love at the deepest and highest level.

See how elements of the soul family and core soul unit intertwine in the next client account.

Maggie: A BROKEN HEART

I am outside on a cold, rainy day. I wear a suit with a jacket and hat. My shoes are T-strap pumps. The wind is blowing, and we are dripping from the rain. My young son and I go into a shop to have coffee and hot chocolate. It is warm inside. My son sips his drink and smiles.

I am there to meet a man that I do not know well. I notice the man come in and I get up to tap him on the elbow. He is French and he looks so sad. His family is dead. They were part of the Resistance. They killed his wife and children. He joins us at the table. I have papers with a false ID for him. I am also a member of the Resistance. The year is 1944.

Later I am home. My son is on my lap. A man at the shop saw me pass the papers. I am nervous. They grab at me and take me away. As I am dragged out of the house, my feet are getting cut. I cannot do anything for my small son. I am thrown into the back of a truck where it is dark and smells bad.

My husband is French and I am German. We were at the center of the Resistance. We came to help. They drag me out of the truck to someplace. I am hit in the face and asked many questions. The interrogator won't listen to me. He keeps hitting me. I tell him I do not know, and this is not right.

I've been separated from my husband. I do not know what will happen to him.

Now I have a strange calm. I am in a stone room with only a hard wooden chair in it. I see a Nazi flag and pictures of Hitler and Göring. The man who hit me returns with papers explaining charges against me. I tell him to go to hell because I cannot answer his questions. He steps on me and kicks me. Later, I am still alive in a cell on a cot. There is a bucket beside me for a toilet. I am sick. I cannot eat. My hands have been ruined.

Now it is my final day. I am lying in a bed against a wall. There is someone there who is my sister-in-law. Her name is Madeline. I know her in my present life. My brother is there also. The war has ended and I have been freed. I am very ill. They want to put me on a boat and go together to the south of France near the Mediterranean. I do not want to go. Every day I get weaker. My brother sits on my bed. He and his wife are so sad as I die.

I see my body below me as I exit that life. I look like a fossilized bird with grey hair, and I am only thirty-eight years old. I feel sad because I died of a broken heart. I am worried about my son. My brother will care for him. I recognize my brother in the past life as my son of today. My sister-in-law is my first love in my present life that I have not seen in twenty years.

As I travel into the spiritual realm, there are people there to greet me. My mom of today died seven years ago and is one of them. She is so happy to see me. My father of today is there also. He's less overt than my mother, but he's still proud of me. I did the right thing in spite of the cost.

Then my spirit guide arrives. He has a long face and nose. He wears a cloak. He welcomes me. He is very reserved. He is a little disappointed in me because I let myself die of a broken heart. He thought I would push on further in life, but he does not love me less. He puts his arm around my shoulder. He says I need to relax now.

My spirit guide takes me to a hot bath where I can readjust. I feel the pain floating and washing away. Now I am happy. My spirit guide is there just talking to me about remembering that I am home. I feel peaceful and safe. My "old bones" are gone. I feel radiant and remember who I am.

Now it is time to meet everybody at my welcome home party. My spirit guide is here. My son from that past life is here. He will be okay. I admire him. He is so anchored. He does not let things blow him off his path. My current life sister is there. I have missed her. She reminds me of a delicate Grecian urn.

My first love in my present life (my sister-in-law in the past life) is also there. He is quite distant and feels badly about not being able to help me more in the past life. I forgive him. I tell him that down there in life we do not know the whole picture. My current life brother is there too. He is very busy and not much of his energy is here with me. There is a friend here that I do not know in my present life. He is the soul with whom I am the closest. We have spent more lives together than with any other soul.

It is nice to be here. My soul family laughs because I am so emotional. We all want to transform and to progress. Some of us are further along than others.

My spirit guide talks with me again. He wants to know what I would have done differently in the past life. I say that I would have gotten on the boat. My brother wanted me to travel, but I was afraid. I should have gone. I would have lived longer if I had gone. I would have seen my son grow up. I would have gone to the United States. I do feel that I was useful in the past life. I saved some lives. Still, I let my anger get in the way. In my present life, I want to get past all that.

My spirit guide and I go to talk with the soul who is the other component of my core soul unit. The three of us sit and talk. This soul's name in the spiritual realm is "Neck-en." He has concerns about me having a life without him (my present life). He is training as a spirit guide. He is going to help me from the spiritual realm. We have not done this before.

"Neck-en" tells me that I am going to be okay in my current life. I will feel him. He is afraid I will be upset with him for not being here. He has not been in body in my last two lives. I will go back to earth very quickly. "Neck-en" will assist me to plan my next life (current life).

Maggie elicits in clear-cut fashion some of the fascinating elements that can be present in past-life regression and between-lives regression, both in her description of the between-life scenario and events and through her clear understanding of who the past, present, and in-between identities are in her lives.

While the World War II portion of Maggie's past life may be painful to read and absorb, regression hypnotherapy indicates that only those souls of more than average experience can and will be allowed to take on such complex events and hardships. Powerful transformation at the soul level can be, and often is, an outcome of dealing with horrific life circumstances in earthly incarnation.

Clients who uncover a difficult past life or horrific death circumstances (like being drowned or burned at the stake) are generally not thrown into a state of pain. Instead, the surfacing of such past-life details frequently explains client phobias, feelings, and thoughts that have been present for years, and creates an opportunity for them to dissipate.

In focusing on her soul family, Maggie discovers an added dimension to the depth and quality of her current life relationships, in that people who were dear to her in her past life are significant others again today. Maggie's brother in the past life is her son today. Her son of today was the uncle who cared for her past-life son after she died. The former wife of her current son was her first love in this lifetime ... The tapestry of past and present weaves a gorgeous and intricate design.

There are absolutely no accidents when a new life is being scripted prior to incarnation. A host of relationships involving the same souls are traded around from one life to the next. Members of Maggie's soul family in her current life so far include her son, her sister, her first love, and her brother.

Maggie's mother and father of today do not appear to be part of her soul family, which is not unusual. Yet as one of the gifts of her regression, Maggie experiences the blessing of having them arrive together to greet her as she crosses over into the spiritual realm. Clients often report this same happy occurrence during the initial stage of a between-lives soul regression.

Maggie's spirit guide appears next. While he would have preferred that she had let go of her emotional pain and lived on, he is no less supportive and loving of her. He helps her to understand the significance of some of the choices she made and to deal with her regret at having decided not to live on and board the boat. He also validates the great contribution she made in risking her life to save those of others during the war, something she herself tended to downplay.

Next comes "Neck-en," a key figure in Maggie's core soul unit, the one she has most bonded with. He has information for her that is critical: he will not be sharing this lifetime with her in the flesh.

Deciding to enter a life without the soul or souls with whom we share the utmost emotional involvement and connection can create an existence where one feels very alone. We must determine how to best function during such a life and discover value in other aspects of our day-to-day living. For Maggie, being aware and accepting that "Neck-en" will be with her energetically can be of great benefit and solace.

Our core soul unit is a powerful relationship. Another client states that she "yearns for the other soul" who comprises half of hers and is also not in body during this client's lifetime. He does, she says, "come in (energetically) while I am doing my work. I just need to think about him, and he is there. We have worked together many times. We had to be separate this time. Work is going to be my love. This is why I can feel the other soul in my core soul unit when I work."

Another complex cast of relationships emerges in the next client account:

Evie: A SOUL-FAMILY REUNION

In the final scene of the past life, Evie is pleased to share her son's wedding. Joy abounds as she recognizes the depth of love these young people have for one another. Soon after, in the manner of an experienced soul, Evie views her life as complete, and with the ease of a bird taking flight, she comfortably exits the life.

I see little lights going somewhere, just like me. Some of them are wandering, but I know where I am going, and I am excited. I am back! It is such a relief from having been in a small, tight space in body. I felt caught— stuck—and could not get loose.

Now I am in a garden. There is a big man there who is happy to see me. He is so bright—purple in color and also white and glowing on the edges. He is my guide, "Lou-neem." He asks if I want to rest or to go see everyone else. I go on my own. I know the way.

I meet up with my soul family of five to six souls. Jim, my dear friend in life today, is there. He is dark blue in color. He says, "What took you so long?" We were not together in my last life. He was somewhere where there was war. He returned first to the spirit realm, before I came. His last life ended before mine. He's very caring, attentive, and funny. It is his eternal soul nature. He wants to play more on earth. He does not want war or fighting.

We have so much to talk about. Jim seems to be more excited to see me than any other member of my group. We have not incarnated many times together. The two of us have different knowledge, different learning, and we talk a lot about that.

Both Jim and I are dark bluish-purple in color. (This color would indicate a high level of soul experience for both Evie and Jim.) Jim is more methodical than I am. He is patient and allows things to unfold. I am more impulsive. I do not always get the methodical part.

Now I see Mary, who is dark and similar in color. She is an acquaintance in my life today. Mary's learning this time is to discover how people get stuck from the inside, how they get themselves stuck in life.

Then I see a woman with long red hair who is dark in color. Diane, my best friend in life today, is there also. She is just a little lighter in color than Jim and me. She comments about the garden. We were neighbors and gardened together. Jim drives her crazy. She is more free-spirited.

I have incarnated many times with Diane. She is part of my soul family. She is the soul with whom I have incarnated the most. Together, we make up a core soul unit. We are more familiar with each another. We are closer with one another than with any other soul.

Evie exits her past life and quickly comes upon the uniquely experienced group of souls with whom she spends the bulk of her time in spirit. She is a soul with significant experience, perhaps at the eight or nine level on a scale of one to ten. While she once spent much time with her original soul family, she is now less involved with the group as a whole.

As a soul, once we reach an advanced rung on the ladder of soul progress, we tend to socialize and work amongst a smaller group of souls who have a

similar degree of knowledge and with whom we are clearly the most connected. As in our earthly families, though we may grow up with four soul
siblings in our present life, we can later choose to spend more time with just
one or two of them with whom we share a similar view on life.

Evie's ease in leaving her past-life death scene could also be considered a
clue to her advanced soul standing. Frequently, souls who have a high degree
of experience will "die" easily and effortlessly, and are quickly ready to jump
the hurdle between the earth plane and the spiritual realm.

As the next client example arrives to meet her soul family, she discovers
that the members of her group include a current life mentor, grandmother,
brother, husband, and friends. There are no rules regarding who will be part
of our soul family. We may or may not find that our children in current life
are included. It is not actually common for both of our parents to be members. Another client finds that her first husband (from whom she is divorced)
is in her soul family. Her spirit guide explains that he served as a bridge to
assist her to move away from the family she was raised in.

So many scenarios can occur. During a between-lives soul regression, we
may learn that a beloved friend or family member who seemed to die too
soon is a member of our soul family. This can be a bittersweet moment since
we also continue to miss the person in daily life.

Often there is a member of the client's soul family whose identity comes
as a big surprise. Some clients are in complete shock when they come upon
a soul they never expected to find in their soul family. Others simply marvel
at how right the new information feels. The uncanny accuracy in the details
that surface during the session is always a powerful validation.

A particular soul may appear in our soul family with whom we have a
complex and conflicted relationship in current life. Perhaps we scripted an
agreement prebirth to behave toward one another in a way that will jump-
start some long-overdue soul progress. We may have married a member of
our soul family, only to discover in current life that we are not compatible.
This too may stem from a prebirth agreement to prod one or both of us to
get on with fulfilling our soul purpose.

Josie: A CORE SOUL UNIT MEETING IN THE OFFING

My spirit guide, "Koo-nah," wants to take me now to see other souls. I am in a big, open space. I see other groups of people near my group. (These would be adjacent soul families.) I am with my soul family now, and there are eight other souls. I have been away for a long time. I would like to watch them from a distance. I can identify some of them, but not all. I used to spend more time with them in the past. Now I am most often with a group that has more experience than some souls in my own group. We help other people. We often discuss life.

My primary companion soul (who makes up the rest of my core soul unit) is incarnate, but I have not yet met him. Doing so before I am ready to would be pointless. I need to strengthen my soul first and overcome my high-strung human body so that I can relax more easily.

Josie is another example of a soul who has accumulated more than average experience and does not reside in her original soul family. She spends the bulk of her time in an advanced specialist group. A clue to the therapist is that all members of the advanced specialist group share a common soul color, and it will be in the upper reaches of the spiritual spectrum.

Josie is a powerful example of weaving together complex goals preincarnationally into a kind of checklist of accomplishments for an embodiment. She quite clearly discerns there is a plan. Once she learns to cope with the human emotion of intense anxiety and adjust to the temperament of her "high-strung" body and brain, she will be blessed with the chance to meet and develop an affective relationship with a familiar and intimate soul friend. She knows she will get to experience life with a member of her core soul unit when the time is right. The perspective we gain through between-lives soul regression can help explain the challenges we face in daily life and thus provide incentive to hasten our soul development.

Many clients arrive for their session with a burning desire to find out "who is" or "where is" or "when will I meet" the other primary soul or souls in their core soul unit. We live in a culture that romanticizes discovering and living happily ever after with the perfect mate. Chapter 14 sheds a little light on this need.

Abigail: ON EMOTIONAL BALANCE

I refer you to the story of Allen in chapter 7 on free will, who, in a previous [female] incarnation, cut off all emotion after the death of her father and then married just to have a place to live. In Abigail's present incarnation, her parents divorced before she was two years old, and her father was neither physically nor emotionally available. Her favorite grandfather, with whom she was closely bonded, kept telling her that "all would be okay," but he himself died while she was still a child.

Abigail comments that she "wallowed" during the past life, allowing the emotional austerity she forced upon herself to bleed over into her everyday existence. In current life, Abigail (in her forties) has lacked for a father all her life and is living out a story that parallels her past life in other ways. In a lengthy committed relationship today, she has chosen a man who is described as "not emotionally accessible."

During the between-lives portion of Abigail's regression hypnotherapy session, she states:

I am in a garden. (This is a common setting for meeting one's soul family.) There are fifteen members of my group, but only twelve are here. (The remaining three soul family members may not be energetically available to be present, or perhaps Abigail is not to meet them at this time.) They are in little groups in front of me. The group to the left is three souls who are friends of mine in present life; they are the silly ones. I am a bit frustrated with them, so they hang back. They tend to laugh everything off.

There is a group in back. They are my father, stepmother, and stepfather in my present life. These three souls have not progressed very far. They let their body overpower their soul. They succumb to emotions. I am told not to try to assist them at this time. Then I see a group right in front of me. There are two souls, my brother and his son in current life. They are both loners who try to help each other out. My brother chose a difficult body with emotional troubles.

The rest are just milling around. My grandmother is there. She is very nervous about crossing over. She is afraid of being alone when her time comes and worried no one will be there for her. She was widowed at an early age. She will be crossing over soon in order to learn that she will not be alone.

Then I see my mother in this life. The intensity and drive of her spirit is obvious. She has progressed but is holding herself back. She also lets human emotion override the progress of her journey. I can help her. She chose to be strong-willed but can be insecure with men. She compensates by appearing independent.

I chose this soul as my mother to learn that having strength can be both positive and negative. Mom chose me to learn from me. I chose my dad's soul to be able to get past rejection in my present incarnation. I needed to learn about self-worth and not to follow how others feel.

I no longer spend much time with my original soul family. I have progressed beyond that. It is time for some in my soul family to move along faster. They need to seek their calling. We all needed to advance at different levels, at different speeds. We need to learn from those both ahead and behind.

Briefly, I spend time with my advanced specialist group. There are three souls in the group. Two I recognize as very dear friends today. The third soul I do not recognize. I will meet this one. I must be ready to accept him into my life. I may not know him at first. I will see the laughter in his eyes. This is the soul with whom I have incarnated the most.

This is a special group where we like to travel, explore, and be adventurous. We all feel great joy in being together. We share tears now. I am home. We help those along the way in order to help ourselves. We are to listen and to be objective and humorous.

Abigail, on the soul level, seems to be working on loss issues, particularly related to men. The focus in her past life on the loss of her father and seeking a husband, not for love but to simply have a home, indicates that she is not good at valuing her own emotional needs.

Abigail's team has a great desire for her not to repeat the pattern of allowing emotions to control her life. It catapulted her into depression and despair in her past life. Believing that she can be in an equal romantic partnership in this lifetime seems to be the hurdle she must overcome this time around.

In meeting with her soul family, Abigail does not find present all fifteen souls in her group. This is a common occurrence. Our team brings forward the souls who are most beneficial for us to encounter.

Abigail is a rather serious soul and person in her present life. She has progressed as a soul, not spending much time any longer with her original soul family. Clearly, she wishes the first three friends she meets to be less silly and to focus more intently on their soul growth.

When Abigail comes in contact with her father's soul (along with the souls of other family members tied to her current embodiment), spirit elucidates how any one of us can allow our human emotions to stand in the way of our soul's journey. Learning to create balance by acknowledging our emotions without becoming waylaid or embedded in them is the key to soul development.

Finally, we get confirmation that Abigail is an advanced soul when she comes upon her advanced specialist group. These soul companions are intent on learning but also enjoy adventure and humor. As happens with Abigail, spirit repeatedly teaches clients to balance one's focus on soul growth through both seriousness and play.

Jane: INSIGHTS DURING THE INTERLIFE

I am moving through the clouds. There are cloud shapes around me. I am back in my cohort (soul family) to be known as I am. I feel accepted, not judged. There are seven to nine people (souls). There are two to three interacting with me. They say, "It is good to have you back." They all say hi. Now I need to go be debriefed. The three go with me. I arrive where my past life will be processed. There are three entities inside, and we go over things I had done in my past life.

I did not choose the right person to marry. I let my head get turned by a pretty girl. The woman I should have married was plain but solid. However, there is no completely wrong choice. What I did take away from my choices is to have paid better attention to my gut. It can affect others also if I do not pay attention. That life was about how to handle disappointment and learn to make the best of it.

These three who are assisting me to evaluate are Anita, my guardian angel, my mentor, and there is a fourth one who is more detached, like a witness. They suggest that I just rest now. They are going to take me to a warm place with a waterfall that will wash away the previous life. They say I need time to meditate.

I am there now at the waterfall. There is an energy mist. It feels good to breathe it in. I needed to release something from the dying in that life. It smells good, like alyssum…a honey smell. Now the waterfall runs clear. I am done, they tell me.

Now I go to a room that opens to nature. I am to be in touch with my intuition and awareness. Then I will make better big choices. I will be in balance. My cohort plays with energy and moves it. This is not my beginning cohort. Three of us from my original soul family joined this special group. Later there will be an even smaller cohort.

This special group I am in now deals with getting the basics having to do with healing…to help others heal. Victor, my son in my present life, is one member of this group. There are others groups nearby like this group.

The different small groups interact with each other so that when you put together a life, you might choose from different groups near you. You can choose someone from a different small group to serve their needs or yours. My husband and son in present life are both there. They play with energy like I do. My current grandson is from another cohort. He is connected through my guardian angel. She watches over him too.

There is one member of our cohort whose color is now blue and who is preparing to go off to do something different. My own color does not indicate that I am ready yet to leave this special cohort. It has only a few other souls like me who are green with a little blue in color. We all have a permeable outer skin.

The teacher for our group stops by. She has us play with emotions, like playing with energy. Emotions can help us to learn and experience. Emotions can be unpleasant. We are to move at a slower pace so that we will see the nuances. We will miss the importance of the emotion if we move too fast. I am told that stress can affect my health, so I am to go slow and pay attention to what is important. They want me to approach most of life like play.

Jane is the recipient of powerful advice on how to focus on life. We are to listen to our gut and not have our head turned by beauty. Someone or something that lacks outer loveliness may, in fact, indicate that the person or life is solid and strong. If we follow our emotions and take time to examine things, we are likely to discover what is of greater value in life. Including play is critical.

In addition, this soul regression provides significant detail about how we progress from our original soul family into one or more progressed and synchronized smaller soul groups. To recap, we begin our soul's journey interacting with our soul family, a group of souls numbering approximately eight to fifteen. The members of this initial soul family advance at differing rates of soul development, which leads to the formation of subgroups.

Eventually, we work with three to five selected members of this team as an advanced family cohort. Ultimately, we join with two or three souls to form an advanced specialist group with a designated task. We may also form core soul units with one or two souls we incarnate most with. Our soul color indicates how far we have progressed toward greater soul wisdom. Always, the mandate is to love.

chapter 6

> Say not, "I have found the truth," but rather, "I have found a truth." Say not, "I have found the path of the soul." Say rather, "I have met the soul walking upon my path." For the soul walks upon all paths. The soul walks not upon a line, neither does it grow like a reed. The soul unfolds itself, like a lotus of countless petals.

> —*Kahlil Gibran*

Life Script or Purpose

*E*ach life is another play in which our soul is an actor. Imagine the soul as the one who agrees to read the script and prepares to step into a specific role onstage. As a soul, we take on a physical vehicle in order to begin a new life, and we arrive on the world scene as the particular character we have agreed to play.

The actor has a core personality, just as the soul has an immortal nature. The character we embody in each life play is temporary, while the soul carries our everlasting note. In order to step moment by moment through the life we are to live, the soul must gain some degree of symbiosis (in some plays more, in others less) with the body, melding its true, enduring temperament with the style of person indicated in the script. The person in each play, or lifetime, is thus an amalgamation of eternal soul nature and human personality traits attached to a dispensable body and brain.

This chapter presents the life purpose and script of each embodiment and includes an examination of the value and effects of life events on both ourselves and others. In addition, we will discuss how and why each life plan comes to be created.

Consider the process actors move through as they decide to accept a particular role in a play or movie. Tom Hanks has played a thirty-five-year-old kid, a simpleton from Alabama, a sullen soldier, and a lawyer suffering from AIDS. Many comment that Hanks possesses an all-too-rare nice-guy charm in all of these movies.

Could this relate to Tom's soul nature rather than his personality in his present life? We have no way of telling without interviewing and regressing him. Generally speaking, however, it does seem likely that the roles an actor chooses to portray in life have a relationship to both his current personality and eternal soul nature.

Consider also the effect each life has on soul progression in general. Just as each role an actor plays would seem to affect both the actor himself and all those who are party to the movie or play, be they cast or audience, so too does each incarnation create a result for the human person in question and their soul, as well as a spin-off effect on those who are touched by the current embodiment.

"Why did I come into body this time, and how am I doing?" is the most common question that comes up in a between-lives soul regression session. I hear it over and over again from clients seeking to discover the reason and overriding intention for their present incarnation.

At this juncture, it is critical for me to explain that we have some lives where there seems to be a very specific plan. The "reason" for others is more general, and possibly even much less evident, but no less important. As a result, clients may complete the between-lives soul regression session with crystal-clear detail in their conscious mind as to their current life purpose. Others come away from the session with a general sense of having decided to come into body this time round to serve, say, as a healer in any manner of their choosing.

Jed: SOUL FOCUS

Jed arrives for his regression seeking answers to a very clear question: "What are my lessons to learn and unlearn in this life?" As the between-lives portion of the session progresses, he appeals to his council of wise elders to know more about his life purpose. Their response is, "Your overall purpose this life is to nurture. You are to live simply. You are to have a relationship with and be connected to animals. You are to speak your truth. Be conscious. Just live in the moment. Do not judge. Be with people where they are at any point in their life. Take in warmth and sunshine. Let yourself grow."

Jed then receives profound, relatively esoteric detail concerning his life purpose. This is not unusual. Many of my clients are provided with deep personal guidance, and Jed is perfectly comfortable with such direction. He is aware of himself and of the perspective on life that he has developed as he nears fifty years of age. No frustration arises as he is handed details to follow in the continuing days of his productive working life and into the future with his retirement.

Although Jed is not directed toward any particular employment, he clearly comprehends spirit's intention for him. Career decisions and commitment to work have never been a big struggle for him, as he is quite aware already of his passions in life.

Jed's soul color (indicating his level of soul progress) is discovered during his between-lives soul regression. It ties in perfectly with the details offered about his life purpose, indicating that Jed is a fairly advanced soul.

Catherine: A MISSION AND A VOW

Catherine, at age eighty-eight in her past life, leaves her body easily and journeys "across the veil" into the spiritual realm. She finds herself as a soul above her past-life body, communicating via energy with her daughter, who has been by her side during the dying process. Catherine relates:

I am somersaulting in space. It is light, and I can see all the planets. I fall into a cloud of light, and it envelops me. Other spirits and I are chasing each other. It is fun. I love to just float around. I play with a cat.

Now they want me to stop playing. Tall, skinny people arrive. They look like four kings. They are like the "hand of God." They tell me that I do important work. They say that not all souls wish to come to earth. It is a labor of love to come here. It is a sacrifice to come to earth, for there is trauma here. Trauma spurs change. You can choose trauma, more or less, during an embodiment. You can sacrifice self so that others are inspired to change. There is often physical pain involved with coming to earth.

In order to shift the third dimension (life on earth) gradually, we must have souls incarnate on earth. We must have people there to do that. Souls will wish to return to earth if the experience there is one of love. "You, Catherine, can make change on earth. You have to remain focused, with your hand on the rudder. We will give you ample support." I like to play in the clouds. They nearly make me go back to earth, but I am willing.

"The money you will need in your life today will flow with the right intention. Your intent is always to solve actual environmental troubles on the earth." (This comment by Catherine's team is directly tied to her current work involving soil and water.) "You have done this work before. You serve as a 'doctor to the universe.' You are to help the universe remain functional, both in literal and figurative terms. Continue with your work as it is now.

"Dark energy is where there is no energy. You are to help keep the universe alive. You are to help keep energy alive. God is a structure of energy. Love is pure energy. When the structure of energy does not flow, there are kinks. The kinks cause us to feel negative emotion. You can help repair the kinks. We need to bring positive intent back to the earth. This will open the flow of positive emotion, the flow of love.

"We will be sending new people to you to assist with your work. As you work directly with the elements of the earth, more people will feel love. The healing, both literal and emotional, will occur. Souls with significant power will create a blanket of energy. All need to feel love much of the time.

"The pleasures of incarnation are to be felt. You must both work and play. It makes us ill to restrict our play. Look at work as play. There are no failures.

"We will now show to you the soul group to which you belong. There are fifty who are the helpers, such as angels, teachers, and guidance counselors. The four souls who look like kings are the coordinators of your large soul group. They are your council of wise elders. Some have been with you since the beginning of your soul's journey and some have not."

Catherine is an example of a person with a powerful and profound mission in this lifetime. Both her past-life soul regression and her between-lives soul regression sessions reveal fascinating information on who she is at the soul level and why she has taken up her current life's work. But all souls have a strong purpose, no matter what the script is for their present incarnational experience and regardless of their degree of soul development.

I have included content from Catherine's session in part to illustrate how we can make a vow or put a pledge in place prior to taking up a lifetime. Her regression was significantly useful in supporting her continued focus on environmental issues in the present life and explaining the depth of her commitment to her work. Furthermore, the actual words Catherine spoke while closely linked with her soul via hypnotic regression were like an oration, or speech, from the other side.

The esoteric detail conveyed through Catherine about our planetary needs is both profound and critical. From the standpoint of our earth and its atmosphere, we have only to examine the environmental news and the growing evidence today to become aware of the ecological damage that is occurring. The natural order is increasingly out of sync.

The universe can also experience pain in an energetic and metaphysical manner. Examples cross our human paths daily that there is not enough love on this planet: crime, drug abuse, social injustice, political turmoil, racial hatred, genocide, increased divorce rate, and more children caught in paternity disputes—the painful and nasty litany could go on.

As a hydrologist, Catherine seems to have agreed to serve literally in healing planetary earth, air, and water. It would appear that she now works primarily with a group of souls (the "helpers") who are not her original soul family. During her regression, she is instructed to work with the flow of love energy. She is truly an angel in the guise of an everyday person, offering love to both the environment and to individuals.

There are many souls presently embodied that have taken up life on earth to instill various aspects of love and positive intent here. Groups of souls that have reached a level of soul development well beyond the mid-range may carry a strong and demanding responsibility. (Chapter 5 presents a discussion and examples of soul families.)

I invite you to examine your own life, and ask yourself, "Do my life and focus stem from the highest order?" The universe, in its infinite generosity, allows us to shift our aims without penalty. Whatever our previous behavior, we have the opportunity to realign our deeds and to move into more loving conduct.

Susan: BRIDGING THE KNOWLEDGE GAP WITH LOVE

As a soul, everyone has a purpose. I am no different. We are all here to help and influence others. Each soul adds a particular influence. My job is to link, making souls feel that they belong, that they have a reason and a purpose for being here.

It is all about love, no matter what. I am to join people together so they do not feel alone. To do so, I listen in earnest to people. I become their friend and give them a feeling of belonging. I help them with realizations and answers. Then I move on. I always leave behind the interaction that I have had with someone.

I am to talk to people who are unsure and unhappy. Many of these people have phobias and difficult attitudes. I cannot stop what happens to people. Often they have to go through difficult experiences.

I have not had life in this sphere for hundreds of lives. (This statement would seem to indicate the client has incarnated in locations other than on earth. This is not a rare occurrence; I have heard this same comment from other clients.)

I am here to experience this type of life and gain a better understanding. I am to influence others in an unobtrusive way. I came to earth to experience what pain feels like. I did not know what pain was before; there is pain in many different forms, and it is caused in many ways. It is a life lesson for me to gain this knowledge and take it back to the angels. The angels know there is pain on earth.

I am thanking them (my spiritual team) for being there and for allowing me this realization, this life, and this precious learning experience. They tell me that I cannot cure all ills. I am not meant to be able to resolve all pain. The biggest thing of all is love.

Susan has recently retired from the computer industry. She has spent much of her working and private life talking with and supporting those with whom she comes in contact. On the surface, her life would not appear to be a powerful reflection of Susan's life purpose as described by her spiritual team.

Nonetheless, she, like many other souls, has come into body with a profoundly spiritual intention: guiding others to believe that they are not alone, that they fit in and are here on earth for a distinct reason, is inexplicably important. If we believe that our human existence serves no purpose, we are likely to feel bereft, like a boat floating in the water without an engine.

Susan assists many people whom others might avoid or misunderstand. Suspending judgment, she offers love where others would be critical and withhold it. But coming to understand the trauma of others' lives is Susan's cup of tea. Her task on this planet is just the opposite. In other words, Susan's mandate for her present life is to come to know and comprehend the depth of pain that many people face and to carry the energetic imprint of that complexity and difficulty back to souls in spirit.

It has been explained in numerous regression hypnotherapy sessions that the job of certain incarnate souls is to facilitate learning in the spiritual realm. Souls there may have not incarnated in a very long time, if ever. The density of the earthly laboratory where we gain soul development can be intensely painful and too complicated to endure. And so, in order for there to be adequate coordination and understanding between the spiritual realm and earth, particular souls appear to have agreed to serve as gatherers of awareness, bringing such knowledge to the higher levels of the universe.

Many clients are not offered a great deal of detail in regards to their life purpose. Simple, concise comments from our team are often enough to imbed the essentials, as demonstrated in the following client accounts:

I am to transmit, awaken, and explain. I am to teach, to write, to heal, and to explain. They have sent many people to me to remind me of why I am here. I am supposed to stop pretending that I do not know what I am here to do. I must be willing to shine. They say, "Be big, not small." I am to claim my inheritance from Source. They love me. I am to be gentle with myself.

The above client, like many other incarnate souls, has difficulty accepting her capabilities in life. Why do so many of us deliberately avoid, devalue, and dishonor our person through self-effacement when Spirit clearly instructs us to "be big, not small"?

Were each and every one of us to respect and project our gifts and proficiencies (both inward and outward) for the benefit of others, imagine the flowering of wisdom there would be on this planet! Allow and assist the overall intelligence and understanding of this planet to advance by accepting and sharing the acumen you have gained through many lifetimes. You hold so much more wisdom and expertise than you have ever credited yourself for.

Another client describes her life purpose as follows:

> I am being told by my spirit guide that the healing ability I carried in the past life as a Native American girl is to be brought forward into my present life. I live near the Rocky Mountains, where I lived before, to be reminded of my healing skills of the past. I should help people to practice the ancient healing arts once again.
>
> My life purpose is to move forward in my soul progression and achieve advancement closer to that of other members of my soul family. I tried to make it before (to a level of greater soul development), but I let my anger get in the way. I want to get past all that in my current incarnation.

Many people in past centuries served as healers in the broadest sense, being the equivalent of acupuncturists, massage therapists, herbalists, naturopaths, etc. The long-standing means of improving physical, emotional, and spiritual health that they practiced were not labeled "complementary" and "alternative" medicine as they are today.

But things are getting better: many people are reaching the point of remembering they have provided health assistance in prior lives. Denying our passion serves neither ourselves nor the general public, so I urge you to pay attention to any such emerging gifts you may sense and discover in yourself.

There are many other approaches to explore. Anger, for example, is an emotion that can block our positive energy and impede our spiritual progress. In coming to understand the true foundation of our anger and transmuting resentment into a constructive force, we allow our souls to develop and lead our human lives toward a place of comfort and greater usefulness for all.

Without question, our parents play a significant role in our lives. The following client describes the soul contract she made in selecting her father in the current life:

> I chose my dad to be able to get past rejection. I needed to learn about self-worth and not follow how others treated or felt about me.

In early childhood, we look to our parents for a "looking glass" onto the world. Whether they mirror reality for us in a positive way or look through the glass darkly directly influences how we grow toward adulthood. The same applies to our soul journey overall. The style of parenting we receive early in life can provide either a "leg up" or an extreme damper as we seek to ascend into our core self and move forward in each embodiment.

During between-lives soul regression, clients may define complex and challenging circumstances to which they have agreed prior to birth. Such contractual agreements with other souls are written into their life script as important hurdles to overcome without completely tripping up and "breaking a leg."

Jean: THE SPIRITUAL "MATERNITY WARD"

Jean is a woman in her forties who has cared for many foster children. She has a biological daughter who is a toddler and a school-aged son whom she adopted as an infant. "In the hospital, when I initially laid eyes on both my newborn daughter and my adopted son, I knew their little faces. In my heart of hearts, I recognized each of them from lives before," Jean volunteers. Her son was exposed to drugs in utero and requires special attention on a regular basis.

Having been raised in an aristocratic style in more than one country, Jean lacks little from a monetary standpoint. Caring for children, whether biological or not, has been a great yearning for her. Children and animals are her true love. Her soul regression brings a startling correlation to light:

I am now leaving the scene where I died an old woman. There are babies floating by. These are babies that want to come to earth. This is the area where babies come to earth. I can communicate with them. I help to see if they are ready. They talk to me. When I am in the maternity ward in spirit, there is not yet a determination as to where they are going. This is like a holding tank before a decision has been made.

I am a nurse who assists these babies who are either in the process of deciding or have decided that they will go to earth. I feel sorry for them because they do not know what they are getting into. The earth is tough. Each of these babies can determine on their own when they will go to earth. Once they have decided to go to earth, they are excited. They do not remain in this holding tank for very long. They go straight from here to the mommy's tummy.

It is my primary mission to reach children. I am to let them know they are not alone. It is important for children to have hope and to know they are not alone.

As a soul presently incarnate, Jean carries an extremely important responsibility, which could be described as both a duty and a labor of love. The "maternity ward" is the central location where souls who have yet to incarnate on earth are either deciding or being prepped to travel into the pregnant mother's womb to grow and develop as a human embryo and fetus.

Ensouled and enveloped in the essential earth capsule of a physical body, we arrive with a first breath, and often a wail, to our first moment on earth. The moment of birth, the dawning of a new child's life on our planet, is a sacred occurrence. Forgetting for a moment the focus on technology and endless progress today, let us take time to recognize, witness, and honor the soul's arrival once more at the gates of earthly learning.

Jean's spiritual script and earthly responsibility is to assist souls to decide and then put their energy in order prior to stepping into body at the time of delivery or before. As the between-lives soul regression progressed and an explanation was offered about her core soul task, it was suddenly clear why Jean is so attached in her present life to fostering biological and adopted children. The decision to function from the earthly plane of existence is more complex than we may realize, yet souls like Jean are everywhere to assist and support our choices.

Data from between-lives soul regression indicates that embodiment on earth provides a dense, difficult-to-traverse energy matrix where we have the opportunity to catapult our soul progress toward higher states of wisdom. The pace of our individual advancement is for us to determine. We can opt to climb further up the ladder of soul development or, with weary legs, we may lag on a given rung or even climb back down.

If we appear to regress during a lifetime, the next "go round" in embodiment can nonetheless demonstrate our past level of achievement. For example, if the ladder has ten rungs and we backed down from rung five to the bottom, during our subsequent life we may easily climb from the bottom rung to rung six in short order. Our amassed wisdom is always available for our use and benefit.

Jessica: FORGIVENESS AND SELF-ACCEPTANCE

My life purpose is to learn how to forgive. I need to forgive myself and others. I am not to get caught up in my mind. I need to follow my intuition. I am left-handed in this life, which helps me to use the right side of my brain. Otherwise, I would be too analytical. (The right side of the brain is the creative, intuitive side of the brain.) I need to live alone; otherwise I cannot listen to spirit. I try to fit into society and be normal. My team are always telling me to accept who I am, to not worry and just get on with it. My team is very funny. They tease me. "As humans, we take everything too seriously," they say.

Jessica received more than one good piece of advice that applies to us all. First, the willingness and ability to offer forgiveness to ourselves and to others is likely as important as experiencing self-love and receiving the love of others. Further, loving oneself and others is the foundation for forgiveness. Forgiveness and love are interrelated, just as earth, water, and air are all required for the plant kingdom to survive. Forgiveness does not exist without love, love does not exist without forgiveness, and both allow a soul to advance to higher states of wisdom.

Secondly, intuition (via the use of our right brain—our soft, feminine qualities) allows us to feel and know aspects of life through telepathic communication that is tied to the unseen world. Intuition—that sense of knowing there is more than what we experience with our five senses—unveils the truth of our core as a soul. Having some form of regular spiritual practice—meditation, hiking, music, dance, having a spiritual community, and the like—is critical if we are to remain in communication with the spiritual realm.

Finally, two vital elements of life are discussed with Jessica: we are to accept ourselves more fully, letting go of that critical mindset that says, "I am different. Others will not understand me and will either criticize or devalue me as a person in some other way." We are who we are. Our core self is what it is. Self-acceptance provides rich soil in which we can grow onward. To become less demanding of ourselves and to find joy through fun in our everyday existence is an injunction repeated over and over during regression hypnotherapy.

Chris: A WAKE-UP CALL

I am a guide incarnated on earth. I have served many times in this way, but I do not remember any of this. When I am on earth, I feel very human and do not remember that I am a guide. I am used physically as a healer. When people need it, they are drawn to me. There is a master that I now see at the top of a pure crystal mountain. He is robed in luminous light.

The master allows me to see what is neverending, the eternal energy of Source. It seems I am further on (more advanced) than I thought. I have spent many eons of time on earth. When I return to earth, it is as though I have never been away. I need to make a stronger connection (with spirit) when I am on earth.

This is a major piece of work for me in this life. They tell me that if I did not have the expansion or level of development of my soul, I could not take on the difficult challenges in life that I do. At the same time, one does not need to be a celebrity. You can choose to work unobtrusively. Souls like me are humble and shy. Therefore, I have a difficult time recognizing my level of soul purpose. It is time for my work to deepen and for me to truly know who I am on the soul level.

Chris has moved through numerous physical and family-related traumas in the sixty years of his present life. He is a profoundly capable and experienced soul. In fact, it is unique that a soul whose level of development is comparable to Chris's continues to incarnate for personal soul expansion and for the benefit to other incarnate souls. Chris's life purpose is to determine a stronger means to be consciously tied to spirit, as well as serving as a healer for others.

During his between-lives soul regression, the panorama that is the universe at the higher levels of wisdom is exhibited to Chris. He feels a sense of push/pull: on the one hand, he strives to honor his experience as a soul; on the other, he experiences great humility, stoicism, and a sense of reticence as concerns his degree of spiritual insight and advancement. Many people will have difficulty appreciating what the struggle is for a soul like Chris. While he is being requested to honor his status and his vast experience in this life, he is also continuing to serve on earth in the role of an esteemed yet humble teacher.

Mary: THE LIFE PURPOSE SCRIPT

My life purpose is to create love and trust. I am to model love. I am to use fewer mood-altering substances. Using these drugs is my way of hiding from spirit. It is like hiding in a closet. I cannot be my full self if I do not stop using the drugs. My full self is truly beautiful. I am to bring joy to the world, like bringing light into a gloomy room.

I am told that I am presently in two bodies at one time. Not many souls can manage that. When I feel not grounded is when I am not paying attention to my current life. When it is more difficult to pay attention is when my soul is very busy in the other life. I am told to not be troubled over it when I feel not grounded.

The plan for my life, my life purpose script, was put in place before I was born with two other people. The three of us agreed that I would come to assist my dear friend when she was dying in her fifties. This is the only way that my friend's husband could accept me as his second spouse. He would be too scared to be with someone younger than he. I have incarnated before with both my friend and her husband. The three of us are quite close as souls. My friend and I were lovers in another life.

Mary has a simple-sounding duty—to model love and create trust. Yet trust and love are not easy to fully achieve in life, nor to adequately portray. The spiritual realm has explained to Mary that her use of mood-altering drugs is a means of avoiding who she truly is on the soul level. She is to honor, not dishonor, herself. This same message has been presented in other cases in this chapter.

Our soul energy can be subdivided, or split, such that we can be incarnate simultaneously in two different bodies. Only capable, experienced souls can manage to balance two concurrent lives. Often the two lives have only a brief overlap in regard to human time (chapter 14 has more on this topic). Being told that her soul is residing in two different bodies seems to help Mary, as she can now comprehend why she at times feels ungrounded and "spacey." This insight can lead her in turn to be less critical and concerned.

A profound story unfolds as Mary describes the events of the last few years. Her dear friend was diagnosed with a lengthy, debilitating disease, and when Mary heard about some of the problems the illness was creating, she knew she must offer to assist both her friend and her friend's husband. Mary joined up with him, and together they became a smoothly operating team that cared physically and emotionally for her friend until the final day.

Mary knew in her heart of hearts that "only time would tell" what would transpire in her friendship with her friend's spouse following her death. Learning that all three individuals have known one another in past lives and that they belong to the same soul family provided further support for what Mary intuited to be the case. When she heard from spirit that a plan for Mary, her friend, and her husband had been instituted before Mary arrived in body, it was of great assistance to her.

Carolyn: LEARNING FROM PAST-LIFE CIRCUMSTANCES

There was a good reason why I lived a past life not being connected with my mother. I had to develop myself. I am gentle and courageous to have taken on such a tough life. Three guides come forward. The one in front is the spokesman. I call him "Old Man." He wishes to talk; he is caring and connecting. He lets me know that it takes great courage to be what we are no matter what we do not receive. It takes great courage to know what we do not have. I have learned to be nonjudgmental about people and who they are or are not.

Carolyn comes to realize that living a past life without her mother openly demonstrating love and affection had a purpose. In that life, she developed the capability of being loving and came to know her own true value despite the lack of positive reflection and feedback from her mother. She was able to move past it all, and in her adult life, she became a caretaker for children, exhibiting love and caring on her own.

Carolyn recognizes that her mother in that lifetime was managing children without the support of a husband and father, and she is able to forgive her. She dies in that life with her siblings by her side, feeling a sense of pride that she struggled and "made it through." Carolyn experiences great solace during her regression when she learns she had the capacity to provide steadfast, loving nurturing in the past. She recognizes these ongoing abilities in her present life and feels gratified.

Faye: SELF-NURTURANCE

I am to carry the light. I am a soul with much experience. I am to create peace where there is chaos. I am told, "Do not give too much of your power away. Nurture yourself first. Be brave. To carry the light is not easy. You must nurture yourself more." I will be guided to where I am needed to hold the light. They say, "Nurture yourself so that you can hold the light. There is a huge potential for the earth. The earth needs the light you can provide."

The key message for Faye is twofold. First, there is her ability to offer light as an advanced embodied soul. Faye takes care of many people, both in her personal and work lives. She provides a loving and spiritual environment, replete with nurturing. Many people like her are in need of caretaking themselves: they make huge demands on their personal life and do not nurture themselves well or often enough.

The spiritual realm makes it abundantly clear that if Faye does not absorb adequate nourishment for herself, both literally and figuratively, she cannot and will not be able to offer what she is so capable of providing to others. The message that we need to be aware of on a daily basis is that none of us is a bottomless pit of resources.

Self-nurturing is a crucial message that needs to be heard and absorbed. If we empty our bank account and do not save for the future, we will lack the revenue to provide for our daily existence. Human energy functions in the same manner. We must receive emotionally, physically, and spiritually in order to be balanced individuals before we can offer ourselves to anyone else.

The term *life purpose* is very broad-based. From their spiritual teams during soul regression, the clients included in this chapter have received an array of intent, advice, and instruction for their current incarnation:

- nurture yourself and others;
- live simply;
- live in the moment;
- speak your truth;
- do not judge;
- inspire others to change;
- balance work with play;
- work with the flow of love energy;
- heal the environment;
- help souls to feel they belong;
- transmute pain;

- teach, awaken, and explain;

- be big, not small;

- provide healing skills;

- gain self-worth;

- nurture children, yourselves, and all others;

- feel joy; and

- forgive yourself and others.

Were we to honor and follow even two of the life goals listed here, surely the spiritual realm would be well pleased. We would be advancing both our own soul development and serving as a model of loving support to others.

When we awaken to the core knowing that we personally are a soul in incarnation and that every other embodied human is too, we come to view life from a more profound yet simple vantage point. Too often, we create our lives to be more complex than they need be, and we lose track of our true power. When we boil it down to the one basic kernel of truth, we are purely soul energy of love and joy.

chapter 7

Cultivating right effort helps us to give ourselves
energetically to each day, no matter how difficult,
and to avoid shrinking from life's challenges.

—*Life and Teachings of the Buddha*

Free Will

$\mathcal{T}$he Buddhist concept of right effort speaks to our power to act or behave in whatever manner we choose. We have an unlimited range of possibilities to select from, based on our free will. We *can* choose to spend money like water or to fill our bellies with fast food, even though we know that neither of these choices is likely to benefit us in the long run. In terms of our relationships, we can focus solely on our own gratification and trample over family and friends, assuming that we have unending credit at the Bank of Human Relations.

From the vantage point of higher spiritual behavior, practicing right effort means choosing actions that create the greatest benefit for all. Feeling that we "deserve" something frequently translates into action that is a disservice not only to others but to ourselves as well.

So how do we remain focused, knowing we are allowed to push our cart down the grocery aisle of life and fill our basket however we choose? Large and small opportunities to use our gift of free will present themselves daily, moment to moment, all through life.

For example, I was once scheduled to fly from Colorado to California for a work commitment the following day. When I arrived, however, my luggage was nowhere to be found, even though I had flown only two hours nonstop from my home city to another major destination.

My first reaction, of course, was that I needed the clothes and personal items in my luggage in order to function and present myself the next day in the style to which I am accustomed. But as I looked a little deeper into the situation, it seemed to me that I had three choices:

- to struggle and fret over the current circumstance, worrying that I'd be "judged" for not appearing at my best;

- to believe that there was some profound lesson I was meant to distill from this predestined mishap, like realizing for sure that my physical presentation is not the core of who I am; or

- to believe that there are no coincidences and to rise above and "let it go," knowing that every incident originates in the higher realm of spirit and the divine reality of truth and purpose, even the loss of fresh clothes for tomorrow.

My point is that each of us has the power to choose to how respond: it is *we* who attribute meaning to the occurrences of our lives, both large and small. It follows, then, that we can consciously opt not to be constrained by outside forces and operate from a victim mentality. Our vantage point on life can either serve or not serve our greater spiritual focus, depending on how we think and feel about every event that affects us.

When we are able to grasp that all is perfect just as it happens, that each detail of our human being serves the highest good, we are truly in alignment, not only with divine flow but also with free will. As above, so below; as the embodiment of divine souls, we can find ways to transcend our outer circumstances.

(As it turned out, the airline did not locate my bags for another thirty-six hours. I purchased some basic toiletries and an appropriate blouse for the next day, and had the above realization to share with people at the conference.)

The following regression hypnotherapy session illustrates free will. Note-worthy in the current life of this fifty-year-old female client is that she suffered physical abuse as a child. As you read through the following case synopsis, watch how current, past, and between-lives elements coalesce to form a clear example of our total and complete freedom to choose how we respond to life circumstances.

Bea: UNDERSTANDING CHOICES

It is night, and I am in a carriage. I can hear the horses' hooves on the cobblestones underneath. I have on spats—black, shiny shoes with white gaiters on top. I am wearing black pants and have on a white, frilly tuxedo shirt. I'm approximately twenty-three years old. There is a woman in the carriage with me. She is my beloved. She is with child.

Someone tries to rob us. I need to take care of my wife, but I am not sure I am equipped to do so. I step out of the carriage to reason with the robbers, who are laughing. One robber tries to get to my wife. I grab him.

I've been shot in the heart. I am on the ground and do not want to leave my wife. She is crying and holding me. There is blood on my chest. I try to say that I am fine. I die. I am now able to comfort her energetically, like being a blanket around her.

(From the perspective of her current life, the client takes time to evaluate the past life. She talks about not knowing how to stand up for herself.) I haven't cared for myself well in my present life. I don't feel I have truly been in love. I care for everyone else but myself. Early in the past life, I felt confident, but when I learned my wife was pregnant, I did not feel prepared to care for a child.

(The client re-experiences another past life.) It is day. I am outside in the country. I am wearing boots, a bonnet, and a dress. I have two or three young children that I am raising on my own. I am trying to bring in wood. We do not have enough food. Life is a struggle, and I feel empty and sad. I fall and cannot get up. The oldest boy goes to get help. The other two children try to care for me. I die.

I am above my body now. I had a hard life with little help and felt alone. Energetically, I tell my oldest son that it will be okay. He recognizes my communication. Suddenly, there is light. It is like the Milky Way. It feels familiar and peaceful. I see the "eyes." They are always with me to support me. My guide is here now. I feel safe and loved. I am home.

I am now in a room of white, surrounded by those who have come to heal and help me. There is silence now as the healing is happening. They place a liquid gold gel in my throat. (This client is a singer and healer in her present life.) They are transmitting messages into me to transform my energy. They place healing energy in my heart. My guides and teachers say, "Physician, heal thyself."

Now it is time to move into the area of trust in what I already know. They tell me that I know what I know, and that I am supposed to stop pretending that I don't. It is time to stand up and stop being afraid (as I was truly afraid of the robbers or of being a father in the past life). I am afraid because there has been much violence and loss in my lives. I bring this valuable information as learning for myself and others. I can show others that rather than being afraid and avoiding life, there is another way to cope.

I am to teach the expansive nature of love. Violence is nothing but energy. Violence can beget violence, or violent energy can be transmuted with love. The violence has no power unless we give it power. Others need to hear this message. It is up to me to decide how to live my present life. It is my choice to behave in whatever way I choose. I can be afraid, or I can be not afraid. My purpose is to transmit love and awaken others. It is my doubts that get in the way.

This client was given an important message from a high level of wisdom. It is that we can actually *give* power and energy to negative behaviors such as violence. If the violence we experience in life is retained within our emotional and energetic selves, the end result can be to distrust others, believing deep down that violence will occur again in our life.

The opposite choice is also available to us. Maintaining an attitude of love, no matter what the behavior of others, can serve as a source of transformation for our self and our perspective on life. Fear can be the end result of experiencing violence. Holding love as an even deeper truth and the foundation of all life allows us to relinquish our fear.

Free will allows us to do this. Free will is a heavenly gift. Like the chisel in a sculptor's hands, it is the tool we use to mold each life into something beautiful to behold, something acceptable to our eyes and the eyes of others. In other words, each of us—through our choice of thoughts, feelings, and actions—has the ability to use our loving, pure soul-self energy to design a life of goodness and providence.

Circumstances that we would rather not face in life do inevitably crop up. We are free, however, to respond to them in whatever manner seems most appropriate. What we feel, what we think, and how we act are completely within our determination. We should aim to be proactive rather than simply being reactive to events or hiding.

In the previous example, the client relates how doubt, fear, uncertainty, and lack of belief in her abilities each became a major roadblock at some point in her soul's history and prevented her from opting to transmit love in order to assist others.

Becoming proactive in life suggests being optimistic and moving forward to obtain what we want by owning our capability and power. How we arrange our priorities as we behaviorally and energetically focus on what we desire ties in directly with our use of free will.

Benedict: DUTY FIRST

For this next case study, it is useful to know the client is male and in his late forties. He has never married nor had children, and describes himself as having a fear of attachment. As you read through the account, listen (as I do during a session) for the moment-by-moment clues that allow us to discover how the present life forms interrelationships with the past.

I am outside on a spring day. I am wearing riding boots and a grey uniform with no jacket. I am bald with a full beard, and I am in my middle twenties. I am standing on a porch in a small town on a windy day. I carry a sword on my hip. I am going to be leaving for war very soon. I'm waiting, feeling somewhat depressed and anxious. I want to delay leaving. I am standing here waiting to meet someone. I have been waiting for a while. There is no one here but me and my horse. I am walking back and forth.

I am waiting for a woman. I leave and am sad that the woman, for whom I have romantic feelings, does not arrive.

I go to the state capital, where I am in my full uniform with a grey feather in my hat. I hold a leadership role. Many are excited about the war. I am pleased and worried at the same time.

I am at Gettysburg. I am at the top of a hill looking down at farm fields. With my troops, I am going to defend the hill. Now I see opposing troops coming across the field toward the hill. They come up the hill, and fighting begins. There is smoke and shooting. I cannot tell how things are going. There is more screaming and people being hit. I am in charge of my troops. The opposing troops are now turning back. Now it is quieter. Some of my men are casualties and some are fine.

It is the next day, and I see myself on a stretcher. I've been shot. It is a sunny day. I am on the same hill. I was exposed, and there was a very intense surprise battle. I have died and can see my body. My death was honorable, but I feel very sad.

My sadness is because of the woman who did not come to the porch. We were not married, but I had known her for a long time. My life lacked purpose. I wish I had a family and a woman in my life. A family would have made me more worthy. I have made some mistakes in my life. I made the choice of duty. The woman that I loved felt I was committed to duty first. She thought she was not a priority in my life.

This client made a free will choice, opting for his role as military leader and soldier to be the principal focus in life. Notice how the next client places duty above love or free will. A fascinating detail of this client's current life is that her father was a military officer during World War II, and that he was described as being honor- and duty-bound to his country.

Natasha: MORE REGRETS

I am alone outside in the country, wearing short pants, a light shirt, and sandals. I am in my twenties, male, Asian, with black hair. I am a farmer working in the rice paddies. It is the early 1900s in China. I'm feeling okay.

The work is easy and boring. This is all that I know. Often I work with my wife. I don't know where she is now. I cannot find her.

I learn that my wife is in labor. She is in a hut with other people. I am concerned. My wife dies in childbirth. I never even touch the child. This is my first child. I feel devastated and hurt. My wife and I were very close. I leave the child for my wife's family to raise. I go to the city to work at menial labor.

I am angry about my life. In my middle sixties, I become very ill. I still have never seen or touched my child. I die on a cot alone. As a soul, I am floating above my body now. I feel disappointed in my life. I allowed my wife's family to take the child. My pain and grief over the loss of my wife were with me all of the time.

My guide, in a male body, appears and tells me that even in my present life, I still grieve the loss of that wife and child. He says I need to forgive myself. I feel that I failed my wife and my child. My guide explains that the death of my wife was meant to happen so that I would have the choice of being responsible to my child or not. Now I must learn to forgive myself for my decision. My anger over my wife's death got the best of me. Then I just shut down. In my life today, I am blocking myself from having romantic relationships by being so busy.

Our guides and teachers are always benevolent. They offer us unending opportunities to forgive ourselves as they forgive us. We are allowed to repeatedly alter our current behavior in light of past behavior, transforming those past choices by virtue of today's behavior. The following male client, of his own free will, has chosen fear and anger over trust and love.

Allen: ON CUTTING OFF EMOTIONAL CONNECTIONS

Allen was one year old when he experienced his parents' divorce. His emotionally detached father visited him only infrequently afterwards. In addition, Allen's loving grandfather, having assured him repeatedly that "all would be okay" though his parents were no longer together, died when he was only eight years old. His past-life regression takes him to the mid-1800s, somewhere in the American Midwest.

It is night, and I am in my simple room wearing an off-white muslin night-gown. I have long, light brown hair. I'm in my middle teen years, female, and feel very sad. There are no windows in the room where I am, and I am alone. I never leave this room. I have imprisoned myself here.

(The client is instructed to go back in time to the event that led to the self-confinement.) We were all very happy. I was very close to my father. Then there was great loss from a death—my father died. He fell ill after a horse-and-buggy accident. Now I can see my father lying in a bed, where he is very sick. My mother is not in the room. Now he is very still and has died. I was unable to help.

Now I am at the funeral for my father. Everyone is wearing black. There are horses and a hearse. I am standing with my little sister, and there are many people. My father was a very prominent, respected businessman. My sister and I are alone now. I don't know what happened to my mother. I am fourteen years old. This is the age where I imprison myself in my room.

I am eighteen years old now and have gone away to school. I am still alone. I am shy and have no friends. I spend much of my time by myself. Then I get married to have someplace to live. Lawyers arrange this for me. There is no real joy. My husband is very reserved, and I am not close to him. It is just a life with someone.

I die when I am sixty-five years old. My husband died ten years ago. I am alone in a chair. I have no children. I feel and see my soul leaving my body in that life. I have allowed myself to be a victim of life circumstances and wasted it. I let the emotional loss in my childhood control the rest of that existence. I die of a broken heart, having been alone for most of my life.

The client is currently in a long-term romantic relationship with a partner who is emotionally unavailable. Though he cares deeply for her, he realizes that the past life and his current life are a continuation of the same pattern: he does not have a fulfilling love relationship and continues to neglect his need for intimacy and belonging.

Pulling back the curtain and finding out how our past-life experiences affect our life today can provide significant clues and insights. All three client cases in this chapter need to relinquish their fear and stop avoiding deep relationships in life. Shielding themselves in fear as an emotional breastplate against further loss in the current life will likely serve to isolate them yet again from receiving love and experiencing valuable emotional attachments.

The information a client is offered during the soul regression session seems to be deeply correlated to that individual client and to their life. I would even go so far as to suggest that which specific past life will be shown to the client is meticulously selected at a higher spiritual level. It is almost as though the team of guides and teachers who love and support each client meet up in the Akashic library, where their records of past lives reside. After some deliberation, the team plucks the book of choice off the shelf and opens it for viewing by the client.

After the soul-regression session is over, what the clients do with the cognitive, emotional, and behavioral insights it has generated is completely up to them. Some people choose to block it out altogether; in that they have repeatedly avoided close relationships, this has been the case so far for the three clients profiled above. For others, the regression is a wellspring. While we are a spark of the divine embodied, we have free rein to continue the bumpy ride along the past and current life "ruts" imbedded in the road, or we can opt to approach life in a different manner.

Some of our choices we make preincarnationally. The data repeatedly states that before stepping into a new incarnation, we design our next embodiment experience with our team of experienced guides and teachers. At times, we may be strongly prodded by our team to take a specific path. Free will is a constant, however, and for all intents and purposes, we retain the power to determine our destiny both prior to and during each embodiment. The next client example will illustrate the kind of choices we are afforded prior to stepping into a body.

Katya: CHOOSING FERTILE GROUND

My guide, "Shah-Meesh," has taken me down a long hall into a room where a jerky, old-time movie reel is being shown. First, I see lots of swirly colors on the screen. My mind seems blank, almost as if the details of my next life have not yet been determined.

Then I see the choice I did not take for entering my present life. I could have lived in New York City, but there was not enough nature there for me. Instead, I was born in Iran, where my American parents chose to live. My dad, as a physician, wanted to work in a country where doctors were needed.

I was raised as a Presbyterian in an Islamic world, being encouraged to be open to all religious and spiritual belief structures. I have always felt that religions all come from the same source. I chose my family and the place where I was born so as to learn about different cultures and have the opportunity to grow up being open-minded and nonjudgmental. I am to continue working on loving myself and being more accepting of the diversity and behavior of others.

Dinah: ABANDONMENT ISSUES

I am a little girl, aged one or two years old, outside on the beach. I have on a pink bathing suit. I am walking with both my parents holding my hands. Then I build a sand castle sitting on the sand. Then I begin to feel uncomfortable. My parents are verbally fighting. They are ignoring me. I am crying. They are volatile. They fight a lot. The water comes up to where I sit. I get wet. They are still fighting. The water is taking me out into it. I am going further out into the water. I am faceup in the water. My parents do not see me. I start to go under. I feel abandoned. I wish they would see me. I feel very sad. I have drowned.

Now I am floating. It is all white. This place feels good. It is almost like fog with lights of many colors. I am floating down a corridor where I know I need to go. I have the sense of others here and there. I come to an intersection and go down another corridor. I am coming upon a group of people. They are all around me in a circle. There are ten or twelve people.

Two come out of the circle. They take my hands. They welcome me back. One of these two souls is my husband in my current life, who has been my husband before. We are good friends. The other one who welcomes me is part of my soul family and does not wish for me to know who they are. My guide, "Bar-Thel," is here now. He is always here when I need him.

Now I am going down another corridor. I come to a building that is white with columns and that feels Greek in style. I go past other souls who are blue. I go up some steps and into the building where there is a library. There are rows of books, but I do not go in there now. I go the other way. There are souls milling around. They are guides in training. They are yellow. The blue ones are teachers already; they are guides.

There is now a set of doors. I ask and receive permission to enter. I feel nervous. I am going to meet the "big guns." There is a long table, like in the Supreme Court. There are three people in robes with hoods. I am asked to sit in a chair in front of them. They tell me that the life where I drowned was not an important life for me. I agreed to have a short life to help my parents. This was their lesson because of their fighting.

I have lessons to learn about abandonment, which will be my focus in other lives. I am to learn to transcend feelings of abandonment and that we are never truly alone. The next step for me is to decide when I want to go back into life on earth. I have the choice of resting awhile and thinking about when to go back.

I just need to breathe but will go back into body very quickly. I want to keep growing and progressing. I am to learn about overcoming difficulty and about being the highest self I can be. I can lift others up. I have lots of choices for the work that I can do in my life today. I need to follow my heart.

As I have already stated, free will remains a constant, both before and during a life. From a strictly human perspective, we would probably agree that while it may not be the most popular plan of action, choosing to be born to American parents in Iran (Katya) is less complicated and much less of an atrocious fate than opting to drown at a tender age (Dinah). For close family and friends, the early death of a child is an unmitigated tragedy, something painful beyond all comprehension.

One or both of the souls who have chosen to serve as parents to the little girl in the pink bathing suit may rarely or never have experienced a cohesive and loving romantic relationship in previous lives. Therefore, prior to the daughter's incarnation, her death *may* have been orchestrated amongst the

three of them as a potent opportunity for the parents to consciously transform their relationship style.

We are blessed with free will, and whether we use it to forge happiness
or sadness rests on a decision as thin as a hair. Will our glass be half-full or
half-empty? Knowing that it is always we who decide should help us to keep
things in perspective. Rather than feeling tossed around in life like a tennis
ball, we can adjust our perceptions and attitudes. We can be happy without
elation or sad without despair. Equanimity is available for the taking.

Many people believe in the Law of Attraction. In simple terms, it states
that positive intention begets positive outcome. But we do not have to rely
on magnetic attraction alone, nor confine that attraction solely to our own
desires. In remembering that we are fundamentally divine, in honoring our
soul self as the eternal principle behind our human self, we can choose to
align our thoughts, emotions, and behaviors through free will and right effort
to create the very best outcome, always and for all.

Dennis: MOVING BEYOND THE VEIL

It is day. I am outside. I am a male on a ship. I have spiked-looking blond
hair. It is sunny. I notice a plane in the sky. Something is dropping. There
are explosions. Ah, &^%$#! I wish there were a way to get out of this. We
are at Pearl Harbor. I see the docks. There is nothing left to do. It is dark
now. I see my body below me, against the side of the ship. I am seventeen
years old when I die.

I am like a globe of light moving higher. It is peaceful, and I am enveloped by energy. I feel supported and healed. It is hard to feel unique here,
even though I died at Pearl Harbor. I feel other intelligent energy. There is
an effort to heal my heart. I died so fast that it was difficult for my spiritual
heart to expand. I am okay now.

Here is my guide, "Al-Woon." I am floating, like in pea soup. The light
is growing more intense. This feels good. In this place, you are clarity and
peaceful. I am being taken by the shoulders to view my own soul. I am told,
"Remember the flow of the river; become like the river." I am born of heaven
and flowing to earth. I am to always connect to the flow of the One.

My soul family is filled with teachers. We have an important job to bring spirit to earth. I wanted to be a woman this time. I wanted to touch the earth as a woman. Many of the souls here have come through difficult past lives. Now we have peace and joy. I am told that I am whole and am loved.

When we become fully aware that we are a pure, divine soul having an incarnation, and not the other way around, life gets easier. It sheds a different light on the choices laid out for us, both before and throughout life. We understand that we can use our free will to create and move deliberately through any experience whatsoever.

For example, we may choose to die of leukemia at the age of twelve. Even when we are eleven years old and experiencing the trauma of chemotherapy, we have the opportunity to accept our circumstances, knowing that all is perfect just as it unfolds. In a similar vein, prior to embodiment, a soul could plan to leave the body by committing suicide at thirty-five years of age for the express purpose of it serving as a teaching tool for his child.

From a human vantage point, the circumstances just delineated seem heinous and painfully difficult. Nonetheless, free will remains a constant both between and during each of our incarnations. In addition, our guides and teachers will be there to advise and support us as we determine our behavior and related responses.

chapter 8

I know the price of success: dedication,
hard work, and an unremitting devotion to
the things you want to see happen.

—Frank Lloyd Wright

Dreams pass into the reality of action. From
the actions stems the dream again; and this
interdependence produces the highest form of living.

—Anaïs Nin

Life Direction

*A*ccording to numerous research surveys, well over 75 percent of people are doing work they find distasteful and unnatural. What a sad state of affairs! Clients repeatedly arrive for their between-lives soul regression session wanting to know how they should be spending the "gainful employment" portion of their lives. In addition, many wish to know if they are on- or off-track in regards to their work life, how they spend their free time, and simply how they are living life.

Either concerning our work commitments or during our spare time, it is crucial to our well-being to be engaging in activities that serve to fill our core need for pleasure and creativity. When we follow our visceral, profound interests and the desires stemming from deep within our soul self, we are never off-track. Regrettably, however, there seems to be an unspoken or tacit message in our culture that we need to behave differently, to do something else besides "following our passion."

Messages we receive, both within our families and from society at large, have many of us grappling with the following injunctions:

- I must take up whatever profession or work my parents want me to.
- I should follow in the footsteps of my parents and grandparents to carry on the work they have accomplished in their lives.
- I can never make enough money to be successful.
- People will frown on me and turn away if I follow my passion in life.
- I should spend the bulk of my time doing paid work. Having playtime and creative time is not important.

During her past-life soul regression, Enid waxes and wanes painfully between believing she has something to offer—by teaching others the benefit of loving support for children—and the depression of her own childhood abandonment. Note the level of detail she spontaneously provides.

Enid: A TEACHING STORY

I am living in an institution. I have been standing at the front of an empty classroom for three or four hours. I am twelve years old, wearing boots, a long skirt, and a blouse of some stiff material with wide sleeves and buttoned up to my neck. I look a bit dirty and plain. I have green eyes, and my face is pale and kind of despondent-looking. I have long, messy hair. It is bright-colored and haphazardly pulled into a red ribbon.

I am facing the empty classroom chairs, feeling left out, which is not unusual for me. This has occurred many times before. I am used to being alone, and I don't mind. I sit down at a desk in the front row. The room feels big and empty, but peaceful. I like that.

Now I leave the room and walk into the hall. There is a non-threatening male standing off to my left who emits grounded, loving energy. I walk out of the building through large double doors. It is very bright outside, and the sunlight feels harsh. My clothes are much too heavy for the weather. I do not have a mother to dress me and care for me. In fact, no one cares about me. I am an orphan.

(Enid's life moves forward to age sixteen.) I look a bit more "put together" but am still rough around the edges. I have a job serving food in the cafeteria in the orphanage. The light outside doesn't bother me as much. I now feel more comfortable in my own skin, too. There is a lady teacher here who has seen past my appearance and is giving me support and caring. I am not just another charge to her like I am for most of the people here.

I have no parents now. They could not deal with me, so they put me here. But my special teacher has helped me to gain social skills and given me hope. Now I feel loved. This woman has helped me to come into my body.

In my early adult years, I become a teacher and speaker, sharing my story about how different life can be when there is someone who truly cares for you. I so want to help other children and adults to find their true potential. But somehow it doesn't work out.

By age forty, I am thin and not physically or emotionally stable. In fact, I am despondent again. The older woman who has been my lifeblood is gone. We no longer have any contact. My brief joy in life has faded, and I cannot keep up a positive outlook. I am unable to get past the pain of being abandoned as a child, living in a small dorm room and feeling alone. I came in by myself, and I will leave by myself. My job is to sustain, rather than having a spiritual or passionate focus.

While most past-life soul regression clients are able to focus on the final day's details, Enid is unable to view the scene of her last day. She sums up her life as follows: My death comes around the age of fifty. My life was harsh at the beginning. There was a short, bright glimmer of hope in my teens and as a young adult when someone loved me, but ultimately she left, and I fell into depression for the rest of my life. I just did not have the tools to sustain the optimism, pursue my own transformation, and continue offering my message of self-worth to others.

Enid has not had the nurturing love of a mother in early life this time either. She was raised in a foster home where there was little joy or loving guidance. Thus, she often felt alone as a child and stayed in her room for long periods of time. In her current adult life, however, Enid has a support system that includes a loving husband and family as well as a strong spiritual life. She states, "I have sunshine in life today, and I take charge of my own life and my own happiness. I have even taken up acting for the fun of it as I enter my early forties."

During the between-lives soul regression portion of her regression, as Enid journeys from the ending of her past life into the spiritual realm, her guide, "Teek-moh," steps forward. He illumines the need for her not to be so abrupt with herself, but to allow the "graceful unfolding" of her true soul nature in its own time:

> My spirit guide tells me, "You tend to forget your core spiritual and loving nature and be drawn to worry and fear in your external world. It is time now to come out and stop editing yourself. Speak your truth. Be true to your soul nature. Your improvisation is spontaneous and beautiful. Do not put a lid on a boiling pot. Let what boils up come out, and be your natural, passionate, appropriately theatrical self."

Enid's story is representative for many people for two main reasons: many people have what are known as timing issues, or difficulty following their core passions. To explain, there is such a thing as mental timing, as opposed to emotional/spiritual timing, whereby we decide in our head and believe we can force an event or an alteration to occur in our life. How often have you decided to swim upriver and attempt to make something happen, to no avail?

When we can get out of our own intellectual, wasteful brain machinations and shift into trusting that we can manifest what we desire, the river of life will flow, providing us with whatever is in our best interests. As "Teek-moh" points out to Enid, "to everything there is a season." Life holds both grace and grit. When we do not become mired in the grit, the grace will show itself. And when we align with that grace and start living our core passion to the utmost, we are indeed fully on-track with our soul self and life plan.

The words "core passion" evoke a litany of words and phrases. If you have difficulty getting in tune with yours, take a moment to check in and see how you resonate to the terms in the following list. It can be a way of illuminating your passion.

- Fervor
- Zeal

- Fulfillment or satisfaction of our soul self
- Love
- Ardor
- Boundless enthusiasm
- Energizer
- Intense joy
- Fully alive

When we are not living our passion, be it our vocation or avocation, a critical component of soul viability is lacking in life. Reflect on those times when you felt the most alive—remember when you were brought to tears as you experienced an event, an occurrence in nature, a unique time with family or friends, or the like. What are the emotional, physical, and cognitive cues that provide a window to your deepest passions? Find and nourish those sparks so that your soul life, your true self, does not become a pale and frozen shadow of itself.

The question remains as to whether it is possible for our team of guides and teachers to deem us off-track in our current embodiment in regards to our predetermined script, or plan. Furthermore, if we are off-track, what, if any, are the consequences?

Enid's past-life details may or may not have been out of sync with her current life script. Quite possibly, a simple but key learning for Enid in her past life may have been that someone who is able to provide love and caring can come along in your life and fill the inconsolable gap left by the loss of parents. Perhaps she needed to experience a drastic level of abandonment by her biological family and be able to accept love and support from a total stranger before going on to fully experience a loving support network in the next life.

Even her brief time teaching her message of empowerment to others may have been rising to the occasion of her life plan. Though Enid completed her past life in the doldrums of depression and despair, the sliver of time during which she received love—and in turn painted a brighter picture of hope for others—may well be contributing to Enid's current life of joy. Although just briefly, she did follow her passion to help others realize that all is not lost without parents.

Enid currently basks in the arms of a full family life. Now entering her fifties, she is progressing even further in allowing herself to follow her passion for acting. Once again, she is demonstrating something important to others: it is never too late to enjoy an activity you have wanted to participate in all your life.

As humans, we often require ourselves to evolve without making allowances for slip-ups, or mistakes, though there is no better way to learn. Many of us are far too self-critical. We make up standards of behavior and attitudes that are nearly impossible to meet, and we hold ourselves mercilessly to them. The expectations that we lay on ourselves frequently seem to be far greater than any our guides and teachers would impose.

It is not uncommon for clients to arrive expressing concern before their between-lives soul regression. They fear that their council of wise elders will label their present efforts as "not up to snuff" in keeping with the preset life purpose and plan. Many believe they may be completely off-track or worry that their elders will threaten or even chastise them if they do not shape up. Specifically, they are convinced they will be faulted for not being sufficiently committed to following their life plan and for not working hard enough to accomplish the tasks they set for themselves prior to this incarnation.

Nothing could be further from the truth. It is not the role of our council of higher wisdom to designate or denigrate us as failures. Fear of failure is a human-induced apprehension based on societal and familial standards, even though we may be carrying over some of our fears from past lives. Our council is ever benevolent, loving, supportive, compassionate, and advisory, as in the next case study.

Cassie: NOBODY'S PERFECT

Cassie begins to move away from her body at the completion of a past life. During this portion of her soul regression, she comments:

I like both dimensions, earth and spirit. I do not have more attachment to one over the other. I am at peace in both places. The life I just completed was not of specific importance. I completed what I needed to do. Each life is like a bead on a string. My soul is the string. Now I am gathering my self that has been dispersed while I was in body. I am reconstituting. I can feel my energy body. I am floating past a type of "doorkeeper." He is familiar and feels like a shepherd of sorts.

Now I am entering a city which is like a community of loving souls. Everyone is very busy. There are many buildings where people study. There are teachers here who consult me about individual cases. Now we are coming to a temple that looks like grey marble. I am excited as I ascend the steps. I have a lot to talk about and a lot to learn. I go past the room where I work with a research and study group. It is like a center for fellows who are like a think tank. I will not go in there just now.

I am going into a room where I find my council. My guide, "Pro-meet," who has been with me, steps aside. My job is to raise the consciousness of the planet. The council members laugh and joke with me because I am "high strung" about my intent to move quickly toward my goals.

I am focusing all my energy to make progress toward my vision. Given my level of soul experience, it is ironic that I have such an intense personality. I am told that in my soul nature, I am thorough and determined. The worry and self-doubt that I experience now are simply part of my current human personality that stems from the biology of my brain.

My council is very supportive and understanding about my human personality. They tell me that it is important this life to have self-doubt because of my human brain, and to learn how to heal my lack of confidence. That self-doubt gives me empathy. I am moving away from having a small picture of myself into gaining an acceptance of my experienced soul nature. The council is encouraging me to relax and reminding me that I need balance. I pressure myself too much and need to take more time for relaxation.

Cassie is an experienced soul who continues to fine-tune with each incarnation. Her visit with her wise council begins with them reiterating the high degree of standing she has already obtained. But the elders also remind her that most, if not all, souls retain human characteristics like insecurity, no matter what their degree of advancement. The persistence of such traits is simply a symptom, or indication, that further soul refinement is in order.

Greater purity, clarity, and enhancement are always possible. Council input and advice are there to provide Cassie with the support, understanding, and guidance she can use.

Such symptoms stem from our human personality being in charge as opposed to our taking leadership from our soul self. Perfection does not exist, no matter how advanced our souls. Thus, we are shown once again that it is impossible to be off-track in our soul journey; neither the concept nor terminology will ever be used by our higher wisdom team. To strive for greater soul clarity is ever permitted and encouraged.

The teachings of mystical Kabbalah tell us that the universe was created perfect and subsequently blown to smithereens (as in the big bang theory), its sparks of perfection scattered to the winds and hidden by husks that comprise today's reality. The duty of humankind is to gather the sparks back together, returning our soul energy to its pure form, one that is capable of residing in body and in spirit simultaneously.

Planet Earth appears to provide good ground for the ripening of our incarnate souls, the ideal environment for our souls to progress in. If we accept the spiritual premise that our soul joins a body for the express purpose of peeling back the husk that locks away, or hides, our true nature, then we move closer to knowing why we journey over and over again to this dense, and at times difficult, place in which we live.

We are never off-track. We are simply becoming and progressing… becoming and progressing. Each life can move us further along the path of return to our purest nature. The challenges we create from incarnation to incarnation and the means by which we face these challenges are what determines how far we have come. Love is the energy of our core soul nature. Judgment, guilt, and fear are human delusion and illusion that block our awareness of the divine love we carry within our very cells.

In meeting with their wise council, many clients receive important messages to help them along life's path. Communications from the elders are often intended to bolster a client's confidence or to foster an ongoing belief in oneself and the power of using love versus judgment as the touchstone in life.

Sample Council of Elders Statements to Various Clients

- "People cannot yet do what they cannot yet do. It is better to hold to the possibility or open to an occurrence rather than creating false expectations or pushing in vain to have something particular happen."

- "Some current life bodies and brains can *experience* all emotions but do not have the ability to *polish* all emotions."

- "It is better to see what you do have rather than what you do not. It is better to recognize what you are than what you are not."

- "You claim to believe in divine providence, yet you doubt. Do not, however, put down doubt, because using your mind to doubt clears up your faith."

- "Do not make decisions based on fear—make them based on love."

- "You can transmute pain into joy. This requires patience. Pain is not permanent. There is an unlimited field of possibilities."

- "Stop worrying so much, and go with the flow."

Our council is always loving and forgiving. Unfortunately, living "in the flesh" teaches us that life can be anything but. Instead of fostering our creativity and our childhood sense of awe and wonder, parents and societal institutions are often geared to drumming into our hearts and minds that we are "good" if we do this and "bad" if we do that. Much conflict can arise, not to mention mixed messages.

We are even taught in a roundabout way that we have the power to control others and manipulate their emotions to our ends by behaving in certain ways. A child soon learns that by throwing a tantrum at the supermarket checkout, Mommy is practically guaranteed to buy him candy. Is it any wonder that many of us come to mainly experience fear, guilt, and blame instead of love and acceptance from others and for ourselves?

The list of council missives you have just read invites us to always go with the positive rather than cling to a negative or demeaning view of our behavior. Even when we have committed serious transgressions, such as rape and pillage, in a given lifetime, there is an opportunity to restore the balance by adjusting our actions and behaviors in some subsequent life.

As we have seen with Cassie, even human frailties like feelings of self-doubt and guilt can serve a valuable purpose when they lead us to question our ways and solidify our virtues. Still, one thing the elders would have us keep in mind is that nobody is perfect.

If and when we truly listen, we will receive the guidance we request from the higher planes, provided the timing and content we desire are suited to our true needs. Believing in our intuition and leading from the heart as opposed to the head will keep us ever on track. When the rational, or "monkey," mind takes over, we are at risk of blocking the valid and valuable input that is continuously streaming to us from our guidance team.

It is important to recognize and heed the subtle thoughts that arise in our minds rather than ignore or dismiss them. If you are like me, you have suddenly felt almost compulsively driven to do something like weeding out your closet when something much more important was left dangling, like a stack of calls and emails to return, bills to pay, or a creative project to finish.

I have learned to listen to these out of the blue, crazy notions. Whatever the thing may be, it is usually just spirit's way of hitting me over the head with an activity that will prepare me energetically for a shift, or new commitment, that is just around the corner.

Logan: ATTENDING A COUNCIL MEETING

It is time to go to see the four who watch over me. They appear as four columns open at the top. They are not saying anything out loud, but I sense I am doing well. They knew I wanted to see them, to meet with them. They tell me when it is important for me to have a bad day. Then they help me get over the hump. I must trust that I have the answers. They are there to catch me when I fall. Now I understand why I don't receive many answers. I have to figure it out on my own. This life is about making a huge shift. They do not want me to give up and lose faith. They tell me to have fun with this and explore who I am.

Logan describes the beauty of trusting the guidance from our council. When a difficult day occurs in our life, our elders are there to assist. They are a steadfast and omnipresent support system. The key element is for us to trust that we will be supported. Quieting our human minds and tuning into the purpose of whatever event may be happening in life helps us to know how to proceed. At the core of our knowing, we always have the answers, because we never operate in a vacuum. The love and providence of our guides and elders light the way forward.

When human nature takes us into that frantic, what-in-the-world-do-I-do-now mode of operating, then we can easily block out of awareness the "how and why" of everyday life events. In rough times, we may be tempted to ask, "Why do I have to experience this trauma? What shall I do now?" Trust and faith, along with the information we receive from our spirit guides and teachers, will remind us that we are never off-track. Our higher wisdom team is there when we falter to tell us there is a purpose for each event in our life. The answers are within; we are capable to discern them, and we are always guided.

I want to present an interpretation of the council statement that "People cannot yet do what they cannot yet do." Our soul capabilities grow sequentially. By this, I mean that as we advance on our soul's path, we layer one level of soul development upon another, just like a diamond cutter polishes a fine gemstone, starting with what appears on the surface to be nothing but a chunk of rough rock or stone.

As we trudge through one lifetime after another, facing myriad human experiences, we develop coping skills, grace, and understanding, and we eventually become more loving and forgiving. Our hurtful, self-centered, and fearful behavior gets whittled away like the dross it is.

All of us start in first grade, moving forward as we learn the ABCs of soul development and fine-tuning our soul quality as we climb each rung of the evolutionary ladder. If we are not in eleventh grade, then we are not; we are in sixth grade or second grade, and that is that.

Expecting ourselves or expecting someone outside of ourselves to operate in the manner of a soul nearing the wisdom of a guide is unrealistic and can be detrimental. *We are not off-track if we appear less stable or evolved than someone else;* we are simply at the point in our journey where we are, which is exactly where we are supposed to be.

Eileen: A LIFE WELL LIVED

I see myself lying on a street. There are people standing around me. There has been an accident. I am in my thirties and have died. Now there is a feeling of lightness. There is a long tunnel, and I feel happy. Two souls join me now. They are wispy, playful, and twirling around me. They serve as my escorts. There is a crowd of souls to greet me. I see Aunt Dot and Esther. They are happy and greet me joyfully. My guide, Lloyd, is loving and caring. He holds his hands out to me. He is bluish-purple in color.

Lloyd shows me a building with columns and many rooms and halls. I am just being shown around. I see many rooms with souls who are talking or studying or joking. I will come back later, but Lloyd wants me to rest. He takes me to a meadow with flowers where there is a lovely cottage. I am very tired, and I rest.

Now I am going back to the white building with columns. I go into a bare white room with a U-shaped table. There are eight souls sitting there in white garments. They are my council of elders. Lloyd sits at the head of the table. I am welcomed back. I am told that I belong to a group whose task is to send healing energy to the earth through the message of love and compassion. I am to offer peace and empathy to others. I also help people have a good death. My job is to take away fear, which is an element that can hinder the spirit in leaving the body. I am a gentle soul, and I open hearts.

The council reviews my past life. They say it was by agreement that I died so young. They felt I needed to learn to benefit the earth, to emanate kindness and compassion. I had completed this task. They are pleased with my work.

I chose a life this time, my current life, with a number of struggles, such as lack of money, difficulty obtaining my education, and not being pretty. They are pleased with me. I have always been afraid before to meet challenges. This time I am facing my challenges, meeting them face to face with confidence. I am conquering my fears, learning to have confidence and trust.

I need to trust my instincts more. My instincts are better than I realize. I have carried forward many fears from other lives. I must continue to not

lose faith and not be afraid to be hurt. My council will always support me
by being nonjudgmental.

We are always guided and supported and loved. What we might label as a
short life, such as dying in our thirties, is in no way viewed as failure by the
spiritual realm. In fact, this may well have been a prebirth agreement, or we
may have completed the script for that life. We may even be slated to experience an early death for continued soul development.

During our council meeting, we are given a progress report. Generally,
we are both patted on the back and offered direction for the future. We are
reminded not to focus solely on what we believe could have been handled
differently. We are strongly advised to examine our achievements. Whatever
our circumstances, we will always be honored and directed as to what might
be our next steps to further our soul growth and expansion.

A council may explain to the client that each life is somewhat like a play
where each person is an actor: "When someone in your life is acting poorly,
do not take it personally. Sit back and observe from a place of introspection."
An individual who needs to develop inner strength may choose a mother
who is not outwardly nurturing or supportive and who may even be frequently hurtful, someone who has trouble showing love and never laughs.

Whatever circumstances life presents us, we have the option of learning
the lesson now or living in denial and experiencing another chance at it in
the future. We always have free will. Being off-track is a misnomer—we are
afforded a second, third, and potentially infinite number of opportunities to
try it again.

It is human nature that steps in the way of our progress. When our thinking brain becomes the master, we are at risk of diving into the deep end of
the pool and forgetting to come up for air. When we are under the water,
trapped in our intellectual machinations, all we do is criticize ourselves.

Once we begin swimming toward the surface, however, the growing light
of day entices us to continue rising faster and faster. When we break through
the surface of doubt and fear and breathe in a gulp of fulfillment and nourishment, it reminds us of the divine nature of our loving and graceful soul
self.

Imagine a tall, sturdy oak tree deeply rooted in rich earth. Its hardy trunk, filled with healthy branches and masses of deep green leaves, rises proudly toward the blue heavens. Each of us has the metaphoric potential of being such a great tree.

Trust that you are riding the rails of life and advancing steadily and securely on-track. As you daily move forward, trusting that you are guided and cannot make a permanent mistake, your roots dig ever deeper, absorbing the nutrients of life on earth.

The body of your healthy tree moves your thoughts and feelings day by day toward the truth of your soul self. You never forget to value yourself and others. The crown of your tree reaches tall into the sky to receive the never-ending, ever-present light of divine love and guidance. By examining each of our experiences for the cues and clues tied to our soul progress, we will continue expanding our branches, and reflexively, the environment will be richer for others.

chapter 9

A new moon teaches gradualness and deliberation
and how one gives birth to one slowly. Patience
with small details makes perfect a large work,
like the universe. What nine months of attention
does for an embryo, forty early mornings will
do for your gradually growing wholeness.

—Jalal ad-Din Rumi

Soul Progression

*B*ased on data gathered from approximately 8,500 cases of between-lives soul regression, there is strong evidence that we choose the specifics of our minds and bodies before birth, as well as our life circumstances. Our mind can also be termed the brain or personality, while the bodily attributes we select include height, ethnicity, bone structure, visual or auditory acuity, facial traits, and numerous other traits. Life circumstances include any number of variables.

To reiterate the case-study findings about our physical being, each soul is afforded the opportunity to visit a limited "supermarket" where, say, Caucasian, Chinese, 5 foot 1 inch, club-footed, and exceptionally intelligent bodies and minds, to name just a few, are there for the taking. A support team of spirit guides and teachers make themselves available to offer explanations and counsel regarding what can be difficult decision making.

We make our preincarnational choices with certain evolutionary ends in mind. Specifically, the body and other life attributes and circumstances we select are designed to optimize our learning in the next incarnation. For example, opting to be African-American in the mid-1800s in the United

States established the potential for experiencing ostracism, standing up for one's culture, and/or living a life of poverty.

Consider the infant whose in utero development has been compromised due to the mother's use of drugs. Resulting complications the child could experience include a range of learning, behavioral, and congenital maladies, as well as greater stress throughout life. On the flip side, such children may also accomplish in one lifetime a depth and breadth of soul development not available to others.

In simplest terms, incarnating is the assemblage, comingling, and coagulation of three essential elements: body, brain/personality or mind, and soul. Without a container, neither brain nor soul can color, or animate, a human. If we lack a physical body, we are either dead or in some other form of nonphysical existence—a term open to discussion or debate, depending on one's understanding and perspective.

So how and why does each of us piece together the particular humanoid attributes that we do? Clients report learning from painful experience. In addition, they say that each life is useful, whatever the circumstances that are played out, so not everyone will opt to be born a poster child.

Appreciation can grow strong out of lack. Often our advancement, our drive, is accelerated by deprivation. For example, being orphaned due to rampant epidemic conditions, a common fate in centuries past, is an experience a soul who wishes to bolster an appreciation for ongoing family ties might consider.

Consider Bobbi's story, a case that summarizes many of the relational elements at play in the reincarnation process.

*B*obbi: CHOICES HONORED

I am taken by my guide to the area of books where I can learn how I chose my mother and father. The books are energy. There are many books. "Zareenah," my guide, tells me that I wanted a mother who was independent so that I would learn to do things on my own. I chose a mother who was independent to a fault.

My father chose me. He wanted a daughter who was fun, smart, and would become accomplished. He wanted someone better than himself. I

needed to learn how it feels for someone to be proud of you but never tell
you so. My dad is a young soul.

Then I meet with my wise elders. They are pleased with me. They say I
am learning and transforming. They tell me I am on the path where I need
to be. They say I cannot help my children to gain confidence; they must do
this on their own. These are their lessons. I cannot live their lives for them.

Bobbi's soul regression highlights a powerful understanding about relationships with immediate family members. We do not necessarily choose
souls and circumstances with our close family members that will make life
simple. Our time in body is not meant to be a piece of cake; soul progress
is the agenda. We select, or agree to be selected, in order to climb the rungs
of development or to assist another soul to ascend. Being able to further
develop a stronger, more inner-directed sense of self is crucial.

Bobbi receives a pat on the back on her journey toward greater soul
accomplishment. She is reminded, however, that no matter how steadfast our
love for them or how intense our desire is to assist our children in avoiding
tripping and falling in life, they must cope with their own traumas themselves. She recognizes the value of learning to stand on her own two feet and,
likewise, the essential requirement for her children to do the same.

In the early part of the soul-regression session, I guide clients backward
in time by having them revisit significant events tied to chronological dates
or events such as birthdays in the current life. We follow through all the way
back into the time spent in the mother's womb. The process is too techni-
cal to explain, but the ultimate goal is for the client to access earliest soul
memory in this lifetime.

Upon conception, the human being can be described as an expanding
cellular structure destined to become an integral physical being outside the
womb. The data shows that, most commonly, the soul has made first contact
with the new body between the third and sixth month of pregnancy. Very
seldom do I hear of it happening before the third month.

In addition, the occurrence of first contact does not always mean that
the soul remains with the body from that point forward. For many, there
seems to be a time of moving in and out before final attachment to the fetus.

Imagine your soul trying on a new body just like you would try on a new pair of pants to figure out if the fit is good or not. This point comes up fairly often at the beginning of the soul-regression process when the client is guided to journey back in age.

The following are examples of client responses to questions I have asked about being in the womb prior to or immediately at the time of birth into the current life:

Miscellaneous Input on Prebirth Conditions

I feel not 100 percent wanted. There are muffled voices and concern from my mother, who is worried she might bring the child she is carrying into the world with a serious condition called stenosis, whereby the child could die before six months of age. This is going to be a difficult life. I don't like feeling my mother's difficult emotions while in the womb. Where I come from, there is unconditional acceptance. I joined this body at five months.

My legs feel cramped but my head feels okay while I am in the womb. I can hear my mother's heartbeat and her voice. I know my mom's emotions. My mother is worried about being a mom. I am eager to try out the body. I look forward to flexing my limbs. I bring awareness and expansiveness to this new life that is unique to it. My soul melding with the body has been fine. I have an intelligent brain that is eager to be activated. I first joined the body of the fetus at seven and one-half months and moved in and out for about one month. Once I am born, I will whip things into shape.

In the womb my legs are okay, and my head feels like it is in a tight space. My mother is both joyous and sad. She and my dad do not get along. The body is a good match for my soul's consciousness. It is both strong and gentle. I joined the fetus at six months and have remained since then.

My legs and head feel okay. I joined the fetus in the fourth month. I do not want to be born. I will feel alone when I am born. I don't feel alone in the womb. My purpose for coming into body is to find a way back home and to take others with me. We are part of everything, like being wrapped up like a ball. When we come into body and when we leave, we rediscover the wonder of it all. It is all like magic. I don't want to forget the magic of it all. It is meant to be fun.

In the womb, my head is bent to the right. It is okay. My mother is stressed, but I cannot help her. I have a new, strong, and willful body with a lot of life force. I am healthy and sensitive. My soul integrated easily with the new body. I have extra synapses in my brain that are multidimensional. My soul made a good connection with the lobes of the brain and the base of the skull. There is an energy grid. I am a receiver of information, a receiver of galactic energy. I can join dimensions to assist others and ground the frequency to this place on earth. The earth is changing its vibration. Those who match the new frequency will stay.

The between-lives regression includes a somewhat brief age regression moving from the client's present age back in time into current childhood. This practice is accomplished for the sake of assisting the client to relax into an altered state for the purpose of memory practice of only positive or neutral memories in order to enhance and aid the regression. Ultimately, the client is guided into the time period when they are in their mother's womb during their current lifetime. In the womb, clients may gain profound detail about themselves and their family.

Some of my clients speak of an energy grid tied to the spiritual realm. Sacred geometry is another term to describe this grid, which archaeologists, anthropologists, and mathematicians maintain encompasses the religious, philosophical, and spiritual beliefs that have sprung up around geometry in various cultures during the course of human history. It is believed that there is a geometric relationship between the spiritual realm and earth. Many ancient spiritual symbols and buildings can be described through geometric formulae attaching the literal form to mathematical ratios, harmonics, and proportions that are also found in music, light, and cosmology.

As the earth's vibration is changing, between-lives regression clients describe their involvement in the process of shifting that is occurring. Apparently, some of us have bodies and brains that are capable of assisting with the ongoing alteration of energy that is described by many at this time. It is highly likely that more people will learn the "what" and the "how" of their involvement in the energetic enhancement on our planet.

Marie: PROGRESS IS AS PROGRESS DOES

A recent client, Marie, aged fifty, describes herself as "belonging to a tight-knit Catholic family" from childhood up till today. By contrast, however, she says she has refused to attend church on Sunday since she was a little girl, and she has never married nor had children.

As a therapist, I could be wondering about other surface contradictions. Why, for example, is Marie showing up for a between-lives soul regression, a form of spiritual inquiry, when (a) she has completely disavowed the formal religion and teachings of her childhood, and (b) she has never developed a formal meditation practice or any alternate means of communicating and receiving from spirit.

Lacking a primary romantic relationship, she continues to be strongly tied to and supportive of her parents and four siblings, and she has a full-time career in the business field that requires a lot of linear structure. During her initial interview, she says her main reason for doing the regression is to find out what her life purpose is.

Upon questioning her spirit guide, Marie reports her life purpose to be serving as a "light force." Henry, her guide, kindly refuses to explain what the term means exactly, and he offers no insight as to why she is not married and doesn't have children. Instead, he recommends that she learn to meditate (for example, by guiding herself into a relaxed state with candles and aromatherapy), and that she not allow doubt to get in the way of focusing on her path.

If she follows the aforementioned steps, Marie will come to understand her soul's path related to light force and various other aspects of her soul's intentions in this life and beyond. "Light force" would seem to indicate possessing and transmitting the energy of the divine, the energy of pure love.

It would appear that Marie moved away from traditional religious structure to be more attached to pure spirituality. And yet she seems no further advanced in her quest. Thus, she is encouraged to deepen her "knowing," her intuitive ability to access her soul self.

From the vantage point of a between-lives soul regression therapist, combining the data from Marie's interview and her regression, I believe she is likely to be a soul of more than average experience. Other signs of advancement become apparent to me as I examine various interrelated components of her life, such as:

- choosing to experience past-life soul regression and between-lives soul regression;

- rejecting traditional, structured religious practice at an early age;

- never marrying or having children, which is a preincarnational necessity at some stage of soul development;

- maintaining a close family relationship; and

- being instructed by spirit to develop her intuitive capacity, her awareness of an attachment to the higher power.

It would seem timely for Marie to become more conscious of who she is as a soul in order to be better able to serve in her role of light force worker.

Soul progression is a very complex matter. Stepping into the marketplace of body/mind choices during the interlife is a part of scripting each life. Imagine arriving at your small neighborhood market with a team of respected teachers who will offer direct support and instruction on better and worse options for your dinner tonight—or in this case, on your menu of possible identities and next-life experiences.

The market is small, with a few aisles presenting limited available bodies, minds, and numerous other life aspects in order to create your next embodied intention and structure. The team of advisors moves along each aisle, explaining possible selections, which you can place in your cart or not as you sketch in the details of your upcoming lifetime.

The specific design of each new life tends to reflect to some degree the level of soul development. For example, my forty-five-year-old female client who has struggled with two life-threatening illnesses and the death of a parent when she was only twelve is not likely to be a very young soul. In order to withstand numerous and significant losses, an embodied soul has generally had to live through many incarnations and developed much wisdom.

On the other hand, not all "advanced" reincarnations are fraught with hardship. There are sometimes lives where we are given a reprieve from intentional progress to simply rest and regroup; I call these "sleeper lives." Nor are well-known or outwardly powerful, carefree, or privileged people necessarily that advanced. Many seemingly ordinary people are—we all just erect various circumstances to evolve within: "Rich man, poor man, beggar man, thief; doctor, lawyer, Indian chief."

Between-lives soul regression offers a special vantage point from whence to confirm one's soul standing. Here's how it works: soul energy emanates a perceptible color that is in line with the point of soul evolution. To explain, each color of the rainbow, beginning with red and ending with violet, demonstrates an increasing vibrational frequency and therefore heightened advancement. Thus, orange vibrates faster than red and would show more spiritual development, yellow vibrates faster than orange, and so forth.

During the session, the client can be asked to observe and report the color of their soul energy. Such was the case in our next client study.

Edward: SOUL COLOR AND SOUL ADVANCEMENT

In the body, I was constricted. Now I am beginning to feel a white, expansive space. It is important for me to know that I was a compassionate, good soul. Now it's bright and expansive. My butterfly wings will unfold. I feel joyous, and I am reveling in it.

This is not like earthly joy. I am returning to a rainbow—there's a spectrum. I can't get back to my band of color. Everything feels ethereal, not contained. I am part of something bigger. I know where I belong.

To go back to earth would be like going through a membrane of clouds. I am seeking my place in the rainbow. I'm moving toward a purple band. I know where I belong. If I stood still, the purple band would coalesce around me. I'm just regrouping. I've done this before. I know how to let the molecules settle.

The purple band is home. I have been in every part of the rainbow. I have progressed. There is no set number of lives to get to the purple band. You get there when you are ready. Each band of color has a major emphasis.

In the purple band, you are positive and experienced. It is like reaching the higher grades in school. It is about kindness and compassion there. It is not about money.

The spiritual realm is aware that our earthly worries may center on materialism. Guides and teachers recognize our day-to-day human concerns. Frequently, regression clients receive messages that underscore and remind the individual of their capable behavior of compassion and kindness.

Note that no hierarchy is attached to or inferred by the soul color. The colors of the rainbow, red through violet, do not signify that color number four is better than color number one. Being in fifth grade in school is not of greater value than being in kindergarten. By and large, if we are approximately five years old, we will attend kindergarten, and if we are eleven years old, we will likely be in fifth grade. Our grade level is simply a fact of our age, emotional maturity, and knowledge. Such is also the case for "soul grade level," if you will.

With the understanding that the concept of better versus worse is irrelevant with regard to soul progression, we'll now explore various aspects of diverging core soul color. In the soul choice marketplace, advice and encouragement is offered by one's team of advisors to select appropriate next-life details that dovetail with our current soul capability. Thus, the offerings of body, mind, and life circumstance are aligned with previous experience and whatever is necessary for the soul's continued advancement.

At the same time, it seems that certain souls request, or are gently coerced, to plan next-life details that will push the soul's ability to the edge of comfort and capability. Although the spiritual advisory team may prefer not to have the soul dive into a complex and demanding life, two factors intervene: (a) permission can be given nevertheless, and (b) the soul in question is further allowed to "forge" or "trudge" through the upcoming life at its own preferred pace, even if it has chosen difficult circumstances.

Our soul may be faced with all manner of human challenges, such as complications with physical/emotional health, death of critical family members (including the loss of parents during our early years), childhood abuse, and numerous other harsh realities. Projecting how well we may do at facing and coping with the traumas of life is a bit like checking the gas tank reading in a car. If the soul experience gauge registers full or at least beyond the middle mark, the soul/person is generally capable of managing a life with more—and increasingly intense—hurdles than might seem the norm.

More than eight thousand between-lives soul regression sessions attest to the fact that the soul progresses. And just as the soul ripens and expands through ongoing development, the universe as a whole seems also to mature; the one mirrors the other. Numerous clients in the course of their conversation with their guidance council of wise ones explain that their decision and purpose to incarnate has been to assist the spiritual realm in understanding life on earth.

Earthly incarnation is a "proving ground" where we, as souls, cycle through the thick and thin of life experience in order to deepen our grasp of higher wisdom and higher perspective. This book presents various tools and components of this learning and progression. The age-old expression, "As above, so below," holds true, as does the converse: as we each advance as a soul, so too does the spiritual realm.

Returning to a further explanation of soul color and soul energy expansion, let us focus on the age-old topic of young soul versus old soul. Let me reiterate that young or old means nothing on the scale of better or worse. We're all students, we're all teachers, and we're all learning and sharing.

As we begin our soul's journey in a body on the earth, frequently we are naïve, immature, and relatively unable to focus on life's trials and tribulations with any perspective. "Newbies" almost always need people around to validate them and are more concerned with daily trivia than more global and humanistic issues.

Soul progression occurs in many individual steps. If we continue placing one foot in front of the other, moment by moment and day by day, we will progress. The most effective means I have discovered is to turn absolutely every experience into an opportunity.

You likely know that the Chinese characters for "crisis" also denote "opportunity." Viewing life as everything being divinely inspired will offer you a window of opportunity. Summing it up, a wise philosopher once said, "Each and every fork in the road is to be explored."

Michaela: IT'S ALWAYS LONELY AT THE TOP

Michaela arrives for her between-lives soul regression seeming a bit lost. She has resigned a very responsible position, sold her home, and moved across the country. Michaela points out that she feels empowered having "jumped out on her own," and also that she enjoys spending time alone even though she loves to entertain. In fact, she actually sequesters herself but admits she is afraid of knowing her core self.

In the course of the regression, much is revealed about Michaela's core self, including information on her inclination to live somewhat in seclusion. Following the ending of a past life, Michaela experiences her soul exiting the body in a kind of "whoosh" that is as simple as taking another breath.

Michaela's guide appears immediately upon her bodily release. He leads her to a circle of her closest soul friends. Following a brief reunion with her core group, which has been together since the very beginning of her soul's journey, Michaela experiences boredom and mediocrity.

Her guide then leads her into a darkened library and encourages her to open a door where she steps out into the moonlight. Michaela states, "I feel privileged to be allowed to just be, not being forced into a further learning situation and not bound by rules." Nonetheless, she continues to feel agitated, lacking something and at the same time needing more surprises.

Her guide then escorts Michaela to her council of wise beings. Surprisingly, the council members remove their formal robes and suggest Michaela do the same, which is not at all a routine occurrence.

The overall purpose of Michaela's current incarnation is to research her unanswered questions. She is told by her council, "You have had the privilege of being in the human realm experiencing earthly struggles, and you recognize the divine nature of incarnate beings. The beauty of life is a symphony with many surprises and disappointments. You will be a more effective council member having planted seeds that lessen human pain. You can be an instrument for change. Your need for aloneness and separateness is due to the difficulty of being too close to people and their emotional distress. Yet it is difficult for you to support feeling so distinctly different."

Suddenly, Michaela begins to sob, explaining that she "sees" her council in everyday clothing sitting cross-legged on the floor. Her soul color is described as purple, indicating that she has reached a high level of soul development and experience. The separateness she feels is tied to her advanced degree of soul wisdom. She learns she is a council member herself and feels she needs to be given permission to honor her divine nature without feeling like a "freak."

Having such marked soul knowledge, awareness, and divine wisdom often leads to an incarnation of great loneliness and lack of understanding oneself. Michaela carries the awareness of her advanced soul standing as a secret. She is not to feel superior or more capable than anyone else. Experiencing a between-lives soul regression and coming to recognize one's level of soul experience, no matter the degree, assists in self-acceptance and moving forward in daily life.

To present another perspective on soul progress, let me focus for a minute on the term *expansion*. The opposite of expansion is contraction, or reduction, or tightening. The soul has a natural desire, or impetus, to expand, or grow. Whether it takes 100 or 1,000 or 10,000 lives to lead us to higher soul wisdom, we seem unable to lose or reduce our soul progress as it is developed.

The road is long, nonetheless, and the increments clear. Just as a toddler needs to master basic physical skills and essentials before intellectual development takes center stage, so too does the soul seem to begin by climbing out of fear and powerlessness at the initial stages of soul development, and then moving toward discouragement and frustration at the "toddler" soul level in the first of many steps to full actualization.

The soul can also amass knowledge by residing in other galaxies and dimensions. Apparently, many souls who are at an advanced level of seven and above on a ten-point scale of soul development have gathered experience somewhere other than on earth in prior embodiment. A recent client whose soul color indicated a high degree of knowledge was informed by her guide that she had stepped through thousands of lives but had not lived in this earthly sphere for hundreds of lives.

"You are here on earth to experience this type of life, to access better understanding, and to influence others in a nonobtrusive way. You have spent most lives with certain angels who assist you, and you belong more where these angels reside. On earth, you can experience how pain in different forms can feel. Pain is caused in different ways. It is a life lesson for you to gain knowledge of pain and take it back to the angels."

Charlotte: LIGHTENING UP IN THE YELLOW BAND

A client we'll call Charlotte steps out of body at the culmination of a past life and describes the experience of being incarnate as similar to "being in sludge." The spiritual realm is characterized as infinite space. Charlotte's guide, "Sheeraah," arrives to assist by creating a cool waterfall to provide both healing and transition from her past life into the interlife.

Suddenly, Charlotte is delivered to her soul family, who are like "precocious children" darting hither and yon, demonstrating great joy. "We are energetic, silly, and adventurous in a mental way," Charlotte says of her group. "On earth, we are all so serious."

Charlotte's core soul color is defined as yellow. Following the soul family gathering, "Sheeraah" takes her to a classroom where the lesson being taught is how to be "lighter" on earth and not take things so seriously. "We are instructed to be more creative on earth … to be faster and not so heavy, making life easier," Charlotte adds. "'Sheeraah' discusses how I cannot blame myself for all the times I was not as loving as I could have been."

As the soul gains progress, the core soul color moves through the shades of the rainbow. Moving beyond red and orange on the soul path, we arrive at the soul color of yellow, and so forth. By simple arithmetic definition, I suggest the following soul scale:

RED		ORANGE		YELLOW		GREEN		BLUE	PURPLE
I *	2	3	4	5	6	7	8	9	10

To explain the ten-point soul scale in greater detail, the blank cells between colors would indicate the stage of soul progression as red mixes with orange, orange mixes with yellow, and so forth.

Remember, I am not attributing any better/worse hierarchy to the progression. However, by stages nine and ten, or blue and purple, the soul appears to have developed infinitely more perspective and wisdom than at previous levels. The glass of life goes from being half empty at the earlier stages of the journey to being half full and more as we progress and the soul becomes more actualized.

To describe the maturation process as a linear evolution, I suggest a short list of terms describing our travels from stage one to stage ten:

Fear and powerlessness lead to ... discouragement and blame, progressing to ... worry and disappointment, moving on to ... impatience and feeling overwhelmed, proceeding onward to ... hopefulness and optimism, allowing us to continue gaining ... enthusiasm and happiness, which advances us toward ... passion, joy, and love at the highest levels.

Lest we believe there is some "final" end point, let me revisit the notion of being and becoming. As each soul progresses individually, so too does the entire universe evolve, and in similar fashion. Our human minds cannot fathom where the ongoing advancement may lead. Consider the most wondrous sunset and you may have an inkling of such purity.

chapter 10

The Vintage Man
The difference between a good artist and a great one
Is: The novice will often lay down his tool or brush,
Then pick up his invisible club on the mind's table
And helplessly smash the easels and jade
Whereas the vintage man no longer
hurts himself or anyone
And keeps on sculpting
Light.

—Hafiz

Life Themes and Common Threads

*E*ach of us is capable of being like the Vintage Man as we journey from one life to another and in between. Each life is a pearl on an exquisite strand of jewels that comes in all shapes and sizes. Every life serves a special purpose, honing and enhancing the kaleidoscopic beauty that is our distinct soul.

The length and quality of the strand grows as we dive deep into the learning experiences of each life and add on the "pearl" of progress that ensues. If we were to examine the "necklace" of an advanced soul, we would find that although no two pearls are exactly alike, some would be similar in shape, color, or clarity because of the commonalities, or characteristic themes, in that particular soul's nature, purpose, and journey.

At the highest levels of wisdom, where the lessons of life have been transmuted, the strand is ultimately worn inside our heart, reflecting the distilled wisdom of our myriad incarnations.

James: ECHOED THEMES AND DEMEANORS

James arrives for his soul-regression session stating that he wants to know his current life purpose and receive guidance on making a career change toward something "more spiritual." He confides that he fears rejection and that he has never been able to sustain a primary relationship.

In the past-life segment of his regression, James is Cassandra, a girl between seven and ten years of age, living a comfortable life around the beginning of the twentieth century. She is wearing "Buster Brown" shoes and short pants. As she gets a little older, Cassandra feels alone in the world and misunderstood. "There is much more to life than what we live in the world," she says. "Everything that we do here is fake, and nobody takes the time to be who they are."

At age twenty-four, Cassandra begins to travel. She has family money and can go wherever she wishes. She now views herself as an explorer and travels in Africa, but she continues to find people's behavior mundane and is often lonely. "As people, we miss the mark," she says.

On the last day of her life, at age fifty-three, Cassandra is still in Africa. "I have gotten used to being here in this life. I felt some attraction years ago to the man who is my husband and stayed. I am very fond of my son. I am not very used to being here in this modern world. I haven't been in body in a long time."

Like Cassandra, James exhibits the desire for things in life to be deeper and more meaningful than they are on the surface. He is seriously considering switching from being an airplane pilot to assisting people who are seriously ill. Clearly, flying allows him to be an explorer of sorts, as he was in a past life. But he does not want to "miss the mark" or waste time in getting on with his soul purpose in this lifetime. Not surprisingly, he has never been married, but he does have a child with whom he is quite close.

James begins his discovery of another past life by reliving its final day. Frederick (James's past-life name) is on an English airfield in 1944, along with fellow pilots, assembling to prepare for another strategic flight during World War II. (This would make Frederick and Cassandra an example of "splits" of the same soul living parallel lives, a concept that is discussed in greater detail in chapter 14.)

There has been much loss. We are going back to do the same thing. We will fly to Germany. I feel apprehensive and disturbed. This is all being directed toward destruction. I love these machines that we fly. Why can't we do something beneficial with these planes? I am very loyal. I worry about what people will think of me if I question what is happening. It is too late now. People depend on me. Now I am flying. It is instantaneous. My ship is broken. It's over. I am falling.

Now I am above my body and the planet. I can see the English Channel. I chose chaos and conflict. I send love to my fiancée. I can communicate with her but only to the degree that she can receive. Many cannot receive another's energetic intentions like this. I send her love. I realize that my mother in my current life is my fiancée. I will come back to earth very soon. Now I feel intelligent energy coming toward me. As we relax into our impermanence, we relax into our true nature. I need to awaken my inner knowing.

James comes to understand that everything changes over time and that he must accept it as the natural order. He recognizes how much the frustration he felt as a pilot during World War II is contributing to his desire to immerse his present life into work of a more spiritual nature. He also realizes that his avoidance of an ongoing romantic relationship in this lifetime is tied to having left his fiancée prematurely in his war pilot's life, coupled with his unsatisfactory marriage as Cassandra.

Past-life soul regression and between-lives soul regression are designed to offer the client a broader perspective. As we examine the related pearls of this and past lives, key elements coalesce for us to paint the picture of our soul's journey over time, and we come to recognize our higher self.

During soul regression, the client will always experience more detail in thought, feeling, and vision than can be captured in words. Both transformation and transmutation occur under regression hypnotherapy, and they are experienced consciously as well as on a deeper level and higher plane. The process thus affects both the current embodiment and the soul level, and it is no surprise that regression hypnotherapy can assist both the soul and the human "being" of the client in many inexplicable ways.

Heather: CARRY-OVERS

During the pre-regression interview, Heather tells me she often experiences a strong sense of insecurity and a fear of loss. She particularly worries about car accidents and wants to discover if her past-life or between-lives soul regression can provide any explanation why. Here is what her session reveals:

I am an adult female in my late twenties. I have long, curly red hair, freckles, and light-colored skin. I am wearing a yellow sundress and standing on a cliff overlooking the ocean. It is early evening, and I can hear the water below.

I have lost somebody. It is a man, my fiancé, whose car went off the edge of the road and over the cliff. He was by himself and driving carelessly. This is a huge loss for me, and I am feeling very sad.

(As the therapist, I ask Heather if she recognizes the soul of the man who drove off the cliff. Instantly she responds affirmatively.) The man I have lost and my current fiancé are the same soul. I have also seen the face of my present fiancé in my mind during my childhood.

I am older now, married and with children, but I continue to feel that a part of me is lacking. I am still missing the man who died.

At age forty, I am outdoors where my two sons are playing. Suddenly I realize that neither of them is to be found, and I panic. They have been playing by the river. One of them has fallen in and drowned. I become hysterical.

I now feel an even stronger sense of emptiness than before. I die in my early forties, ready for the pain of loss to end. I fall while I am in a field and something sharp pierces my chest.

I felt so alone after my son died. In my present life, I spent much time feeling alone until I met my fiancé, Walter.

Heather learns during her between-lives soul regression that Walter is the soul with whom she has incarnated the most. Her soul has contracted with his to share numerous lives for the purpose of joint soul progress.

Heather has been married twice before in her present life. She was pregnant and married in her teens, subsequently divorced, and married again in her mid-twenties. Through her regression, she is able to gain a clearer understanding of the depth of her ties with Walter, and she comes to realize more fully her previously unexplained fear of loss.

Life is often not a smooth progression. We may be forty, fifty, sixty years old or older before reaching a vantage point where we understand something of our learning objectives for this incarnation. Nevertheless, many—though not all—of our lives are woven around a common theme that is designed to help us evolve.

As a regression therapist, I have had the privilege to witness both past-life accounts and communications during the time between lives, where profound insight is dispensed from the soul level. This has provided me an expanded perspective on several topics. I have come to believe, for example, that souls can come together for a common purpose during specific world events.

One such time period is that of World War II and the Holocaust. In examining my regression research, I have found that quite a number of advanced souls reincarnated very quickly from the later 1930s into the middle 1940s and now work in some domain connected with emotional, spiritual, planetary, or physical healing.

Sheila: QUITTING COMPLACENCY

I live in a small Polish village. My husband had gone out, and I tried to hide. They had already shot my husband, who went outside to try to distract them, and they found us anyway. I don't understand. We are simple people not doing anything to anyone. They are frightened of us because we are different.

I wanted my husband to stay. Why didn't he stay? Nothing would have made any difference. They had a deep fear that we knew something they did not. We knew how to live. We knew loving was important. We looked after each other. We did not want to change them.

Now I am bare and lying down. There are people on top of me. They are dead. They killed us all. We are in Germany and are Jewish. We are all squashed. It is a dreadful sight. My child, who is also my child today, is my dead baby son lying next to me. I tried to keep him safe. The dying is not important. This was a demonstration for people to learn to feel horror. They have to be shocked out of being complacent.

This client's life today is focused on assisting others to know themselves in greater depth. She is what I would call a healer. This client has also uncovered another past life where she was burned at the stake for being different from others while living a spiritually focused life. Luckily, a healer in today's world can work either professionally or as a layperson and can openly practice any number of modalities to help people to mend physically and/or emotionally.

Norman: HEALING AND REDEMPTION

I am inside, and it is cold outside. I am an adult man with boots on. I am a Nazi officer in a high position, looking out a window. I see a smoke stack with smoke pouring out. We hate the Jews, but I also feel some qualms about what we are doing.

Another train of people comes in. There are dogs there to scare the Jews, the gays, the Catholics, and all the other people we want to annihilate. We want to throw them off balance and keep them frightened. The people are put into different groups. There are the healthy ones. The women and kids go to the gas chambers. Those that will die are lined up. Sometimes I am there when they go into the showers.

The Allies have come now to liberate the camp. I am taken as a prisoner to a Russian camp. I don't care about much of anything now. I lost my soul long ago. All that I saw and participated in was too much. I am involved in an attempted escape. I knew this would be a type of suicide. I am shot and die. I have great global remorse. Now I see the heavens and the great expansiveness. I am accompanied by spirit as I fly over the Himalayas.

Norman is told he has been a "shadow carrier" through many lives. At the soul level, we can accept the responsibility of transmuting negative energy for ourselves and for others.

I came back into body very fast. I needed to redeem and transmute the Nazi energy. I chose my parents specifically to assist me to release the energy of my Holocaust past life. My father had a compelling and unstoppable need to help others, including me.

I have completed nearly 90 percent of my redemption. But I am still working on forgiving myself. I am told that I have been a monk many times. My guides tell me that my work with clients is for our reciprocal evolution. "You are on the right path. Continue with your healing work. You are doing very well."

Once again, we discover a client who has served as a spiritual person (as a monk) in past lives and continues to provide healing in the current life. While certain events in history (such as the Holocaust) may appear on the surface to be completely heinous, there may or can be a redeeming purpose such as that described by Norman.

A world incident can have the profound effect of shocking us into action and altering social structures and behavior. In no way am I suggesting that the loss of life and the brutality that happens at such times are unimportant; on the contrary. As humans and as souls, we often avoid learning until a significantly traumatic event occurs.

Studies on people whose past-life sessions indicate that they lived during the Holocaust and World War II suggest that many such souls returned relatively soon to life on earth. Furthermore, these souls frequently seem to be more advanced than most, and are often dedicated to serving in present life as healers and teachers in a variety of capacities.

The next case addresses what a large number of clients discover during regression about ending life by suicide. It would seem that it is definitely not a preferred transitioning mode of our guides and teachers.

Immediately after being informed that a past life ended in suicide, some clients are instructed to begin discovering other means with which to face life's complications and cope during incarnation. Others are assured by their spiritual council that they have already completed this task and successfully developed the wisdom to grapple with daily life by rolling more smoothly over the hills and valleys of earthly existence.

Eleanor: LETTING GO OF NEGATIVE EMOTIONS

Eleanor, currently in her early fifties, explains that when she was fifteen years old, her father ended his life by committing suicide. She points out there have been a number of times during her current life when the idea of doing the same has crossed her mind, but she has never developed a serious plan to carry through. Given her father's suicide, Eleanor wonders whether the major lesson to be learned in this life is her father's or her own.

I am a short woman, aged thirty-five, and I have on a full wool skirt and matching jacket and lace-up leather shoes. I have dark hair that is neatly piled on my head. The day is hot, and I am afraid to go home. I am worried about what might happen. I think about killing myself.

I am standing on a dock, and I jump into the water. I cannot face the humiliation. (The client offers no detail as to what the humiliation is.) I need to tell him I am sorry that I am leaving life so abruptly. I feel shame. Now I am quickly moving away from the scene of my dying. I am moving through blue light. This feels like a spiritual car wash.

I feel the need to be forgiven for taking my life. Suddenly, my spirit guide, Gavin, is there. He is trying to assist me to let go of the shame. He explains that shame is a soul issue. I have a fear of facing how I died. In that life, I was also holding fear. I am told that holding fear and shame is not productive, and that feelings are part of being human.

In my current life, I do not hold shame so tightly. I have moved through it better. My father in this life agreed to take his life in order for me to gain an altered perspective on suicide and how his choice to end his life in this way has affected the family members. My father's soul was able to take on this agreement because he is quite advanced. I need to learn to not feel alone in my present life.

Suicide is a theme for Eleanor, a core component that she still holds within her cells on the human and soul level. Past-life soul regression serves to bring into her a conscious awareness of a tightly linked chain of events from one life to another, where the key that unlocks the door and sets the soul and human person free has yet to be found.

It is difficult, if not impossible, to fully understand exactly what it is that unlocks the door and allows the individual to be set free of a previously imbedded trauma. However, following regression hypnotherapy, many clients attest to having let go of emotions or physical symptoms they have been carrying for years.

There are other themes tying past lives to the present that are as potent and significant as suicide, though perhaps less dramatic or more subtle. The client's spiritual team chooses the best messages to convey. They may want to nudge a person to alter something about the present life, or they may simply wish to support the client to maintain and enhance the course of the current incarnation.

Before regression hypnotherapy, a good thing to do is to imagine your team of guides and elders arriving in a library with your name on the door. The walls of your library contain shelves of beautifully bound books, each volume containing the story of one of your past lives.

Your spirit team has your highest good as their intention, and perusing these books with their higher wisdom, they come to a collective agreement on which life story to unfold before you during your past-life soul regression. The particular volume is carefully chosen to serve a profound purpose— offering you the detail of a past life that will greatly assist your soul progress today. Asaph, below, is provided a bird's-eye view into a past life:

Asaph: "I BEEN A MINER FOR A POT OF GOLD"

I am wearing old, worn boots, denim pants, and red suspenders. I have a scraggly beard, and my face is weathered and tanned from being out in the elements. I look disheveled. I am a miner with a pick ax. My life is good. I've worked hard to find gold in the mine, and it has paid off.

I am walking into town, and I feel good about myself. My intuition was right: I have found gold, but I am not going to tell anyone. People in town are shocked to see me. I usually keep to myself, spending the bulk of my time alone, without anyone.

On the final day, there is a cave-in at the mine. All my hard work is taken away. I die quickly with my legs being crushed. No one will care that I died, because I am a loner. Whoever finds my body will claim the mine. Now I realize that along with hard work, it is important to still have a life. As the miner, I kept telling myself I would have more in my life just as soon as I reached my goal. Now I know that I did not truly live my life. I should have had more than gold in it.

I need to energetically communicate with my mother (of the past life). I need to try to tell her that she was loving, kind, and supportive. My mother then is my wife today. In my life today, I have a lot of love with my wife and children. I don't feel a sense of loneliness like I did in the past life.

(The client travels into the spiritual realm at the ending of his past life. He is met by souls who serve as greeters.) I am told "I love you" by the welcoming committee. Many of them are telling me that I did well in the past life, that I gained the experience that was needed.

Each of our lives serves an important purpose, even when we seem to have avoided contact with people who can enrich and enlarge it. Gaining the intended soul learning allows us to continue to "climb the ladder" of soul progress. Our team of higher wisdom is never judgmental or chastising. They continue to support us with infinite love, allowing our choices in each lifetime to create valuable headway towards our becoming more advanced.

The next client, Remy, is male, retired, and in his mid-sixties. His life focus is to uncover his past lives and understand the ongoing and upcoming spiritual change on the planet.

*R*emy: HEALING THE WOUNDS OF A PAST LIFE

There is fear on the part of all present. Something could go wrong. I am an arrogant person and knew there would be terrible consequences. I wear a pale blue velvet jacket and pants with a white ruffled blouse, having a big bow and ornamental buttons. My eyes are brown, nose large, and cheeks sunken. I am thirty-five to forty years old. I dismiss everyone, as I think that I know everything. I am the head of the household, with everyone else being subservient. I am going to speak with the crowd that is gathering. I'll put on a friendly face.

The women come outside with me. The front of where I live is protected by high stone walls. There is a group coming up with torches. There are about a hundred men or more coming toward me. I walk out alone into the yard. I speak calmly to them. I realize this may be more difficult than I thought. They are drunk or angry. I don't know why they are angry. If I talk to them, I can convince them all will be fine.

The women scream and flee. The men opposing me wear red, conelike hats and white shirts with brown, crude pants. Their shoes have buckles. They are not our enemy. Two men are the ring leaders. I see the bony faces of these men who are missing teeth and do not look healthy. They will not back off.

There is a guy in the third row that comes out and pushes his way to the front. He tells me he wants justice. The ring leader reaches for his long dagger. I think he will just threaten me. He plunges it into the middle of me. I am shocked at how fast this happened. My death is fast. He hit a main artery. They carry my body into the fortress, or castle, of which I am the owner.

My life was cut off before my role became obvious. I feel angry about this. I was stupid. I left people to fend for themselves. No one else was hurt. The life was in southwestern France in 1677. I wish I had not made mistakes. I wish I had not been so arrogant. These peasants were just hungry and angry. Suddenly the darkness changes to a white, golden light. It feels like a sunny day, and I feel peaceful. There is a large eagle who winks at me. I am moving into the spiritual realm.

Following a regression session, clients will generally continue to examine their experience, and they often recall further detail and develop a broader perspective on the past life. Remy was initially met by an eagle that many believe represents the power of the Great Spirit, the divine. The eagle speaks simultaneously to being attached to the spiritual realm while being incarnate. During regression, it is common for the energy of a guide to shift and appear in animal form. Shamanic belief would label this as shapeshifting.

Remy explained that during the era when this past life occurred, people with opposing religious and political views were often murdered. He realized that he had reached a point of forgiveness for placing himself and his people in danger.

Moreover, Remy was able to clear up the shock related to his death coming as a complete surprise since it happened so quickly. Following his regression, he experienced no further pain in the area of his solar plexus, which was something that had bothered him for many years in this lifetime.

As many would say, "We cannot heal what we have not yet made real." By bringing to the surface and combining conscious awareness of our soul's history with spiritual and energetic healing, past-life soul regression affords people a means to uncover, release, and heal previous trauma.

Marion: A LIFE WITH JESUS

I am outside near a group of people. I am wearing rough leather sandals and a robe. I have a dark beard and am about forty years old. There is a spiritual man speaking. He looks like Jesus. We are on a hill. We know that we are not going to be allowed to live with God and peace. Now I am in a church or a synagogue. There are animals outside making noise. Jesus is explaining something about spirituality. He says this world is not reality. We are in the world but not of the world. He tells us there is never a wrong way to act.

It is later, and I am in a room with a long wooden table. It is dark and dusty. There are fifteen to twenty of us (men) seated at the table. We seem distressed. Jesus will be put to death. There is no sense to put him to death. People are confused. Jesus tells us it does not matter. He does not care. There is nothing we can do about it.

Now it is the last day of my life. I am under a rock, a boulder. I am alive. There has been an accident. I am alone. I am okay with this being the end. Jesus is gone. I do not want to remain. It is good to leave my body. Now I can see my body below me.

I did not know how profound the life was with the presence of Jesus. I am always looking for that presence in my life now and cannot seem to find it. Jesus wants me to know that he loves me. Jesus tells me to follow my heart. I will be led and shown what needs to happen in my life.

Past-life experiences for the client often come as a complete surprise. Marion found her regression experience to be immeasurably enriching. It is note-worthy that more clients of late are experiencing past-life details that either include Jesus or are tied to the historical period when Jesus lived.

A possible explanation for this is that more individuals living today need to focus on the core teachings that Jesus provided before they were formalized into a religion. Clients who have uncovered past lives at the time of Jesus do not as a rule blindly and dogmatically follow the teachings of modern-day Christianity.

To sew together the seam of this chapter (which is focused upon themes and threads of past lives), consider the image of a weaver at a loom, working with the warp and the weft. The warp is the strong thread, or yarn, laid in parallel fashion, which sets the foundation of the weaving. The weft is the thread that is shuttled back and forth on the warp to create the woven fabric.

The soul is the warp, with the life threads of the weft creating a pattern gradually and over time. The threads that make up the weft can be all one color or can be a multitude of colors representing various themes. Ultimately, they coalesce into a lovely fabric design as we absorb each experience and create a detailed tapestry. Our soul weaves this unique mosaic of elements by distilling the experience, learning, and progress that stem from each past life.

The next client offers a final example of soul progress, where the importance of speaking one's own truth is the core soul learning.

Stanford: A LIFE LESSON

My feet are bare, and I am wearing a robe that falls from my shoulders. My beard and hair are white and grey, and my fifty-five-year-old face has a stoic expression. It is daytime, and there is a large stone structure nearby with columns. I begin to walk up the steps to the building and speak to people about politics and society. We are talking about the Romans, and I incite these people to talk about needing to be free.

Now it is the last day of my life. I am sitting down. There is a friend sitting with me. We are talking about affairs of state. People were forced into slavery. They were subjected to things that should not be. We are teachers. I am tricked. Someone that I trusted was not who he said he was. I am stabbed in the back with a knife. I am not surprised that my life is ended. There was risk because of politics.

I realize that it is important to speak what you believe in. It is important to be free of oppression and tyranny. It is important to teach how important it is to not limit yourself. It is also important to not give up when something becomes complicated or difficult, to keep striving for what is important.

Stanford speaks of the value of standing up for what we believe in. The overall message is to be true to oneself. We can truly never be anything other than who we are at the core. If we attempt to present ourself as something contrary to our soul self, we will likely endure great stress and strain in the process. In addition, others are likely to be able to recognize that we are not presenting ourself in an honest light. In turn, people may either distrust or shy away from us.

Regression hypnotherapy offers an invaluable tool for gathering insight into our past-life experiences and the indelible mark that is imprinted on our soul with each incarnation. Our core self is made up of the detailed moments that our soul has spent both within and without a body. As we pull back the curtain of amnesia and bring into conscious awareness the facets of significant lives, we come to know our nucleus in a manner that was previously hidden to us. Regression hypnotherapists often describe the process of past-life soul regression as identification, dis-identification, and transformation.

During a regression, we must first identify some detailed account of who we were and what occurred. The next step is to allow our self to release the emotional and mental trauma that life placed on us. Finally, through the conscious and energetic process of regression hypnotherapy, it is crucial to transmute and transform the events of past lives into higher wisdom, propelling us forward both as a human being and at the soul level. Our mantra can be "There are no accidents, and everything serves."

I invite you to discover the components of your past lives in order to more fully know yourself. Your realization of who you have been and what occurred will assist both you and the universe to release lost truth. In the resource material at the end of this book, you will find suggestions on how to find a capable, trained, and experienced regression hypnotherapist.

chapter 11

Participate joyfully
in the sorrows of life.
—*Joseph Campbell*

Human Experience

*B*uddhist philosophy, like Joseph Campbell, calls for joyful participation in the sorrows of life. This advice is not meant to suggest that we try to enjoy suffering—rather, it encourages us to recognize that hardship and pain are an unavoidable part of life. If we face sorrow and suffering knowing this, we embrace the experience of being alive. Learning to deal with the specific events confronting us serves to augment our soul progress.

This chapter examines the deeper meaning and purpose of traversing the thorny human circumstances in our lives. These would include serious if not life-threatening illness, serious mental disorder, physical and/or sexual abuse, the death of a beloved friend or family member, suicide, uncompromising addiction, divorce, accident, handicap, and other such hard situations for ourselves or those we care about.

Ideally, our approach would be that when life hands you lemons, make lemonade. But just how does it happen that one person views life's traumas as heinous while the next is able to maintain a more philosophical attitude? Generally speaking, people find it difficult, if not impossible, to face dire life circumstances in a detached way. Those individuals who come to view them as a step on their soul journey are unique.

One well-known example is Viktor Frankl, who wrote *Man's Search for Meaning* about his life as a prisoner in a World War II concentration camp and his ultimate release. Frankl discovered in himself the ability to hold fast to an ongoing belief that life is important despite the cruelty and despair of his captivity.

In this chapter, we will examine case histories in regression hypnotherapy for soul-level clues to the reasons for life's vagaries. We will also examine why seemingly more advanced souls sometimes appear to be saddled with more than their fair share of traumatic life events.

Charlotte: PREBIRTH CHOICES AS LIFE OPPORTUNITIES
Charlotte completes a lifetime and describes stepping into the spiritual realm.

Twinkly lights are greeting me as I leave the body. Oh boy, let's play and dance. I can be a light again too. I can do or be anything. Being in body is like sludge. It feels like I do not get to play much on earth. But here, there is infinite space.

Now my spirit guide steps in like an affectionate parent and says, "Okay guys, let's round up now." My spirit guide is lavender in color, seeming tall and willowy in a white shimmering gown. Her name is Sheena, but her name is not important. We go to a white temple with columns. There is a cool waterfall there. All of my soul family is there, and Sheena says we are like a group of precocious children. The temple gives us an enclosed place to communicate in. My group is energetic, silly, and adventurous in a mental way.

Charlotte delivered a daughter in the early 1970s who died a week after birth. In the same year, she adopted a biracial infant daughter, Karen, who is presently drug-addicted and homeless. Charlotte finds this much harder to bear than Karen herself. "Karen is giving me quite a ride in this life," is her summation.

Karen is a member of Charlotte's soul family and emanates a soul color that suggests she is very advanced. She sees her present life as an experiment in trying on a "non-pristine" life. Her high level of soul development allows her to manage such a complex life.

During her time with her wise elders, it is explained to Charlotte that she needed to be challenged to accept her adopted daughter as not being so good from a traditional standpoint. Karen's journey is a clear example of life circumstances that are scripted prebirth as a means of learning—for both her own soul and that of her mother.

As Charlotte takes time to relax with her soul family, she states:

We are all a team. We help each other. Now I am going with my soul family to a one-room schoolhouse. We all sit at desks. We are learning how to be lighter on earth and how not to take everything so seriously. I am told to remember what I can do. I can just think and it is so. I need to not blame myself for all of the times when I was not loving.

I did not meet any of my soul family (except Karen) until I was well into my adult years in present life. I had to get confident to do it on my own first. My soul family has agreed to be prickly on earth. We won't feel like a team. We are formidable as a team. This time, we need to be individual selves.

We can be so close that we are almost inside each other. Then we come to resent one another and pull apart. We know how to meld our energy. In this life, we must learn to operate separately. In our current life, we are all female but are usually all male. I am told that for me it is harder to be female.

(Charlotte suffered abuse from her father, who molested her repeatedly as an adolescent.) Dad agreed to come this one time. He is on a different path. We agreed to the details of this life in order for each of us to get what we needed. He had to master a dark compulsion. He does not feel good about himself. He failed.

I chose being a lesbian in this life as a challenging means of discovering who I truly am. My immediately family won't see that I am not like them. They are on a different wavelength. I have had to find a way out, to find my own group. I realized that finding out who and what I am as a lesbian would guide me to find my group, and that when I found the light in myself, I would know it in others.

Now I have found myself and my group in this life, but I have not yet let my light shine. I have taken life and its happenings too seriously. If I weren't so fearful, my light would be bigger. I have feared being different. In past lives, I would just retreat and be solitary. In this life, that is not an option.

Charlotte's regression hypnotherapy session reveals a number of circumstances that were scripted prebirth as opportunities for her soul to progress in this lifetime. First, Charlotte has been challenged to accept as a parent that, drug use and homelessness notwithstanding, her daughter Karen has had a meaningful life so far rather than squandering this incarnation. So many of us walk by an unkempt street person and silently sit in judgment and even fear. We could perhaps take a lesson here too.

Secondly, Charlotte suffered sexual abuse from her father. The trauma of physical, emotional, and sexual abuse by a parent can be so devastating that it scars us for the entire current embodiment. In the mind of our emotional self, we tend to blame ourselves rather than confront the unthinkable—that our loving parent could be the guilty party. Low self-esteem and clinical depression are common repercussions.

Charlotte and her father agreed at the soul level to the roles they would play in present life. She experienced abuse as a challenge to her ability to value herself and maintain a sense of self-worth. Removing herself in her late teens from her family home to avoid further abuse became essential.

In addition, Charlotte set in motion other prebirth agreements with her parents. She got herself raised in a socially and politically conservative milieu in order to necessitate a drastic shift in lifestyle. As a lesbian, she was "different" from her family, and that discovery compelled her to move across the country to a new city where her identity was socially acceptable and not criticized.

In sum, Charlotte is the capable, productive person she is today because of her predetermined agreements. She had to separate from the lifestyle and behavior of her birth family in order to become her own person. In finding the light of her core self, she began to meet others like herself and later to form personal links with members of her soul family. At the end of her session, the spiritual realm lovingly directs that she continue diving deep into herself to discover even more of her soul self.

Soul agreements developed during the time between lives are designed for the spiritual growth of all involved, regardless of the level of trauma they engender or the occurrence of seemingly violent events. We may even agree to play a role assisting others to leave the earth when they have fulfilled their chosen life experience.

Many would agree that accelerated deep learning can occur in a situation where two or more souls act out particular behaviors. Horrible as the triggering scenario may be, living the most painful lessons can bring about rapid soul progress, and all souls involved in a prebirth equation can advance swiftly by following through on completing the agreed-upon script.

It is the same in a soul family, where the more experienced souls often tackle the hardest physical or emotional lessons, while the less experienced souls are still involved in seeking balance and more basic learning. You would think it would be the opposite—that things get easier as you progress. But do not consider this arrangement to be unfair to the more advanced souls. The less experienced souls, even as they piggyback on the hard learning of the others, carry their own responsibility to grow and progress.

Ultimately, it is equal work for all souls to achieve their necessary spiritual growth. Just as the first-grade student can simply add, subtract, and multiply, and the fifth-grade student has developed the ability to work out algebra problems, we each have the soul capability attached to the level of learning we have mastered thus far. The spiritual realm functions as a matrix of energy that is finely tuned and egalitarian.

When souls return to the spiritual realm (where all is known), there is a period of elation at having successfully wound up some dense, earth-based, karmic lessons. This is coupled with a spirit of gratitude toward those souls who have assisted in the attainment of one's preset goals.

Mariana: MY BROTHER'S KEEPER

During her between-lives soul regression, a middle-aged client, Mariana, visits the location in the spiritual realm where prebirth choices are made concerning our body, brain, and immediate birth family members.

Mariana is told that her brother agreed to have Down's syndrome and be mentally retarded "to test my loving side." Mariana accepts this explanation of her brother's condition and is greatly comforted by the new understanding.

Anneli: MY SON'S KEEPER

Another between-lives soul regression client, Anneli, wishes to ask a similar question during her session. She explains: "I have a son who is ten years old and whose mental age is approximately eighteen months. He wears diapers, has limited muscle tone, and requires a great deal of care. What is his soul's purpose in this life?"

The chief elder of Anneli's council of wise ones responds by saying, "Let Evan be, and do not struggle with his life. He had just one more thing to try out in the body. He is almost done with his incarnations. He chose you as his mother because of your soul capacity."

Anneli is an advanced soul, and as such, she is able to cope with the life challenges tied to her son's soul choice. During her session, she gains valuable insight into her agreement with Evan, who will soon not be expected to incarnate but who will work at a higher level from the spiritual plane.

Under the heavy burden of difficult life circumstances, when a loved one must forge their way into and through serious physical and/or emotional trauma, regression hypnotherapy can sometimes offer an explanation that tempers the accompanying pain and sorrow.

The following account gives a bird's-eye view of a painful life:

Manny: THE LEAVE-TAKING

We are in a camp. There is torture. I am male and malnourished. I am beaten. I have been separated from my family. (The client detail was spoken in short, painful bursts.) I am twenty-nine. I am at Auschwitz and am Jewish. (The client is now beginning to be aware of leaving the body in the life that is being explained.) I was there seven years. I was used for prostitution. When I was healthy, those evil people used me for certain activities. My guide is watching. My time is near. My guide wants me to trust that I am not alone.

Whoosh, I am leaving that life. Now it is deliciously cool and soft. There is an opening with beams and warm rays of light. A magnet pulls me into the light. I am surrounded by warm energy. The higher I go, the more I feel the cool, soothing, purple-blue universal light.

There is a ship now that hovers to take me to another level. There are beings in the ship who are the receivers of damaged energy. They work with me. My ragged edges are smoothed. They tell me that I will soon be home. It is incredibly quiet here. I have left earth's pull. I am on the way back home. This is all being done by thought—all this repair work is done by thought. This type of repair happens by universal force. A door opens. I am home. It is very bright.

Now I am enveloped in purple and embraced by love. This is truly beyond words. The purple is a high healing color. It is good to be back and to just be at one with everything. I feel totally accepted. If I did not have the expansion of energy, I could not have coped with the pain.

Another client describes in her between-lives soul regression the purpose of human ordeals:

Cecilia: DARKNESS

Trauma spurs change. We can agree to sacrifice ourselves so that others can be inspired to change. It is better to be an example. The Holocaust would show the world what is light and what is dark. Many souls who died in the Holocaust and World War II came back to earth very quickly.

My guide tells me that my soul required the experience of darkness, of being on the receiving end of humanity's base impulses when it is drawn in through mass consciousness. The soul yearns for experiential opportunities at all levels and has the ability to manifest and create these experiences while in physicality. This promotes evolutionary and spiritual growth regardless of the joy or suffering for the soul involved.

Lest we judge the behavior of anyone active in dark periods of history, it is useful, if not essential, to recognize the potential merit of such involvement. On the one hand, we can blame human free will for earthly behavior that we would label detestable. On the other, we may have established at the soul level a willingness to behave in some odious way to trigger, or stimulate, the opportunity to change our actions or attitudes.

Another between-lives soul regression client discerns from spirit input why her father died when she was only four years old and why her mate is chronically ill:

Susan: LIFE MISSIONS

During her session, Susan is told, "Your father could not stay around. Both you and he knew this was the agreement. You chose this and knew it would be hard. You had a short time to enjoy him. He came to do what he needed to do. For Steve (her mate with diabetes), it is about his willingness to receive. For you, it is about the willingness to live in the moment. You are a high soul. It is time for things to move to a higher level on earth. You are one of the souls who are here to help. You have come at this time, as you are needed."

Susan seems to easily comprehend and accept this interpretation. It is as if she already knew at a core level that there was a powerful reason for the challenges she has faced in her present embodiment. For most clients, the soul perspective gained during a between-lives soul regression shines a bright light on the plan for the current life and its intended expansion, and offers relief and release from daily scrutiny and doubt.

Allison: LESSONS LEARNED FROM CHRONIC ILLNESS

Allison is in her early twenties and was diagnosed with diabetes in her middle teens. At the time of her between-lives soul regression, she had become legally blind as a complication of her chronic illness. One of Allison's key questions during her between-lives soul regression was, "What is the reason for having to move through such severe physical issues?"

It is hard for me to take physical form. Each time I do, it is easier. I came to earth this time to stick it out, to be here and not to try to escape. I have come to earth four or five times. I get sick so I can feel my body. This lets me know I am still here, and that I need to laugh and enjoy happiness. I need to always love and not fear that my happiness will be taken away.

My vision issues are to help me let go of ego. (Chapter 12 offers further examples of learning to live with humility and compassion rather than ego.) I become too attached to the physical (corporeal) part of life. I must spend more time going inward. Going inward is my home. My home is not that far away.

Earth is not my home. I came to experience the physical form here. I came for the separation from where I truly belong. I came here for the first time five thousand years ago. I have had lives in other places (other galaxies and dimensions). Here, the veil is thicker. You forget more when you come here. If you did not forget, you would not want to stay. What I am going through is hard and will serve to give me growth and understanding.

The spiritual realm gives me strength. I am moving toward becoming an elder. My council of elders is cheering me on. They say I make it harder than it needs to be. I do not trust them easily. I am told to trust them, and that they will never leave me. I am told to eat more raw foods and to walk more. They also tell me to meditate more. I need to love my body more. Now I am being massaged by light. It feels freeing.

From an earthly vantage point, Allison, in her early twenties, could be pitied for her ailments and her inability to live a "normal" life for someone her age. Examining her life from the soul's perspective provides a distinctly different understanding of her plight.

Rather than feeling sorry for Allison, we can appreciate that people's life circumstances are put in place to give the soul a chance to reach higher, or deeper, levels of spiritual wisdom. She has a golden opportunity in her present life to go beyond the ego, focus on deeper spiritual concerns, and serve as a mirror for the advancement of many others. Many girls her age would be simply materialistic.

Allison describes herself as a soul who has been in human form only a few times. Based on multiple regression accounts, it would seem that many souls of advanced standing have experienced incarnation in dimensions and physical locations other than on earth. Such souls appear to have amassed significant soul knowledge prior to embodying on earth.

Mandy: ADOPTION ISSUES

Mandy is taken by her guide to the area in the spiritual realm where her life choices were made for her present life. She was adopted as an infant and is now in her early thirties.

My (adoptive) mother had so much love to give that she wanted to share this love with more than her one biological child. She couldn't have any more children of her own. She taught me about being upstanding, wanting knowledge, and learning how to love.

My (adoptive) dad wanted to show me there was more than one way to know God. He taught me that spirituality is bigger than God. He taught me how to be quiet and listen more deeply. Dad also taught me how to be self-sufficient and how to fix things. He is doing well on the other side. He is hanging out and playing golf! It is not important for me to know more than that about my birth parents.

Some adults who were adopted as children struggle with loss issues and symptoms of depression stemming from the unsolved question, "Why did my birth parents give me up to be raised by other people?" Other adopted individuals do not experience such pain. Mandy did not learn she was adopted until she was a young adult and found it relatively easy to accept.

During her between-lives soul regression, Mandy received specific information about the soul decision of her adoptive mother to become the primary nurturing and rearing female in her life. Yet, she was encouraged to trust that it is not important or useful to know anything further about her birth parents.

Numerous other regression hypnotherapy sessions have confirmed that adoption is a soul-level choice set in motion prior to birth. If more individuals suffering adoption pangs recognized that this life circumstance is selected prior to incarnation, a greater overall comfort level could prevail. Adoption does not have to represent human tragedy, grief, and loss.

Leigh: LIFE LESSONS AND A FAST RETURN

Leigh asked during her between-lives soul regression session why she had been diagnosed with amyotrophic lateral sclerosis, a motor neuron disorder also called Lou Gehrig's disease.

It is to humble me. It is a way to teach strength of humility and spirituality to others. Often I try to bend things to my will. I love to be in charge. I need to learn trust and have faith on a deep level. I do not believe that I will be cared for.

I am told that I am on a fast track to becoming a healer. I am also told that I will make a quick return to incarnation after the ALS takes my life. Souls are given to deal with only what they can bear. My spouse is also going to learn from the illness that I have. He will be learning about trust and dependency. This was an agreement that he and I made at the soul level. Do not see this as a punishment.

During her between-lives soul regression, Leigh's spiritual team of guides and elders provides her with a profound insight concerning her choice to walk the path of a neurologically debilitating illness that will end her life.

Spiritual contracts are set in motion before embodiment. Apparently, Leigh and her spouse agreed to face this illness and develop important human traits through it. Furthermore, this experience will allow her quickly to return as a healer. The circle of life does go around and around, and each life is but a drop in the bucket.

Madeline: TRUE LOVE AND RELATIONSHIPS

Madeline is a woman in her sixties whose husband had recently died after a fifteen-month illness. He was described as a very intelligent professional man who misused addictive substances and was prone to anger and anxiety. Though Madeline's marriage was difficult at times, she had a deep love and bond with her husband.

Following her husband's death, Madeline became reacquainted with a former love relationship that had been on hiatus for twenty-five years. She arrived for her between-lives soul regression wanting to more fully understand her relationship with her husband (James) and her newfound partner (Carlson).

I meet with my spirit guide, Omega. He welcomes me back into the spiritual realm. I am told that Carlson keeps me from sliding back into my pain. He is a safety net. Now I see Carlson. He is warm and supportive, a special companion. He is less serious than I am.

I tell Omega that what has hurt me the most in my current life is my unfulfilled potential for love with my deceased husband. I am told that James was embodied as a test for him to experience love. He was being tested and refined. He had a great brain and much insight. He could have become godlike. Finding me was a gift because I softened his difficulty.

James was blocked from moving forward with his learning because of his addictions. In his future life, he will have great responsibility. He does know that I loved him. James comes forward to express his gratitude to me. "You did help me," he says. "It was beyond your control to change me. I had to live my life as I did." We go to a special place now where we are able to "touch."

I am told that it is possible to love more than one person. With Carlson, I feel accepted. I am told to go play with him and have a good time. This may be a short or a longer relationship.

I will be with Carlson or someone else. I am to just enjoy Carlson for now. We are very parallel, whereas James is on a different plane. He is a soul on a mission and has moved to a higher level. He is being prepared to be a strong leader. In his recent life, he could not coordinate well. His threads were sticking.

I have known James and Carlson before. James is a very rich and experienced soul. Carlson is joyful. He has intense passion and desire. "Always nurture the friendship with Carlson," I hear. "Be patient with him. Do not try to possess or control him. You are a gift to one another. Be gentle with yourself and others. Never hold back on loving and being loved."

Madeline received a powerful clarification about the important role she played in being married to James. Her spiritual team validates the depth of caring she offered to him and states that it is now time for her to enjoy the calm beauty of her relationship with Carlson as a special, more compatible and equal companion.

The underlying message is that by demonstrating true love to James, she has gained the reward of an easy relationship with Carlson. All of life's experience serves us in one manner or another; nothing is without purpose.

Kathy: PARALLEL LIVES

I am in my parents' bedroom where I see a flowered bedspread. I go downstairs and jump on the couch to see myself in the mirror over the couch. I am a blond-haired, seven-year-old boy wearing a red striped T-shirt and sneakers. I go outside and into the garage. I find my mother in the front seat of the car. She is dead. There is blood everywhere. The car seems modern, like a model in the 1940s or 1950s.

I go back to my parents' bedroom and hide in the closet. My father comes home. He finds me and carries me downstairs. There is a lot of commotion. The police come and put me in the police car. Now I am sitting on a bench in the police station. There is a strange woman in a business suit sitting next to me and trying to comfort me.

Now I am in a courtroom. I am being questioned. My father is on trial for the murder of my mother. Next I see myself at age sixteen. I am walking to school with a backpack. I live with my mother's sister and her family. I hate living here. I don't like their kids. I don't have any friends. I am miserable and angry.

Now I see myself at age forty-five. I have on black suit pants, a white shirt, and a skinny black tie. I am sitting behind a desk. I am a lawyer or something. I hate my job. I have never married. I am unable to sustain lasting relationships. I am a loner. Now I see myself at home after work. I am drinking alcohol. This is what I do after work. Next I see myself lying on the floor. There is a gun next to me. I have shot and killed myself.

Kathy was born in her present life in the mid-1950s. During the discussion following her session, Kathy explains that the images of the past life she has experienced must overlap the time frame of her current life. "*Leave It to*

Beaver-style clothing" is the expression she used to describe the garments she was wearing as a boy in her past life.

Kathy has been presented with two kinds of complexity concerning the human experience. As she recounted the murder and loss of her mother in her past life, she immediately discovered with newfound clarity why her marriage and children of today are so important to her. It is interesting to note that Kathy's current life mother, with whom she was very closely bonded, died at a young age just like her former one.

Secondly, Kathy is a very capable, well-balanced, loving individual who seems to have maintained parallel lives. Chapter 14 explains that souls can create a script in which they manage two lives that overlap in time. They do so to make significant soul progress within a short period of time. Based on regression hypnotherapy case accounts, parallel, or split, lives generally occur only for souls that are relatively advanced, and the overlap is usually rather short.

Lives we label as difficult are not forced on us. Examine the profundity of statements made by client Therese:

Therese: ON GOING HOME

Each challenging experience in each life is very much going along with what we arranged before coming into physicality. I am told that I have free will and can change the course of these events should I wish, but I knew well in advance what I was coming to do. I have chosen the harder way. I am also being told that I have evolved sufficiently to be able to ride the storms of earthly life, to survive the challenges without my energy being traumatized. Each time I come back home, my radiant light is deeper and brighter.

Let me explain something: when you are in body, you are not fully aware of the power of your energy. What you feel and sense very subtly while in your host body is, in fact, the power of the beloved universe working through you.

You have taken on the bitter lessons of this planet. You suffer the pain, and the guides and teachers can only watch this. "We will never sabotage these very valuable opportunities which you experience," they say. "Love is so much more than this, dearest child. Your soul courage is boundless. Don't you know this?"

After each of these challenging experiences, I see angels softly floating toward me. They are robed in the most beautiful, soft, flowing colors of purple and indigo with silver running through. They polish my energy with gentle sweeping motions. As they are doing this, any impurities are swept away and more radiance is revealed. I am sprayed with stardust. I hear tinkling sounds and distant choral music. I see my immortal, luminous self. Oh, the joy, the bliss of this—I cannot describe it in words. My soul dances with ecstasy and surrender as I witness this.

In a nutshell, Therese has provided the core message of this chapter. First, our life challenges, set in motion before we arrive in body, can be altered during our lifetime. We have complete choice as to what does or does not occur. Our soul capability is in sync with our scripted life circumstances. The level of soul progress we have attained is perfectly calibrated to the degree of difficulty of the lesson plan drawn up in conjunction with our spiritual team prior to incarnation.

It is as if we step into our predetermined next climb with adequate hiking boots. Having summited our mountain in each life, we are released from the density of earth, freed to be wearing new boots of a higher quality, boots that will allow us to carry greater wisdom next time. Often, the human life that is ending has been trying, to say the least. Upon our reentry into the all-loving higher realm, our spiritual team offers every ounce of healing and rejuvenation that is required.

Being incarnate can be, and usually is, a mix of agony and ecstasy. As we strive for soul progress, everything we experience along the way serves a purpose. There are moments of despair and desolation for each of us, but sitting side by side with our pain is the vast beauty of human experience.

chapter 12

It is unwise to be too sure of one's own wisdom.
It is healthy to be reminded that the strongest
might weaken and the wisest might err.

—*Mahatma Gandhi*

Love is patient and kind, never jealous or envious,
never boastful or proud. Love is never haughty
or selfish or rude. Love does not demand its own
way. Love is not irritable or touchy. Love does
not hold grudges and will hardly notice when
others do it wrong. Love is never glad about
injustice, but rejoices whenever truth wins out.

—*1 Corinthians 13*

Ego versus Soul, Love, and Humility

*E*go is both essential and nonessential all at once. If we define ego as narcissism, the blind focus on and overvaluation of the individual self, then ego could be considered highly detrimental. If we use the term "ego strength" to refer to a capacity to maintain emotional and mental equilibrium throughout most of the minor and major storms of life, then ego is a priceless faculty to possess. When it provides internal equilibrium along with an egalitarian view of all people, we come to honor the ego in everyone.

This chapter discusses ego where its human face is pride, arrogant self-importance, and narcissistic self-infatuation; where the need prevails to see oneself as separate and more powerful than others at all times, in all places, and under all circumstances. While there are degrees along the spectrum of ego, for clarity and simplicity, this chapter utilizes the initial definition of ego as a detriment.

The expression *soul self* refers to love in the most wholesome sense of the word. At its highest point, love is as indescribable and inexpressible as the divine, its ultimate source. And like the divine, it can only be accessed through emotion and nonlinear experience.

This chapter discusses the polarity between the forces of ego and love, and what lies between. The beauty and intention of regression hypnosis is that the client receives spiritual input from a non-ego-based source.

Mysticism and the ascension experience speak to the communion with our soul self while embodied—grasping the awareness that we are pure light at our core. To be a mystic or to ascend describes the intuitive sensory experience of knowing we are simultaneously a soul in body and a soul in spirit. Embodiment is the height of divine task, a sacrifice even, as our soul must confine itself in coming to live for a time within a container that grounds it to the frequency and density of the planetary laboratory.

In body, holding fast to the awareness of our true, or divine, self can be a struggle. The paradox is that we are thrust into corporeal life precisely in order to advance as souls. We need to recognize human ego as a complex and tenacious mask covering the perfect beauty of the soul, and to strip away the camouflage of our human "warts." In sum, we need to become simultaneously aware of both ego and love to reach the summit and discover our true self.

Eli: FINDING ONENESS

There is a sense of gossamer as I move through the spiritual realm. I am being told that there is more love coming into the world. We will feel it in every cell of our bodies, but it is not the love that we know in our earthly selves. It is not even an emotion. It is completeness. It is simple understanding.

The whole of our human society is about materialism and incompleteness. Now we stand in the gap. We know what needs to be brought in. We must hold on to spirit and to the place or person that we are. We can then transmit the completeness.

Our collective beliefs are evolving. We are all trying to find our way home. This is where we do the changing. Let this key open the door of your heart. Let your "bird" out to fly. Look into your heart. You know the answer too.

Having the separateness of incarnation compels us to work our way back to oneness. We must feel the paradox of separation in order to find our way back and feel the completeness of that oneness.

$\mathcal{L}$ila: ON EGO AND EVOLUTION

"A message from your wise council: Your soul evolution has allowed you to reach a high level in soul standing. Those like you who can put aside ego and serve as a conduit of universal light are usually humble and shy. Such souls do not judge. They have understanding and wisdom, and infinite compassion for each soul. Those with great ego, on the other hand, who need to be recognized and do not honor their deep spiritual privilege, will have their privilege taken back. The laws of the universe must be learned."

Eli and Lila offer a rich depiction of the dichotomy of ego versus soul. Eli's spiritual team mentions standing "in the gap." When consciously unaware of ourselves as a soul self, we are mired in the bog of materialism. Discarnate, we are wholesome waves of light and energy as a soul.

During between-lives soul regression, the "gap" is seen as an inability to merge our corporeal existence and our pure spiritual being. The "bird" that can take flight from within our heart is the inexplicable but palpable love of the soul self. Joining body with spirit is the key to releasing the energy of the higher self. When this union is experienced and exhibited, it creates a fulfillment previously unknown to the being in incarnation.

Lila offers a number of powerfully descriptive words, such as *humble, evolution, high, ego, light, shy, judgment, compassion, conduit,* and *privilege.* To distinguish "love" from "ego," simply remove the terms *ego* and *judgment* and see what remains.

Judgment stems from ego. As our soul evolves, we begin to operate more and more from a perspective of light. This in turn leads to the privilege of serving as a conduit for love, and so we are likely to exhibit compassion and be humble, perhaps even a little shy. Lila's message reminds us, however, that we can also lose the privilege of being an advanced soul. No matter our degree of soul experience, free will is always available to us. We can choose to operate primarily from ego to serve our own needs.

Sandra: GOING FOR IT

Sandra is a highly experienced soul who was not required to reincarnate. Her soul color is purple. She chose to come in order to be a powerful support and advocate for others, but she has initially had to struggle to find inner joy.

Sandra's spirit guide tells her, "You can be as big as you want to be now. The woman who embodied as your teacher in this lifetime could not handle the competition from you. Human competition is a human problem, and in your life as a performer, you have already discovered that competition must be set aside. It does not make for a more accomplished performance. Performers must go beyond. You know what you need to do. Go out and be happy."

Competition stems from ego. To believe in our own capabilities regardless of anyone else's skills appears to be the message from Sandra's spirit guide. When we are following our passion, trusting that we are competent, we accede to a place where we have the ability to operate from our core truth, our soul self. Ego is not truth; it is a mask to hide our human frailty. Our guides and teachers endeavor, moment by moment, to direct us toward healing what is incomplete or inauthentic within us and stepping into the greater purity of our soul self.

Love is the energy of spirit, the energy of the soul. The words *love, spirit, soul,* and *the divine* are interchangeable. Functioning from our ego is not operating out of love for ourselves or others; ego attempts to camouflage our human fears and concerns, and thereby entrenches them. At our nucleus, however, we are nothing less than love, the highest level of spirit.

Our only task in each lifetime is to recognize and come to realize who we truly are. We are a soul residing in a body and having an incarnation, not the other way around. We are pure love that has traveled to earth, arriving in this dense laboratory. We are charged by our spiritual team to experience life moment by moment in order that our pure, loving soul self might advance on its journey. We are souls that are here to progress.

When we shine our loving heart, our soul self, out to others, some will receive it gracefully, while others will stay mired in ego and illusion and not have the wherewithal to perceive it. It is not our job to force anyone to accept our love. Everyone opens to love at their own rate. The more we continue to radiate love unconditionally, the sooner souls trapped in their illusory egos can begin to let go of their hardened human shells and start to soften their hearts. All happens in divine timing. At our core, we are simply pure, divine love.

As we progress in our soul journey, we achieve greater ease, ability, and likelihood of functioning from the soul level rather than out of ego or human personality. Imagine a ladder in your mind or the stairs in your house. There is no hierarchy, no "better or worse" connotation involved. Both are simply a means of reaching a higher floor. Everyone begins their soul's journey toward soul progress on the ground floor.

Chapter 9 includes a ten-point scale depicting the stages of soul advancement. Level one is our initiation point, where we all set out on our trek toward individual purification, transformation, and greater wisdom.

Consider a couple of metaphors for the journey of the soul. One is that the road is circuitous and often rocky. Another involves your closet; consider that you begin your incarnational journey wearing numerous layers of clothing, like two pairs of pants, two shirts, three sweaters, and a jacket. Each garment covers up the purity at our core, just as our ego behaviors block out our soul awareness.

Not only that, but just as a young child might choose to don inappropriate or ill-matching attire, a soul still early on in its journey will quite normally and naturally operate more from ego than from love. To put it another way, our soul moves through innumerable stages of complexity toward greater refinement and illumination, like a light bulb in the lamp of our being that burns brighter as it gathers more and more wattage.

Each descending plane of the universe, from the godhead, or the divine, to the level of human ego, represents a veiling, or diminishing, of the original divine light. The arc is from subtle to gross, with each universal element being spirit, or soul, to the one below it, right down to the physical earth. By the same token, matter and body are ego relative to the awareness above, and our goal while incarnate is to seek a tighter grasp on soul, to spiritualize matter and release more of our ego as we evolve.

Tracey: SOUL LEADERSHIP

This account begins at the point where Tracey leaves her past life and travels to the spiritual realm.

I am being washed with a healing light that goes into all my cracks and fills them up. There are powerful beings moving around me, taking charge of the healing. I feel a beautiful sense of love and home. I had contamination from the last life that needed cleansing.

Now I move on and come to a group of souls who are my students. Most of them have incarnated before. I've been teaching some of them for a long time. Others just come and go. I send information to them via energy. Some of the teaching is even tactile. I worry about being thorough. I teach these students about fear, specifically that it does not have any substance of its own but somehow manages to make us feel transparent. Decisions in life need to be made out of love, not fear. Fear is tied to ego, not soul. This class that I teach happens before these students go back to earth.

I am told that I need to be an unassuming teacher, to have humility. I am not to be "front and center" but rather to work quietly. I am not to draw attention to myself. It is tricky to shine without shining, but the students learn better that way. It is good for my own learning to be in the background.

I am to learn to let out my light. I am not to appear too bright, but I am not to hold in too much either. It is about being steady. I am to remind myself that I am a teacher. I have made the choice to be here. I am not required to be here, and I need to maintain my connection with spirit.

Tracey's comment about feeling love and "home" upon arrival in the spiritual realm is very common in clients at the point of completing a past-life scenario during soul regression. Love in the spiritual realm is a palpable and powerful experience. Notwithstanding, she is a very advanced soul, no longer needing to incarnate. As such, she could be likened to a senior executive in industry or the professions who has gained significant knowledge, experience, and standing.

At the same time, the more developed the soul, the more likely the individual is to exhibit characteristics such as humility, compassion, loving-kindness, and discernment about fear, narcissism, and judgment. As we move up the ladder, we leave behind more and more aspects that are locked into ego and gather feathers in our cap that are related to soul.

Tracey is directed to teach from a relatively inconspicuous position and in a down-to-earth style. She is to maintain ego strength (belief in herself) and portray her capabilities in a modest manner. To be somewhat in the background as she teaches is a delicate balance for Tracey, as she has apparently reached a level of soul development where she was able to choose to come into body. While there are souls with this capability incarnate at this time, such is not the norm.

Soul progression takes time—time to progress by virtue of our lives. As we trudge, swim, plod, and lumber through scores of incarnations, we advance even when life may seem almost unbearable. The more we fall down, pick ourselves up, and comprehend the preferred manner in which we can care for ourselves and others, the further we climb on the ladder from ego to soul self.

We advance gradually and intentionally—but we do advance. Our starting point is that of a new soul functioning primarily from ego, or the earthly personality. Onward and upward we progress, ultimately to view life from a more spiritual vantage point where love is the fuel for our existence.

Dena: ENERGY FREQUENCIES

I am told that it is time to stand up and stop being afraid. I am afraid because there is a lot of violence in my lives. I am to show there are other ways of being and teach the expansive nature of love. Violence is nothing but energy. Energy begets energy. To transmute the energy, there has to be an understanding that violence has no power. If I open my heart, I will move out of my mental process. I love. I am loved.

Dena helps us to comprehend that violence is low-level energy tied to the machinations of ego. Love is the height of the divine, which transmutes and lifts our energy through purification. It is as if we take the energy of violence and place it into a fire, where we alter its power.

Fire is a rapid, persistent chemical change that releases heat and light. By imagining we can transform the intensity of violence into the light of love, we come to understand the resolution of duality and separation. As an incarnate soul, we are pure love at our nucleus. That dimension of love is to be incorporated into our humanity, our corporeal self, as we live day by day.

Without our soul energy, which stems from the love of the Source (another term for God, the Tao, the divine), we cannot reside in the state of incarnation. Separation from the spiritual realm does not exist; the only reality is one of unity, of oneness. Once we come to know there is nothing more at our core but soul energy, we gain the purest perspective on embodied life. We who are incarnate now are all striving alongside our fellow souls to advance, both for ourselves and for the greater good of the universe at large.

To limit and define ourselves as part of a hierarchy, or pecking order, where someone or something "wins" at the expense of someone or something else is in direct opposition to cultivating the power of humility and all its gifts. It is often said that when we take what we do seriously, but we do not take who we are seriously, that is humility.

Marianne Williamson, author and teacher, states in *A Return to Love: Reflections on the Principles of A Course in Miracles* (Harper Collins, 1992): "Our deepest fear is not that we are inadequate. Our deepest fear is that we are powerful beyond measure....There is nothing enlightened about shrinking so that other people won't feel insecure around you....We are all meant to shine, as children do....And as we let our own light shine, we unconsciously give other people permission to do the same."

Carrie: THE NATURE OF HUMILITY

Following a regression hypnotherapy session, Carrie explains:

It seems humility comes out of a sense of having thoroughly examined and made friends with yourself. You've actually accepted yourself and developed a sense of warmth and compassion toward yourself. At that point, you don't have to prove yourself time after time, moment after moment. There's a sense of not having to check yourself all the time to see how you are doing, whether that is in relation to others' standards or in relation to your own. It means you don't have to win or impress others. You could just as well accept loss and blame. Out of making friends with yourself comes a sense of confidence and freedom.

Ego and judgment sit in opposition to concepts like soul, love, humility, discernment, and compassion. They serve to maintain a dualistic worldview of right versus wrong, black versus white, being on-track versus offtt. The spiritual realm does not function from a dualistic perspective; based on regression hypnotherapy, we are never judged as acting properly or improperly, but we can be lovingly advised to alter certain aspects of our lives. Love and acceptance are the coin of the spiritual realm.

As one client stated in her regression hypnotherapy session, "Power combined with wisdom is what we seek." Merging our soul self with our human self is the recipe for combining wisdom and power. When our human self is simply the vehicle to put in motion the wisdom and knowledge of our soul self, we function from our most pure energy.

Darcy and Julie: EGO AND COMPASSION

Darcy is told by her elders, "We are to be in the world (life on earth) but not of the world. War in the world—over whose beliefs are correct and whose are not—is based on ego, not soul. War is senseless."

The profound message for Julie is, "If you are to be a healer, compassion must come first. You will live a series of lives where you are emotionally wounded in many ways. In order to understand and gain compassion, you must feel pain."

As soul progress expands, wisdom is enhanced. As wisdom is enhanced, ego is relegated to its proper place of operating from strength, not "better than." Living daily life with the awareness that we are a soul, consciously walking moment by moment through the hills and valleys of human existence, overcomes dualism. The more we realize that each and every experience in life serves our ongoing soul advancement, the more we are prone to facilitate both our incarnate experiences and the ensuing insights that lead to the expansion of our wisdom and that of others. This last case illustrates how this can be so even under the direst circumstances.

Robert: FROM DARKNESS COMES LIGHT

Robert, a client in his fifties, is a well-known and much-respected spiritual writer and speaker.

I am a woman and am outside at night. I'm in a meadow near a cemetery. As I am walking, I am grabbed and thrown down. A man has me by the throat. I am told to be quiet. He lifts my skirt, feels me, and somebody comes. Have I been raped? I leave the body. Maybe I have been choked to death. Now I am floating above the body. This should not have happened. I know that I must go on. I do not feel alone. I'm called upward. As I move faster, it is getting brighter. I am taken to a place to relax and heal.

A guide comes. I knew him in my current life before he died. He came into my life to help me overcome this past-life experience. I have had many lives being powerful. This past life where I was sexually assaulted left me questioning my validity as a human being. I was to learn the balance between being powerful and powerless. This was an opportunity to develop greater understanding and compassion. Walking through such fire is a means of purging and anointing.

Robert's soul regression teaches each of us a precious lesson: that soul advancement can be augmented through heinous events. Though we often cannot comprehend why such things occur, they are one means by which the soul expands more fully into all there is. As Robert supports others today who may be walking the hot coals of daily life, he becomes even more sensitized to their trauma.

chapter 13

The white American man makes the white American woman maybe not superfluous, but just a little kind of decoration. Not really important to turning around the wheels of the state. Well, the black American woman has never been able to feel that way. No black American man at any time in our history in the United States has been able to feel that he didn't need that black woman right against him, shoulder to shoulder—in that cotton field, on the auction block, in the ghetto, wherever.

—*Maya Angelou*

Men weren't really the enemy—they were fellow victims suffering from an outmoded masculine mystique that made them feel unnecessarily inadequate when there were no bears to kill.

—*Betty Friedan*

Male and Female Past Lives

Androgynous traits are traits that are balanced, traits that harmoniously blend the traditionally distinct male or female. If a culture or relationship is androgynous rather than patriarchal or matriarchal, it will display a lack of rigid gender roles and create a milieu where the people involved can comfortably display opposite-sex characteristics or be involved in activities that are commonly associated with the opposite gender.

Androgyny is a term derived from the Greek words for *man* and *woman*, suggesting a lack of gender identification. The word *patriarchy* comes from the two Greek words *pater* (father) and *arche* (rule). A matriarchal culture is one where the power lies with the women, especially the mothers. History suggests, however, that few, if any, cultural groups are or ever have been matriarchal. While cultures may be matrilocal (the husband comes to live in the location of the wife's family), such groups generally retain a hierarchy where males hold the balance of authority.

Recent studies in human biology have come to support that the brains of males and females are literally different, both in terms of hemispheric configuration and energy patterning. Women are more capable in most areas of right-brain sensory processing and tend to focus on broad-based sensory input. Men are more prone to left-brain abstract reasoning and awareness and therefore operate more in terms of directedness and intent. They tend to plan and finish one task at a time, whereas women are hard-wired to multi-task.

The research into gender-based brain configuration also suggests that neither male nor female characteristics stem exclusively from the realm of biology or the domain of socialization. It's both nature *and* nurture that mold us. Furthermore, humans each have both a male and a female side, though one or the other is usually dominant. In the grander scheme of things, we need both female and male incarnations to develop the androgyny of the soul, which it does as we progress along the path and gain balance through maturation and wisdom.

We do have to recognize that male and female brains are different. Culturally, however, this does not support the supremacy of patriarchal or matriarchal dominance. Respect for gender equality is the ideal in society and culture.

Androgyny exists both in external behaviors and internally within each of us. Conventionally, females demonstrate loyalty, warmth, and shyness, while males are viewed as assertive, analytical, and independent. Traits that seem to oppose the social norms are often squelched in children. For centuries, men have had clandestine emotions while women have either avoided or hid their desire to take charge, particularly in the workplace.

Fortunately, gender roles in the West have become more malleable over the past half-century. The media now routinely portrays fathers being present at the birth of their children, women engaging in careers previously viewed as part of a "man's world," and open homosexuality. We could say "the times they are a'changin'," even though inequalities persist and the alteration is gradual.

What light do past-life soul regression and between-lives soul regression shed on gender issues? Past-life regression clients demonstrate time and time again that whether we are now male or female, we have *all* experienced lives as the opposite sex.

The natural rationale for experiencing incarnation as both male and female would be to absorb both perspectives. In the course of thousands of regressions, I have never once worked with a client who described all of their corporeal lives as having been lived in the current gender. The automatic assumption arises that the spiritual realm has a purpose for causing even a minimum number of lives to be lived as the opposite sex.

Lindsay: FEMALE LIVES OF ACCOMPLISHMENT

Lindsay is told by her spirit guide that she had a life in Europe where she was an accomplished female pianist. Though people knew she was musically gifted, the era in which she lived dictated that she had to put up a big fight to be recognized as a female musician. Lindsay's spirit guide points out the parallel between the musical career she had in the past life and her life today as a professional woman in a man's world.

"Do what you can to shine. There will be no question, as your talent is obvious. You have respect now but do not notice this. In the past life, ultimately you did gain respect. Your performing helped to open doors for other women. You need to come to terms with your gifts and abilities today. When you are guided by intuition, you are always on the right path. Appreciate the joy you feel about your life path."

Lindsay is an example of following our heart into endeavors that create bliss and passion. When we are in alignment with our core nature, creating the work we love, we are in alignment with our soul self. In the area of gender equality, some of us choose to blaze the trail for others. No matter what the prevailing mindset, putting our skills into practice and forging ahead will ultimately bring us achievement and success.

In more than one lifetime, Lindsay has agreed to persevere and increase her capacity as a woman to demonstrate skills previously ascribed solely to the male gender. Planet Earth and its related social structure reaps the benefit of Lindsay's incarnations as an accomplished woman—incarnations she has forged with integrity and truth.

The core nature of our soul self shines brighter and truer than ego. Spirit wants each of us to present who and what we are without judging or demeaning our innate spiritual being. Our soul nature is androgynous, having the power of the masculine and the power of the feminine equally mixed.

Just as ego carries judgment and lacks compassion for self and others, allowing our pure soul light to lead brings androgyny to the human plane. As men or women, we are neither good nor bad, right or wrong, acceptable or not. We simply are who we are. Within each of us is the need to assert ourselves and the awareness of our emotions. Our androgynous soul is gender balanced and gender neutral.

Each life lived authentically from our soul's truth draws us closer to a natural equilibrium. Walking the path of each embodiment, we begin to wrap our arms around the polarity between strength and softness, between masculine and feminine qualities. Changing gender from incarnation to incarnation, we come to understand which traits and behaviors are healthy and unhealthy in either sex, such as leadership versus tyranny in the male or true nurturing in the female versus self-effacement or abject codependency.

Karl is an example of a currently incarnate male striving to integrate and balance actions tied to numerous past lives as a warrior. Karl is a very capable, goal-oriented individual with strong "take charge" skills. It is easy to label him successful, both in his work and family life. Through soul regression, he becomes aware of having lived as a Viking and later as a Crusader. He also learns that he rarely had any long-term romantic involvements because of his incessant travels and warrior lifestyle. In the course of his repeated past lives, however, the meaning of being a warrior got kicked out of balance for Karl.

Men have historically provided for their families and used force when necessary to defend their family and their communities. This Karl can agree with. During one lifetime, however, he discovers that nonstop raping, pillaging, and killing for the sake of it serve only to devalue the warrior role.

A warrior, he realizes, is not someone armed to the teeth, perpetrating violence on others; that is a tyrant. Rather, the warrior is trained, ready, and willing to regulate violence and to meet any threat to his safety and well-being as well as that of his loved ones. He lives as one with his inner soul self, committed to upholding his individual values and the principles that guide and define his life.

During regression hypnotherapy, Karl broadens his view and the understanding of his life today. In addition, he views a point in the life as a Crusader where he defects and becomes a farmer and family man in the Middle East. Karl chose in that life to stop killing for a cause.

The next account is of a seventy-year-old female client, Janice. Her interpretation is totally different as she discovers under regression why she has never been married.

Janice: A WARRIOR'S TALE

I am a powerful warrior with armor, a hood, and a helmet. I come upon the scene of a fierce battle that has ended. There is carnage here, with many fallen bodies and spears. I believe the year is AD 800. I've been gone and have just arrived back. I should have been able to prevent this but did not get here in time. I was away taking care of some negotiations. All that I have worked for has been lost. I feel all alone in the world. My community is gone. This was a neighboring tribe that killed everyone. In those days, this kind of thing just happened.

Now I walk to my village. It is deserted. I go to a wood building and into an elaborate, large room. The bedroom is full of blood. My wife has been brutally murdered. I feel anger and despair. I have to go and attack them. They murdered everyone. There must be some way to get to him (the leader of the community that has slain my wife and village). Though I am sophisticated, I feel violent anger and blind rage.

Now I feel pain in my right shoulder and chest. I am near the other village. I feel all-consuming anger and want to kill him. I run at him with my spear. He stabs me and I feel a flash of light. I'm dying. I am delirious. My death was not a big thing. I believe in right action.

(As Janice experiences her soul stepping away from the body of the man she has been, she is able to process the wisdom she gained from that past life.)

I now understand the reason why I sometimes feel a desperate need in my current life to strike out to protect myself. My present boyfriend loves to reenact battles where he is a knight. This also makes me mad, but now I can identify more with his interest in battles.

As the warrior, I was all-powerful and dominant. I was firm but not a tyrant. My wife was furious at me at times, and I ignored her. I was not close to my wife, though I was very close to my twelve-year-old son. I did feel paternal responsibility then and also great love toward him, but in this life, I have always struggled with communication, particularly with men. I have suppressed my male energy. I need to take back and reintegrate my power.

Janice raises a good point about male energy and power. It is important for the modern man to understand that healthy warrior skills are a critical ingredient in his ability to produce results in life. They generate good health, vitality, and longevity as well as the strength and stamina to combat stress and deal with economic setbacks, career shifts, upheaval in family and other relationships, etc.

Warriorship is not only about physical training and preparedness. It is an attitude and a stance one takes in life, in every arena of experience. Whether we are presently male or female, we must embrace and take pride in our warrior side. The warrior is strong in times of risk and difficulty. Concurrently, the warrior is sensitive to the needs of others as he chooses his actions. Both assertive "maleness" and caring "femaleness" must coexist within the warrior. In today's life and for the future, healthy warrior traits are crucial.

Androgyny is about demonstrating the power of the masculine and the power of the feminine in equal measure. Edie receives input and direction from her panel of wise elders for her personal life as a woman and for her life as a teacher of women.

Edie: ON BEING A WOMAN TODAY

I see a still lake. They tell me that stillness is missing for women, including myself. Men do not need stillness like women do. Women have lost the ability to be still. I need two times each day to be still. I see an open vase. They keep emphasizing that in order to be a receptacle, women must be open like a vase. Women hold the energy of the ages. I love walking a labyrinth maze because it is a vessel of feminine energy.

"You came as a woman this time to continue softening your energy. You have been a woman many times. Your group takes the intensity of energy and finds ways to soften it. Women change the resonance of energy. They bring in a 'curve' to break the sharpness of resonance. Open vowel sounds create a resonance and energy that is easy for the body to track."

The message to Edie provides her with a feminine focal point. In a broader sense, the message serves to remind each of us of the inner need for softness. Stillness and quiet allow us to align, to listen, and to receive from our divine nature. Perhaps there is an unspoken message from Edie's wise elders suggesting that women today lean too far in the direction of the male archetype, being overly driven to accomplish. Feminine energy contains the supple gentleness of the divine that is received through intuitive knowing.

Walking a labyrinth ties one to an ancient, cross-cultural, spiritual practice that serves a threefold purpose. First, by following the circle into its nucleus, we purge, or release, the details of daily life in order to open the heart and quiet the mind. Second, an illumination or a receiving happens through meditation, prayer, and divine input while we are at the center of the labyrinth. Finally, a union occurs as one gradually leaves the core of the labyrinth, retracing one's footsteps outward while remaining tied to a higher plane of wisdom and carrying what has been received.

It is no accident that the pattern of the labyrinth echoes the soft curves of the vase mentioned by Edie's wise elders. As the circle is walked, the sharpness of conscious life can be left behind, and we become a receptacle for higher gifts. Just as Edie is being requested to maintain and enhance the softness within her, we all are encouraged to be open and not rigid in order to receive. The feminine and masculine energies need to be balanced within our being human.

As our soul self is attached to the divine, we are the repository of androgynous archetypal energy in our subliminal consciousness. Deep within human consciousness, the human self, we carry an archetypal image, a blueprint of sorts, of what constitutes maleness and femaleness. Carl Jung, the famous Swiss psychiatrist, used the term *collective unconscious* in referring to the primordial images of masculine or feminine behavior that are at the root of our cultural awareness. These male/female archetypes include gender-specific patterns of thinking, feeling, and reacting that are instinctive.

While Edie has been handed her loving directive from spirit to be softer, another client might be asked to strengthen their ability to enforce limits and personal boundaries if that person exhibits too much flexibility and openness. Softening one's energy and strengthening one's belief in self not only improve traditional male-female characteristics, but in so doing, they also help lead the soul to androgyny.

Accepting the notion that our human self, or ego, is compelled to rise through lifetimes of experience (no matter how slow or fast) toward alignment with our soul self, or love, we examine the common labels or characteristics of both genders. Our ego encapsulates the gender-based design of our consciousness, either masculine or feminine. Our soul strives toward androgyny, toward carrying a pure balance of equal parts.

Classic descriptive words for male characteristics include *strong, assertive, problem solver, provider, protector, achiever, driven*, and *intellectual*. Descriptors for traditional female characteristics include *soft, caring, nurturing, loving, quiet, feeling, supportive*, and *engaging*.

Past-life soul regression and between-lives soul regression clients frequently describe how their spirit guide looks or feels. The description of the guide immediately provides insight into the style of behavior and presentation deemed necessary by the guide to create a specific effect on the client. The following are some client examples:

- There is someone here. He is humorous. His color keeps changing from blue to purple and back again. He feels familiar. He wants to lighten my heart. He understands my sadness and lack of joy. Now he's holding my head and releasing something negative. He is releasing my sadness. He tells me that I am growing into my own power.

- He is cobalt blue and radiant. I feel pure love from him. He says, "Welcome, precious one." He is pleased with the growth in my energy. I am becoming more tolerant of others and of myself. I tell him that I could have been less rebellious in the last life.

- A presence is coming toward me. She is like a blue fairy. She says I am doing a good job. I am growing spiritually.

- My guide says to be more respectful. He is blue and more advanced than I. He's very stubborn. I am so angry because of the sadness. I must let this go; my approach must change.

- I see a blue light. The light surrounds me. I am taken inside it. Do not worry. He is here to help release my lives of violence. He is pure love. I had too many lives where I misused power. I had power without wisdom. He tells me that the blue light is about speaking my truth.

- I die, and my soul exits from my solar plexus. I am going somewhere as I fly quickly. All the pressure is taken off of me. I feel soothing and forgiving. I see my guide, who is meditating, and I hear the sound of *Om*. It is such a beautiful sound. My guide is an Asian monk in a temple. His whole being is beautiful. He is my teacher and deeply loves me. He tells me to simply call him "Monk."

Spirit guides can be male, female, and androgynous. They may present in human or energetic form and can have on particular clothing. In classic shamanic manner, the spirit guide may shapeshift into the form of an animal. The communication style of the spirit guide could be humorous or serious, though never harsh and punitive. The spirit guide may behave in either an acerbic or irreverent mode, which is intended to nudge the client into making some change in life. Whatever the fashion in which the spirit guide appears, there is always a message for the client.

When the spirit guide appears as either male or female, there are elements of the client's current incarnation where one or the other archetypal gender-specific energy is needed. In simple terms, maleness is strong and femaleness is soft. No value judgment is attached to either. When the spirit guide presents as energy, with neither the masculine nor the feminine quality dominating, the client is either being applauded for reaching a balanced blend of human traits or the spirit guide is suggesting that the client focus more heavily on gaining a gender-balanced lifestyle.

Clara is a sixty-year-old lesbian. During the preliminary interview, she says that one of her goals for her session is to get a deeper perspective on her sexual orientation. Upon meeting with her wise elders, Clara explains:

> Being a lesbian is about finding out who I am. I have to propel myself on my own out of the situation I was born into in order to seek others like me. It is like a challenge or a maze with a light inside. The light is covered up, but if you can find the light, then it is possible to connect with it. I must find the light in myself, and then I will know it in others. I was born to good people, but they are on a different wavelength. Now I have found my group. But we do not work as a team yet. We chose each other in order to push off one another. We could make a beacon if we could get together.

Clara's biological family is socially and politically conservative. Realizing that she is a lesbian has been a complex and strenuous experience, but her arduous journey to find support and validation has been successful. The light within herself to which she refers is the truth of who and what she is in her present life.

Clara has latched onto her light and found happiness in doing so. She has also been able to demonstrate her core light to those with whom it is safe. Her task now is to build up comfortable teamwork with others whose light is similar to hers in order for them to meld their truth and project great illumination outward. Androgyny, rather than a feminine or masculine persona, is the core reality for Clara.

Serena: A BALANCING ACT

Serena prepares to leave a meeting with her wise elders. "Use your power with humility and potency" is the final statement from the coordinator of her spiritual team. "We encourage you to seek us out during your meditative times."

Now I am in a very high place. The air is rare. There are lots of lights and colors. The light comes from different sources. There is a sense of excitement. My spirit guide, "Or," is here with a new mix of guides. Before we get to the place where I choose a body for my next incarnation, the guides explain what I am to work on in the next life (the life which Serena is living presently). I am to work on compassion, humility, nonjudgment, and forgiveness.

Now we have come to the place where I am shown the body choices for my upcoming life. The first possibility is a dark-skinned female body that is weak and sickly. The second choice is a female body with substance abuse problems and chemical issues. The third possibility is male and gifted. The first life is too short. The third choice is an affluent but hard life. I have not been more male or female in the past.

I want to be female, although it is easier for me to male. I like the male body because of its mental and physical capabilities. But I need to be female to grow. I need to work on being gentle, to be more compassionate and nurturing. I am to give back and to be of service.

Serena is lovingly instructed by her wise elders to balance her strength with softness of language, suggesting she move through life maintaining androgyny.

Moving on to the between-lives soul regression, Serena discovers herself in a rarified place where pure energy exists. The life script determined for Serena by her wise elders is to place her intention and focus on reducing criticism and judgmentalism and gaining compassion, humility, and forgiveness. From a conventional standpoint, one could label the words provided to Serena as feminine versus masculine.

Having experienced a balanced number of male and female lives, Serena opts to work within the body of a woman in her present life. Though working through the physical and intellectual capabilities of a male body may have been easier for Serena in past lives, she seems to require experiencing her present life as a woman to develop a more kindhearted, concerned nature and to reach out to support others in a softer way. The message from the all-knowing divine is for each of us to extend and round out our soul character.

Darlene is the final example of a mandate to love being explained directly during between-lives soul regression. She describes her current life purpose:

I came into incarnation to expand my love, to learn to open more freely and love without condition. I am to expand my ability to create here. It is harder here to deal with such a dense form. My expansion is a huge part of this life. Balance is critical for me. Balance must be maintained of the right and the left, of the male and the female. The etheric (spiritual) must become stronger to balance with form (grounded reality). These dualities and the power they hold must be utilized with balance.

Darlene and her team of guides and teachers ultimately provide the key message of this chapter. While incarnate on earth, we reside within a literal container, walking in a human form and energetically dense reality. Such grounding could even be said to be hard-wired into our cerebral cortex. The left side of our brain manages logic, rational and analytical thought, spatial perception, and other faculties generally labeled as "masculine." Our etheric, spiritual, or intuitive nature stems from the right hemisphere of our brain, with its synthesizing, subjective, and holistic perspective commonly attached to the "feminine."

Darlene has been instructed to discover balance in her present life. She is to be as logical as she is emotional. The core message telegraphed to Darlene during regression hypnotherapy is of overcoming duality. We are the souls who become human in order to advance both earthly reality and spiritual truth. Being grounded in body and reaching toward the height of celestial wisdom draws us into the awareness of our divinity in body and in spirit.

We are to be both masculine and feminine in one container. We are to be ego and love simultaneously, melding equal parts of yin and yang. The warrior image of masculine, take-charge protection of community serves as

MALE AND FEMALE PAST LIVES

the prototype of strength. The mother image and its feminine caretaking qualities demonstrate the strength and simultaneous softness of being able to set aside one's requirements in favor of the needs of others. Without equal aspects of thinking and feeling, of intellect and intuition, of power and softness, of ego and love, of body and soul, we are not integrated in the truth of who and what we are and can be.

chapter 14

Grief can be the garden of compassion. If
you keep your heart open through everything,
your pain can become your greatest ally in
your life's search for love and wisdom.

—Jalal ad-Din Rumi

Soul Development

First and foremost, we are each an advancing soul. Just as breathing is automatic, we all progress toward greater wisdom, no matter the literal speed measured in earthly time. Our soul is wired to seek greater levels of discernment in life as we achieve a more keen awareness of appropriate judgment and discrimination in our behavior. It is like a soul seedling that first germinates underground, pops its head through the earth, and continues to grow into the sunlight.

Many clients arrive informing me they have been told that they've already lived 583 lives or some such number. The exact number of incarnations we have experienced has no bearing on our level of soul development. Just as some children can count to ten at age two and others at age three, how quickly we progress is not of critical significance. What is important is that we continue to advance as a soul, no matter how quickly.

The Buddha stated, "I teach one thing and one thing only: that is suffering and the end of suffering." To be human is to want to avoid suffering and experience pleasure, but also from a human perspective, we all experience suffering in life. When we are able to accept that each and every detail of our life serves a purpose, then we have the opportunity to view daily existence from a non-dualistic perspective that one is many, and many is one. We come to realize that suffering or lack of suffering, also labeled pleasure, do not exist. There simply is life, moment by moment, with each small element providing the energy to guide our soul development.

When we can ask ourselves the purpose of a given event in our life rather than judging it as good or bad, we are truly moving into higher wisdom. In this chapter, we will discuss how solitude in life supports our soul development, how both pleasure and suffering can be instruments of soul growth, and how the advancing soul may sometimes elect to manage more than one incarnation simultaneously.

For many people, the word solitude connotes spending time without companionship. I am beyond what we call middle-aged and have spent this lifetime living in a family while growing up, living with roommates at college, or being married and raising children. By contrast, I have a close friend of similar age who was divorced many years ago and has lived alone for the better part of the last twenty-five years.

Living alone or living with a mate is neither better nor worse in the scheme of soul advancement. What seems to be essential is to have experienced one life or more where we spend a significant amount of time in relative isolation. And if we do live within a partnership, we need time to be simply alone with our own self.

Prior to embodiment, we have the option of scripting a life where we spend the bulk of our time on our own. It seems that in order to dive fully into knowing who we are at the core, a minor or major degree of alone time is a necessity. Thus, a life of solitude may contribute to, and can be indicative of, soul advancement. One or both are entirely plausible.

I hold a palpable memory of a lifetime I lived as a native woman in the forest, near a body of water, where I spent most of my adult life in complete solitude communing with animals, an herb garden, and the water while gaining a deeper sense of self.

Even as I write, I recall the transcendent beauty of that life. I may have lived other lives of solitude, but that particular existence lived in the wild and at one with nature is emblazoned in my spiritual DNA. In my mind's eye, I can quickly and unerringly draw forward the mental images of the life.

Michaela: THE CASE FOR TIME ALONE

This is the same Michaela that was profiled earlier; different detail from the regression session is offered here to highlight information tied to soul progression. Michaela arrives for her session and explains that although she loves to entertain, she frequently sequesters herself. "Why do I feel compelled to spend a lot of time alone?" she asks in her interview. After completing a past life, Michaela travels into the spiritual realm where "someone steps forward to embrace me. There is a positive and familiar feeling from my guide, Staffordson, who takes me to meet with my wise elders. I am told the purpose of my present incarnation is that I still have research left to accomplish."

Being in the human realm to gain knowledge of the earthly struggles of others is the key element and privilege of Michaela's present embodiment. Because of her advanced soul standing, incarnation is or will soon be no longer a requirement for her.

I am able to recognize the divine nature of all people and feel full of love for them. My task is to examine the beauty of the symphony of life, where surprises and disappointments are many, and bring an understanding of it back to the spiritual realm.

I need aloneness and separateness in order to assimilate the ups and downs in the lives of others. It is hard to get close to people as I gain a sense of the details of their lives, because I am unable to lessen the pain of people. I do not like to be so separate, but this is what I came to do.

I am shown my soul color as purple. It is hard for me to acknowledge my advanced degree of soul standing, though it does explain the separation from others that I feel. There are many of us like me. This is all about love. I am not to feel superior to others.

Michaela is an example of a soul whose high level of wisdom allows her to take on the mission of traveling into body to amass an energetic understanding of human struggles and to transfer such awareness to the discarnate souls who coordinate the spiritual realm. Her service is twofold: she can assist many on earth as they walk the hills and vales of daily living, and in addition, she is a trusted information gatherer for the spiritual realm.

The spiritual realm must remain abreast and aware of the trials and tribulations of embodiment on earth in order for the universe as a whole to advance. The souls who manage and coordinate it serve in an advisory capacity to those of us who continue to incarnate. However, these very advanced beings have either never been incarnate on earth or ceased to be required to do so long ago. Hence the contribution needed from this side by Michaela and other souls like her.

While some may have difficulty accepting that the spiritual realm progresses as does the earthly one, I do believe this is true. We are all divine, whether in body or in spirit, and we evolve whether on this side of the veil or beyond.

Michaela leaves her soul regression with a clear perspective on her role in life, her level of soul advancement, and the reason she needs a certain amount of isolation. Confirming who she is and what she is here to do allows her to breathe more easily. I often notice relief or renewed serenity on the faces of my clients as they complete their time in the "inner sanctum" of my office.

The next account of a soul regression experience provides a potent example of the purpose of solitude in life. With a view to deepening your understanding, I provide here an extensive soul regression transcript for Chase, a man in his fifties, along with his observations weeks and months following the session.

Chase: DIFFERENT STROKES

Chase volunteers the following information about his life:

Most people, it seems, have a drive to get married and have children. I never actually had that drive, though I am very attracted to women. Actually, in recent years, I have thought it would be rewarding to have children. But, on the other hand, I have observed the downside of being married and having children. One just doesn't have the freedom of being single. I've always appreciated being independent and even alone. I don't feel that I need someone's company to enjoy myself. When I'm home alone, I don't pine for companionship. I don't feel lonely.

Chase's soul regression opens as follows:

It's day, and I am flying a biplane that I'm testing. I have on goggles and a brown leather helmet. There's a problem, and the engine stops. I pull the levers but can't get the engine started. The plane sputters and keeps going down. I am scared. The plane crashes.

My soul left before the plane crashed. I designed the plane and am disappointed. I want to tell someone that it's okay that I have died. Spirit tells me that I did fine. My brother fixed the mechanical problem. He fixed something under the steering choke stick. My brother and I worked on this together; I told him what to fix.

Gary, a lifelong friend, meets me as I expand into the spiritual realm. We're laughing hysterically. Here we are again. Gary and I have shared a lot. We've known each other in more than one life.

We pass some structures made of light. This area is important and sacred. There are books along the side. There are people there doing research. They are doing the same research as I am. They are looking at their books. There is a dark blue sky or space inside the books. There is a green-looking guy here who helps people with their research. Some souls need help finding their books. The books are like energy packets.

"You're not from around here originally. It might take a while to get used to it... being on earth, that is." The green guy points to a glowing area that opened up in the book. "That's where you are from. You incarnated on earth three hundred years ago and have had seven lives there." The green guy is tall, with delicate features. It is easier where I am from; people are more gentle and spacious. People do not get in each other's way. I was more advanced on that planet.

I am told that my human body has a nervous system problem because of the adjustment to being on earth. My sleep, chest, and alcohol issues are tied to not being here on earth for very long. I do not need to force the adjustment. I should not smoke cigarettes. It makes me more nervous. The green guy turns up the volume from the planet where I am from so that I can feel my home more.

I am on the edge of greater things. My life purpose is to evolve in consciousness. It is not about a mate or things. It is about greater vision. I must raise my consciousness even more. Even when I drink, I can still develop greater consciousness. I am working with deeper levels of confusion in order to gain clarity.

I am bathed in green light for greater comfort and energy. This helps my liver. It is suggested that I try more art. My life on earth has broken through more spiritually. It is happening quicker than I think.

For each of us as a soul, and for each life, the degree of solitude from which we will benefit varies. Chase's soul regression is a clear example of a life where solitude is the preferred option. He learns that relative isolation in this lifetime will allow him the opportunity to dive deep into spiritual awareness.

Chase is also an example of a soul whose incarnational existence has occurred somewhere other than on earth. Often the individual with such broad-based dimensional experience will have literal physical/medical issues to face, as the soul is more familiar with a different "container," if you will.

Following his soul regression, Chase shared the following insight:

And I think my guide gave me that infusion of energy because he's a healer. He knew what I could take. He plunged me into a health crisis that has compelled me to stop drinking. I haven't had a drink or smoke since I don't know when. I may have quit entirely.

When I was partying, I was actually more in tune with my mind moment to moment in the sense that I am now. Altered states are more of a challenge and more mysterious. I think that's why I was allowed to continue.

Chase provides a powerful bird's-eye view into the benefits and liabilities of using chemical substances to enter an altered state. As many of you know, there are other, more healthy means to do so. Shamanic journeywork is one example.

Listening weekly to regression clients for a number of years, I have never heard a word spoken suggesting the divine shakes a fist or finger at any of us; quite the contrary. Repeatedly, I hear a loving appeal from the teachers in spirit for clients to let go of creating more suffering in life. Instead, they would have us view each occurrence as a means of progression, an event drawing us toward a new and expanded perspective. Why waste our lives blaming ourselves for a litany of things we should or should not have done?

*N*ina: BE WHO YOU ARE

Nina is a female client in her middle forties. In a past life, she is a man in the early nineteenth century, living near a gothic church in a beautiful castle. In the opening scene, he is wearing lovely, rich clothing with long white socks, velvet pants, and a velvet jacket. He sits at a cherrywood desk writing a letter with pen and ink to discuss a philosophical issue.

Later in the past life, the man is in his study discussing war and peace with other noblemen. He feels that he doesn't know enough to offer useful input on war with another country. Words come automatically, and he is surprised at his own expertise. Surprisingly, the noblemen listen to the man, who discovers that his words change the course of what will happen. He is concerned about offering incorrect advice. "What if people die?" he muses. At the end of his life, the man is told by many that he is wise but he does not trust his decision-making.

I am comfortable only with my family and with books. We did make a good decision about the war. I do not feel that I have the right to say the words that I speak. Who gave me permission to say such important things?

Why do people respect me so? Did I do everything that I could? Maybe I have not done enough? Why is there not peace in the world? There has always been a war inside of me with no calm. My loving wife comforts me, but I do not feel worthy of her.

(He dies and begins crossing into spirit.) There is bright light all around me. I have no weight and merge with the light. The wise one speaks, saying, "You are one with the divine. You are nothing and everything. All the knowledge you need is open to you. You opened the door for many."

Now I am with my guide, who is seated on a throne and looks scary. He looks like a warrior with horns. I am told that I resist the warrior in me. I am told that I should not judge by appearances. Suddenly, my guide shifts into losing the horns and appearing as a jester, a clown. He says that I do not laugh enough. I feel safe in his presence. He pulls my mouth out to my ears so that I smile. My guide is not arrogant. He is wise.

My guide takes me to water, where I am to swim. I am to learn to go with the flow. Water has warmth and has heart.

My life purpose is to learn to not take everything so seriously. My mission is to be in the here and the now. I am to ask what each moment is about. I am to appreciate what I have. All else will emerge in its own time. I do not need a goal.

Nina brings each of us a beautiful and profound message: that we should believe in ourselves and not denigrate our capabilities. Her soul regression is a lesson for us all about increasing our self-worth and our knowledge without becoming arrogant. Our inner core needs ego strength, or self-esteem, not ego, being self-absorbed and always in "better than" mode.

In sum, Nina's guide reminds us to be who we are. We can be a warrior without being hurtful or killing others. Swimming through the daily events of life and laughing when we err will serve us much more effectively than being constantly worried that we will make a mistake or not do enough.

The expression "lighten up" may seem folksy, but those exact words turn up in more soul regression sessions than I can easily count. Clearly, the realm of spirit often views embodied humans as too serious and lacking in joy and playfulness.

The following words were spoken by a number of clients during soul-regression sessions:

- My council tells me that I need more joy. It is time for celebration and change. I am moving up a level as fast change happens. I am doing well, but I am too cautious. I always question my motives. They tell me to just go buy the car. They want me to "lighten up."

- I am told to listen to my heart. My talent is obvious. I am respected but do not notice this. When I follow my intuition, I am on the right path. I need to stop being so analytical with my mind. I forget the joy. I need to bring more fun into my life.

- I need to lighten up and not be so serious. I have made mistakes and dwell on this. I have done well in my current life and have worked things through. I need to be working on being more aware of myself and my soul. I am told to lighten up and enjoy more.

- I am taken to a fun place where I find water, birds, and sunshine. A guide tells me this is the "fun side," where I need to go on an adventure with love, pleasure, and good food. My guide propels and encourages me through this area of joy. The darkness of my dad's behavior in current life is to give me a contrast with the light. I am challenged to get to the depth of joy by having such a mountain of pain to climb beyond. My life purpose is to engage my heart.

Each of the four client cases I have quoted speaks of fun, pleasure, and joy. Viewing life through the lens of the heart assists us in not becoming stuck in the mire of our analytical mind, forever labeling things as good versus bad. All that is … is simply what is.

The divine realm recognizes the value of those carnal pleasures that are available to us only as incarnate beings. By viewing the glass of life as half full rather than half empty, we enhance our soul progress. The spiritual realm wants us to understand that all is in right order.

The Holographic Soul

The final topic in this chapter on the advancing soul is a discussion on soul energy being capable of holographic splitting, or subdivision. I have explained elsewhere that our higher self is the portion of our soul energy that remains in the spiritual realm, while a mirror-image segment of soul energy innervates our human bodies during incarnation. We are simultaneously soul in body and soul in spirit.

Based on soul-regression information, our soul can also separate and reside in more than one lifetime at once. An example is Cassandra, the wealthy traveler in chapter 10, who lives concurrently with Frederick, the British pilot who dies in World War II, and who dies herself a decade or so later. One client's words explain that many of us are experiencing two lives at once: "We evolve as a species and as a soul when we are able to manage more than one life. We are raising both our own vibration and the vibration of the universe."

The experience of living in two separate bodies at one time is a bit like being a circus rider with each foot on the back of a different horse, holding

both reins with balance and finesse. It takes skill to maneuver two life journeys simultaneously, but it does serve the achieving of further soul progress.

I have sat and listened to numerous clients as they uncover specifics of
a past life, only to experience a dawning awareness that their past overlaps
with their present. When this happens, they are initially a bit confused; they
wonder if it can be true. Most, however, come to honor their experience and
accept the overlap of two incarnations.

Our souls are capable of inhabiting two lives at once, but they need to be
somewhat advanced to do so. Just like a first grader can add and even perhaps multiply but does not yet have the ability to solve geometry problems,
so too must we gain the soul capability to ride two lives at one time. In addition, the literal overlap in time may be relatively brief, which has been the
case with a number of my clients.

When we elect to shoulder the energetic challenge of splitting our soul
energy in thirds (being in the spiritual realm and two bodies simultaneously),
we may do so to seek rapid progress as an individual soul, but it is also a
means to serve the greater whole.

I invite you to read the following case where the client discovers she has
had a past life that overlaps on her current one. As my client, she is a para-
legal secretary in her late thirties, unmarried but in a relationship. Her parallel life goes as follows:

Melody: MY OTHER LIFE

I am in New York City in the middle of Central Park. There are brightly lit
street lamps. I am wearing a long dark blazer, pants, and high heels. My
hair is pulled back. I am twenty-two years old. There are people sitting on
benches, and the weather is cold and blustery. I'm trying to walk quickly to
fight the strong wind. I can hear the noise of the street as there are a million
people here in Manhattan.

I go across the street through a revolving door into the Plaza Hotel. I am
to meet someone. I see a gentleman in a suit. He waves hello. He comes
toward me and gives me a European-style kiss. I have the sense that I
know him. He puts his arm around me. We sit down at a small table and

begin to talk. I feel very comfortable with him. I take out a binder and go over some plans. This does not seem business-related. We order drinks, laugh and talk, and feel quite close.

It is later now. I am in a sun-filled room with a baby in a cradle. I am quite happy. This is my child. I am now in my middle thirties. I wear pink sweatpants and a black sweatshirt. Nathan lives with me. He and I have married and adopted this child. My life is wonderful. I feel joy and light.

Now I am an old lady all hunched over. I wear a scarf on my head and look like an old-school Italian woman. Outside there are plants and a white fence. There is a gravestone for my husband. I can hear children and a ruckus in the house. I have five grandchildren and am so sad that my dear husband is gone. Life has been full. I face the sun. I relax and simply stop breathing. I feel my soul leave my chest, exiting near my sternum. I am happy. I have had a good life. Now I am ready to rejoin my soul friends.

As the therapist, I listened intently to my client Melody's account of a past life, wondering but not voicing my curiosity about the timing of the life. The clues for me that it could be a life unfolding concurrently were the clothing description, Manhattan, the hotel, and the large number of people.

Moving into the between-life segment, Melody met with her wise elders. "Your soul is split in two bodies. Not many can be in two bodies at once. When you feel ungrounded, it is because of this split into parallel lives. Do not be worried about it. You have sufficient energy to manage. Some of your soul essence always remains in the spiritual realm."

This chapter has presented three elements of soul development that have been gleaned from, and repeated in, numerous soul-regression sessions. One prerequisite for soul advancement is to experience at some point one or several lives without a daily romantic partnership or other such form of companionship. Living in total or relative solitude gives us the karmic opportunity to deepen our link to our higher self and attain higher consciousness.

Another key point is that suffering in life is relative. Being more accepting of self and others leads to being less critical and more forgiving. To err may be human, but "lightening up" about life is part of becoming divine.

Learning to step through the grit of life without drowning in the mire leads us into greater levels of soul progress.

Our final theme in this chapter is that, after a certain point in development, we can choose to handle two simultaneous lives and provide ourselves with the opportunity to progress at a dramatic rate in our climb toward greater wisdom. However, the spiritual realm does not seem to require such precipitated growth. The choice, as ever, is ours. Learning to handle our life challenges from the soul plane rather than out of ego is what speeds up not only our own journey and awareness, but also that of group consciousness and the greater universe.

conclusion

$\mathcal{S}$oul regression is a priceless tool that allows us to touch that inexplicable whole that is our core self. As a practicing regression hypnotherapist, I am deeply moved each time I am allowed to sit with a client and witness their soul journey. Some clients experience their session as a prophetic illumination. Others recognize and intuitively grasp the profound wisdom that is delivered on things like where they need to live or what work they need to be doing to fulfill their current life purpose.

What needs to be received from a higher plane of awareness is exactly and beautifully packaged for each individual. At the same time, no judgmental, punitive, or chastising words ever stem from the divine and none are ever heard in the course of a session. Always, the focus is loving understanding and guidance.

I thank each of you for this precious opportunity to share some of the experiences I have been privileged to facilitate and guide. Whether you experience past-life soul regression and between-lives soul regression or not, it is my sincere hope and desire that these pages have helped you to realize you are a unique and precious soul and to expand your understanding of your invaluable role in the universe.

Through soul regression, we gain recognition of our truth and of the higher truth. It provides a special opportunity to know ourselves as pure love residing at this time in body. We stem from the divine. We are souls having a human experience rather than the other way around. And as we daily live as souls in alignment with the higher order, it is our privilege and our role to help advance the universe itself.

Practitioner Notes

*I*t is truly a blessing to have the high privilege and honor to witness the spontaneous descriptions of the client's nucleus during soul regressions. Still, as the therapist, I breathe a sigh of relief knowing that it is not my job to determine the elements of past-life experience or its significance to a client.

The therapist is responsible for the process of the session, and the content is determined from a higher level of wisdom—the client's team of spirit guides and teachers. The information is received by and through the client, using their intuition combined with an altered state of consciousness.

Thus, the client essentially becomes their own channel, or conduit, for the higher, or soul, self. As such, the substance of the session is not the responsibility of the hypnotherapist. Though an altered state of consciousness is induced, all hypnosis is self-hypnosis and so the client is always in control of the process.

Having the ability to receive intuitively and speak the data of lives one has lived before is an awesome experience for the client. So is the gift of receiving soul-level input relative to who and what we are and are intended to be.

Many scientists believe we use the right temporal lobe of our brain to resonate with energy fields that are timeless—that we have the ability to use our human brain to access timeless, spaceless reality, which quantum physicists label as the "non-local."

Still, it is difficult, if not impossible, to explain the literal and energetic mechanics tied to accessing soul memory, both in past life and between lives. In essence, lessening the arousal or stimulation of our brain through regression hypnotherapy creates an altered state of consciousness that affords an opening to our intuitive, or mystical, processes.

The slower our brain-wave activity, the more able we are to recognize or intuit the specifics of the past, when our soul resided in another body or in the discarnate state. In both past-life soul regression and between-lives soul regression, the process used to access these memories is a form of hypnosis.

Hypnosis itself is about brain-wave shift, also labeled altered state of consciousness or trance. If we wish to relax and enter the hypnotic state, essentially we need to alter the speed of the energetic oscillation of our brain. The brain is an electrochemical organ that produces brain waves, as is demonstrated by the electroencephalograph, or EEG, machine. Researchers speculate that a fully functioning brain can generate as much as 10 watts of electrical power.

Brain waves range from the highest level of activity, or arousal, to the lowest. Beta brain-wave state, when the brain is the most highly aroused, occurs when we are engaged in totally mental, linear, or intellectual thought activity. As our brain waves slow, the amplitude of the brain wave increases and we move into deeper states of nonarousal and relaxation.

Once a sufficient level of relaxation, or trance, is gained via hypnotic induction, the next step is for the regression hypnotherapist to guide the client backward in chronological time, either in the present life, past life, or the time between lives.

Age regression to access the memory of current life events is a standard and common practice in the field of psychiatry. Past-life soul regression and between-lives soul regression are simply an extension of the practice of standard age regression in current life. They were pioneered in the late 1960s by Dr. Michael Newton, author of *Journey of Souls*, *Destiny of Souls*, and *Life Between Lives*. Since the early 1970s, the numbers of individuals seeking soul regressions have grown dramatically.

The "discovery" of hypnotism itself in the late 1700s is most often attributed to Franz Anton Mesmer (1734–1815). In fact, Abbé Faria, an Indo-Portuguese monk who lived from 1746–1819 and practiced in France, was the first to understand that hypnotism works through the power of suggestion and to demonstrate the existence of autosuggestion.

Faria's ideas superseded Mesmer's theory of "magnetic fluid" and brought forward the notion of hypnosis as a completely natural state, a form of lucid sleep controlled and maintained by the client and not the therapist.

In actuality, however, it is over 10,000 years ago that shamans (indigenous healers and priests) began using altered states of consciousness, or hypnotic trance, to access the unseen spiritual realm, or the non-local, for purposes of healing and for gaining a vision of the past and the future.

Using drumming and other repetitive percussive sound to alter human brain waves, shamans have verbally and energetically assisted community members physically, emotionally, and spiritually for countless centuries, and they continue to do so in contemporary times. Thus, hypnosis is neither new nor dangerous, and modern adaptations, like regression hypnotherapy, can be extremely beneficial in multiple ways.

Basic Tenets of Soul-Regression Therapy

*T*he following points consistently show up in past-life regressions:

- The soul is immortal, intelligent energy manifested by waves of light and color.
- Souls gain wisdom during past lives and between lives.
- Wisdom is gained through varied and often complex experience.
- As the soul advances, its vibrational energy increases and moves gradually through the full color spectrum to purple, gold, and sometimes radiant white.
- The soul innately desires to move toward greater levels of advancement, or progress.
- Souls gain wisdom while experiencing incarnation both on the earth and on other planets and dimensions.
- The earth is a laboratory for learning and progress for the soul.
- Souls choose their next physical body, and the soul remains attached to that body until its physical death.

- Each soul has a unique immortal character that melds with the body and personality/brain.

- A portion of the soul's energy remains in the spiritual realm during incarnation.

- As souls begin their path of advancement, they belong to a soul cluster, or soul family group.

- The teacher of each cluster group is the spirit guide for each member.

- Members of the soul family incarnate repeatedly with one another.

- A past-life regression process is conducted by the therapist, while the content of the session is the responsibility of the spiritual realm.

- Nonincarnating souls manage and coordinate the advancement of souls from the spiritual realm.

- Healing via past-life regression occurs in three stages: identification, dis-identification, and transformation.

- Soul standing is signaled by soul color.

- Recurring circumstances or patterns of behavior are sometimes triggered in an incarnate being so that the progressing soul can remedy or improve in that arena.

- Once a high level of experience is gained, souls generally no longer incarnate.

- Free will is an inviolate principle whether we are operating in incarnation or in the spiritual realm.

Between-Lives Soul Regression
Target Questions

*W*hile the client's spiritual team serves as the gateway in the between-lives soul regression and ultimately determines what information will be shared during the session, the regression hypnotherapist can facilitate by asking specific questions that will help the client ascertain background information such as:

- guide's name (usually provided by the guide at the start of the session);
- guide's soul color;
- client's soul color;
- percentage of soul energy brought into the current life;
- how the client is doing with this amount of soul energy;
- members of the soul family;
- primary soul mate;
- purpose for the choice of body, particular talents, life circumstances, etc.;

- purpose for the choice of current mother/father/other significant people;
- how the council feels the client is progressing in this life;
- primary purpose of the current life; and
- overall mission of client's immortal soul.

Between-Lives Soul Regression
Session Checklist

*B*efore the session:

- Review any instructions you have received to help prepare for your session.

- Avoid excessive alcohol and caffeine before the session. (One beer or glass of wine is acceptable, as is one cup of tea or coffee.)

- Get a good night's sleep if possible on the night before the session.

- Eat a moderate amount before the session.

- Prepare a list of the names of five to ten people (living or not) who have had a significant effect on your current life. Write down the first name, relationship, and a few words to describe the personality of each person.

- Prepare a list of one to five important questions that you hope the between-lives soul regression session will answer. Remember that it is your guides and teachers who will ultimately determine the session content.

- Continue your spiritual practice daily, when possible, prior to the between-lives soul regression.

- Preferably, have a past-life regression hypnotherapy session *before* the between-lives soul regression (unless you have had one within the last two years).

Overview of the Between-Lives Soul Regression Session

- The session, generally scheduled for three to four hours, starts with a preliminary interview with the following objectives: to gain a basic psycho-bio-social-spiritual client history, to discuss goals for the session, to explain the between-lives soul regression process, and to create rapport.

- The therapist utilizes a specific between-lives soul regression hypnotic induction process to guide the client into an altered state of consciousness. (The client remains aware and in charge of themself during the session.)

- Next, a moderately brief age regression of the current life culminates in the womb.

- A past-life regression follows, culminating on the final day of the life reviewed. (Often, but not always, the client experiences the most recent past life.)

- The between-lives soul regression begins as the client experiences their soul exiting the body at the completion of the past life.

- The content of the between-lives soul regression varies from client to client (and also each time the same client experiences a subsequent between-lives soul regression) and is specifically tailored by the spiritual realm to meet the current needs of the client.

- The content of the between-lives soul regression is digitally recorded for the future use of the client.

- The content of the between-lives soul regression session comes to a close when the client and their guides and teachers determine that completion has occurred.

- The client is roused from the altered state of consciousness and awakens alert and refreshed, generally within a minute or so.

- An exit interview occurs (usually lasting fifteen to thirty minutes) where the between-lives soul regression therapist and the client process the content and feelings attached to the session to whatever extent is desired by the client.

- The client is invited to join an ongoing email discussion with other between-lives soul regression clients.

Following the Between-lives Soul Regression Session

- The client does not leave the therapist's office before being sufficiently alert.

- The client is advised to have time following the session for quiet and processing. If at all possible, driving a long distance or plane travel should be avoided until the following day.

- The client is encouraged to be aware of intuitive detail that may surface anytime following the session (minutes, hours, days, and even months afterwards), to journal any thoughts and feelings that come up, and to pay attention to the content of dreams.

- The client may notice alterations in their life, both consciously and sometimes only after they occur.

- The client is advised to listen to their between-lives soul regression recording anytime after the session that feels appropriate.

- The between-lives soul regression therapist is available for further processing of session content.

- The client is advised not to discuss the session with anyone other than the therapist until they feel ready for additional input.

The between-lives soul regression session detail and process provided here is by no means a replacement for adequate professional between-lives soul regression training for the therapist. See appendix E in this book for information on how to find a between-lives soul regression therapist or between-lives soul regression training.

The between-lives soul regression induction process is highly specific, with particular hypnotic commands, sequencing, and instruction. Please be sure to receive appropriate training and practice in the methodology before attempting to guide a client to access the soul state.

Finding a Regression Therapist

*I*n order to find the regression therapist who will best serve your needs, I highly recommend that you ask specific questions. However, trusting your intuition, or "gut feeling," is equally important. Be sure to balance out both elements in choosing a therapist.

Here are some of the questions you might ask:

1. In what city and state or city and country is your office?
2. How long have you been a regression therapist?
3. Where did you receive your training?
4. Are you certified as a past-life or a between-lives regression therapist?
5. What do you charge for a session?
6. How soon do you have an opening in your schedule?
7. What led you to decide to become a regression therapist?
8. How long is the regression session?
9. How many regression sessions do you suggest?
10. Are you available for follow-up questions and discussion after the session? If so, what is the fee?

You may experience a past-life or a between-lives soul regression only once in this life, so factors like proximity to where you live and fees may not be all that important to you. Once again, however, do be sure to heed your gut feeling.

One means of finding a regression therapist is to consult your local alternative magazine. Such publications can often be found at coffeehouses and bookstores. Another excellent way to locate a regression therapist is to search the Internet.

I highly recommend that you visit the website of the Ravenheart Center, www.ravenheartcenter.com, and the International Between Lives Regression Network, www.iblrn.org. Here you will find individuals who have taken formal intensive training and completed the requirements to become certified in past-life and between-lives soul regression. Further information regarding soul regression can be found at www.bringingyoursoultolight.com.

Between-Lives Soul Regression
Hypnotherapy Training

*A*nyone can become a skilled between-lives soul regression therapist provided certain conditions are met.

- First, it is not essential that you intend to have a full-time private regression practice, but you must have an interest in, and perhaps a fascination with, the work of guiding the client into moderate or deep trance, into a past life, to the final day of the past life, and into the spiritual realm of pure soul energy.

- Second, approximately fifty hours of basic training in hypnosis is needed, which can be taken in person or via home study.

- Third, basic training and experience in guiding past-life soul regression sessions is required.

None of the above prerequisites are difficult to fulfill. The Ravenheart Center offers past-life soul regression training in a five-day intensive program and in-home study format. Both are open to the general public. Between-lives soul regression training is offered in a five-day intensive program only (generally residential).

The Ravenheart Center and the International Between Lives Regression Network co-sponsor soul regression training in various locations in the United States and abroad. Dr. Linda Backman, with the support of experienced soul regression colleagues, teaches a five-day intensive course in both past-life and between-lives soul regression. Included in the program are various practices with a spiritual and mystical foundation to support the experience.

All students will receive a letter of completion at the culmination of the training and will be eligible to complete additional requirements and apply for soul regression therapist certification.

Should you have any questions regarding hypnosis, past-life or between-lives soul regression training, please visit:

www.ravenheartcenter.com

www.iblrn.org

or contact Dr. Earl Backman at earl@ravenheartcenter.com or (303) 818-0575.

references

Larry W. Bryant, *Conjuring Gretchen* (Galde Press, 2007). (Foreword by Dr. Linda Backman)

Ellen M. DuBois, *I Never Held You* (DLSIJ Press, 2006). (Foreword and commentary by Dr. Linda Backman)

Laura Faeth, *I Found All The Parts: Healing the Soul Through Rock 'n' Roll* (Sound of Your Soul, an imprint of Wyatt-MacKenzie, 2008).

Michael Newton, *Journey of Souls* (Llewellyn Worldwide, 1994).

———, *Destiny of Souls* (Llewellyn Worldwide, 2000).

———, *Life Between Lives* (Llewellyn Worldwide, 2005).

Andy Tomlinson, *Healing the Eternal Soul* (O Books, 2006).

Websites:

Bringing Your Soul to Light: www.bringingyoursoultolight.com

The International Between Lives Regression Network: www.iblrn.org

The Ravenheart Center: www.ravenheartcenter.com

These definitions are based on Dr. Backman's knowledge of between-lives soul regression to date.

Advanced Family Cohort: A group of souls (usually three to five) from our soul family who have gained a relatively equal level of advancement and have a specific task to focus on, such as learning and teaching more advanced energetic lessons.

Advanced Specialist Group: A group of two to three highly advanced souls whose task is tied to high wisdom. The members of the group, other than the client, are generally not in body and no longer incarnate. This is the third step in soul advancement, from soul family to advanced family cohort to advanced specialist group.

Alpha Brain-Wave State: An altered state of consciousness characterized by relaxation, creativity, and expanded awareness; brain-wave activity of 8–13 Hz.

Altered State of Consciousness: The brain-wave states of alpha, theta, and delta, as opposed to the general waking-state brain wave termed beta.

Ascension: A conscious awareness and energetic state where we are aware of residing in the physical world while simultaneously maintaining divine consciousness.

Beta Brain-Wave State: A state of consciousness characterized by being alert, sharp, and focused; brain-wave activity of 14–27 Hz.

Between-Lives Soul Regression: Regression hypnotherapy used to conduct the client into the state of the interlife, or the time between incarnations.

Certified Regression Therapist: A hypnotherapist formally trained and experienced in the work of regression hypnotherapy.

Continuity of Consciousness: The recognition that soul energy remains constant from lifetime to lifetime and between lives.

Core Soul Unit: The small group of souls, generally one to three, with whom we are the most familiar due to having more shared lives with them than with any other souls.

Council of Wise Ones: Teachers or elders of high wisdom, generally discarnate, who guide each soul and coordinate the spiritual realm. Each client has a panel of wise elders who often communicate during the between-lives soul regression session.

Delta Brain-Wave State: An altered state of consciousness characterized by detachment, physical healing, and sleep; brain-wave activity of 0.5–4 Hz.

Divine: The highest level of pure wisdom, often described as God, the Tao, Great Spirit, the Source, etc.

DNA: A long, linear polymer formed from nucleotides found in the nucleus of a cell and shaped like a double helix; associated with the transmission of genetic information.

Ego: Defined as the "I" that constitutes the human self, or human personality, as opposed to the soul, or nonhuman, self that innervates the physical body.

Ego Strength: The emotional and spiritual stability of an individual who is incarnate.

Elders: See Council of Wise Ones.

Energy: Source of usable power.

Ensoulment: Refers to both the process and state of the soul being attached, or incarnate, in a physical body; also termed embodiment.

Essenes: An ancient Hebrew sect who held and taught mystical, messianic, and ascetic beliefs.

Free Will: The ability, while incarnate or discarnate, to make decisions with regard to one's experiences and behavior.

Higher Order: See Divine.

Higher Realm: See Divine.

Higher Self: Soul, or divine, self.

Human Self: Ego, or personality, that stems from the human brain.

Humility: A lack of false pride.

Hypnosis: An altered state of consciousness when a subject is in alpha or theta brain-wave state.

Hypnotherapy: The experience of being guided into an altered state of consciousness to benefit at a human and soul level.

Interlife: The time between lives, outside of time and space.

Intuition: The act or faculty of knowing or sensing without the use of rational processes.

Kabbalah: A body of mystical, secret teachings based on an esoteric interpretation of the Hebrew Scriptures.

Life Plan: The intention, or script, set in place for an individual prior to an incarnation.

Life purpose: The overall mission, or intention, for each incarnation.

Love: A deep, tender, ineffable feeling of affection and solicitude, generally felt toward a person.

Mystic: Of, relating to, or stemming from direct communion with ultimate reality, or God.

Parallel Lives: Concurrent incarnations when the soul is split between more than one embodiment.

Past Life: Soul embodiment prior to current time.

Past-Life Soul Regression: Regression hypnotherapy to reexperience past lives.

Regression Hypnotherapy: Hypnotic trance used to guide the client into an altered state of consciousness to access memories of past experience.

Regression Therapist: An individual formally trained to guide clients into the memory of past lives and between lives.

Reincarnation: Rebirth of the soul in another body.

Shamanism: One of the oldest tribal healing traditions, still found in many cultures around the world. The shaman, in an altered state of consciousness, uses forms of journeying to spirit worlds, along with prayer and ceremony, to connect with the spirit animals, or totems, of the client to energetically guide the client to a state of balance and well-being.

Solitude: A state of social isolation.

Soul: The immortal and spiritual energetic body of light that animates all living beings.

Soul Advancement: The soul's ongoing development of wisdom and higher knowledge.

Soul Color: The energetic vibration of soul energy perceived and described as color.

Soul Family: A group, or cohort, of souls who join together at the beginning of their soul emanation for the purposes of interaction, support, and progression.

Soul Progression: See Soul Advancement.

Soul Purpose: The script, or blueprint, developed by the soul with guides/ teachers for each incarnation and for the overall intent of each soul.

Soul Self: See Soul.

Soul Standing: Point of soul evolution. (See also Soul Advancement.)

Soul Therapy: The experience of hypnotherapy to gain perspective on who and what we are as soul; also termed between-lives soul regression.

Spirit: The vital principle or animating divine force within living things.

Spirit Guide: The disembodied soul or souls who serve as our advisor, or "spirit buddy."

Spiritual Realm: The unseen world outside of time and space where souls reside; termed the non-local in quantum physics.

Spiritual Team: The group of disembodied teachers (guides and elders) who guide, support, advise, and direct our experiences and advancement as a soul.

Tao: The ultimate source of power and the height of wisdom, also termed the universe, God, the Way, the Source, Great Spirit, etc.

Theta Brain-Wave State: An altered state of consciousness demonstrated by intuitive, superconscious, and out-of-body awareness; brain-wave activity of 4–8 Hz.

Truth: The core principles and understanding of the higher wisdom of the universe.

Universe: See Tao.

Wisdom: The pinnacle of knowledge.

Wise Elders: See Council of Wise Ones.

index

Free Catalog

Get the latest information on our body, mind, and spirit products! To receive a free copy of Llewellyn's consumer catalog, *New Worlds of Mind & Spirit*, simply call 1-877-NEW-WRLD or visit our website at www.llewellyn.com and click on *New Worlds*.

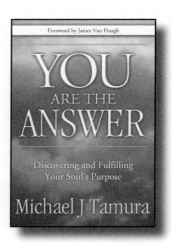

You Are the Answer
Discovering and Fulfilling Your Soul's Purpose

Michael J. Tamura

*W*orld-renowned spiritual teacher, healer, and clairvoyant Michael J. Tamura shares his wisdom in this inspirational guide to true spiritual empowerment.

Hailed as a "beautiful manual for living" by Echo Bodine, *You Are the Answer* brings us profound spiritual lessons, highlighted by the author's powerful true stories. Discover how to use your intuition, make room for spirit in your life, and respond—instead of react—to everyday experiences. As you build a temple of the soul, you'll learn to recognize truth, create miracles in your own life, and find your purpose for living!

This insightful and moving guide also features a "spiritual toolkit" of daily practices and exercises to help you on your extraordinary journey in consciousness exploration, healing, and spiritual development.

978-0-7387-1196-6, 6 x 9, 288 pp., appendices $16.95

Soul Visioning
Clear the Past, Create Your Future

Susan Wisehart

*T*his groundbreaking book teaches you how to create a life of passion and purpose by following your soul's wisdom. Using breakthrough methods such as Energy Psychology (acupuncture for the emotions without the needles), guided journeys, forgiveness practices, and past-life and life-between-lives regression, you'll discover practical, step-by-step techniques to heal the unconscious beliefs that block the awareness of your true spiritual identity and life purpose.

The soul-visioning journey connects you with your higher self to guide you into the ideal expression of your soul in your work, relationships, health, finances, and spirituality. Powerful and inspiring case examples with long-term follow-up interviews demonstrate the remarkable results that Wisehart's clients have experienced from these life-changing techniques.

978-0-7387-1408-0, 6 x 9, 336 pp, worksheets,
index, bibliog., chapter notes $17.95

To Order, Call 1-877-NEW-WRLD
prices subject to change without notice
ORDER AT LLEWELLYN.COM 24 HOURS A DAY, 7 DAYS A WEEK!

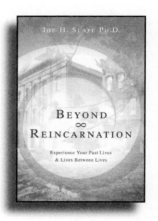

Beyond Reincarnation

Experience Your Past Lives &
Lives Between Lives

Joe H. Slate, PhD

*E*xplore past lives, communicate with the departed, and meet spirit guides. . . . According to Dr. Joe Slate, accessing the spirit realm is not only possible, it's beneficial for our present lives and future spiritual evolution. Past-life knowledge can offer direction and balance, explain fears and compulsions, build self-worth, and promote acceptance of others.

This introduction to reincarnation examines the mind/body/spirit connection and the existence of the ageless soul. Also presented here are Dr. Slate's simple, laboratory-tested strategies for exploring the nonphysical world. Readers can learn how to probe past lives and preexistence through self-hypnosis, astral travel to new spiritual dimensions, and communication with spirits through table tipping. The author's own fascinating experiences, along with personal accounts of his subjects who have tested his techniques, are also included.

978-0-7387-0714-3, 6 x 9, 216 pp.$14.95